WHY
WOMEN
WILL SAVE
THE
PLANET

About Friends of the Earth

For more than forty years Friends of the Earth has seen that the well-being of people and planet go hand in hand – and it's been the inspiration for our campaigns. Together with thousands of people like you we've secured safer food and water, defended wildlife and natural habitats, championed the move to clean energy and acted to keep our climate stable.

This book forms part of our three-year research project Big Ideas Change the World, which aims to inspire a new campaigning journey for Friends of the Earth and others. It is collaboratively researching ten topics, including the future of cities, innovation, women's empowerment and the history of change. It starts from the premise that humans are ingenious and have enormous capacity for collaboration and empathy, even though right now we are doing some pretty stupid things.

Big Ideas Change the World will identify what needs to change to focus some of humanity's amazing abilities on solving the challenges we face and building a brighter future for everyone.

Find out more and get involved at www.foe.co.uk/bigideas

WHY WOMEN WILL SAVE THE PLANET

A COLLECTION OF ARTICLES FOR FRIENDS OF THE EARTH

Edited by Jenny Hawley

Zed Books
LONDON

Why Women Will Save the Planet was first published in 2015
by Zed Books Ltd, The Foundry, 17 Oval Way, London SE11 5RR, UK.

www.zedbooks.co.uk

Typeset in ITC Galliard by seagulls.net.
Cover designed by Kika Sroka-Miller.
Printed and bound by CPI Group (UK) Ltd, Croydon, CR0 4YY

A catalogue record for this book is available from the British Library.

ISBN 978-1-78360-580-4 hb
ISBN 978-1-78360-579-8 pb
ISBN 978-1-78360-581-1 pdf
ISBN 978-1-78360-582-8 epub
ISBN 978-1-78360-583-5 mobi

CONTENTS

ACKNOWLEDGEMENTS

First and foremost, Friends of the Earth and I are grateful to all the contributors who have generously shared their expertise, energy and time to make this book possible. We would like to thank all those at Zed Books for their support in its publication and the staff, volunteers and activists at Friends of the Earth who have championed this book and helped in its production and promotion. Finally, I would like to thank in particular Mike Childs at Friends of the Earth for enabling me to work on this fascinating book, as well as his support and encouragement during the process of pulling it together.

Jenny Hawley

ABOUT THE CONTRIBUTORS

Celia Alldridge

Celia Alldridge has contributed a piece on behalf of the World March of Women (WMW), an international feminist, anti-capitalist movement bringing together organized grassroots women – as individuals or as part of groups, collectives, trade unions or social movements – in the struggle against all forms of inequality and discrimination against women. WMW recognizes the deep relationship between feminist activism and territorial self-determination, with parallels between the exploitation and commodification of women and the environment.

www.worldmarchofwomen.org

Shukri Haji Ismail Bandare

Shukri Haji Ismail Bandare has served as the minister for environment of Somaliland since 2013. Previous to her political appointment, she was an active campaigner on environmental issues and founded a local NGO, Candlelight for Health, Education and Environment. The charity continues to deliver training, education and healthcare programmes with communities across Somaliland.

www.candlelightsomal.org

Quinn Bernier, Chiara Kovarik, Ruth Meinzen-Dick and Agnes Quisumbing

At the time of writing, the authors worked in the Environment and Production Technology Division and the Poverty, Health and Nutrition Division at the International Food Policy Research

Institute (IFPRI). Their piece draws heavily on an article on 'Gender and sustainability' by Meinzen-Dick et al. published in 2014 and extends it to suggest that the Women's Empowerment in Agriculture Index may be a useful tool for understanding this relationship. They conclude that empowerment does matter for environmental sustainability – both for men and for women – and that there are important gender differences to address to allow this to happen. www.ifpri.org/staffprofile/ruth-meinzen-dick

Isabel Bottoms and Amena Sharaf

Isabel Bottoms and Amena Sharaf have contributed on behalf of the Egyptian Centre for Economic and Social Rights, an Egyptian non-governmental legal and research group which works to ensure Egypt is free of all forms of oppression, poverty, discrimination and social injustice, where its citizens enjoy all economic, social, political and cultural rights. It supports campaigns and social movements, including those against the extraction and use of coal. ecesr.com/en

Susan Buckingham

Susan Buckingham is a professor at the Centre for Human Geography at Brunel University in the UK. A feminist geographer whose main focus is on gender and environmental issues, her teaching, research and activist work is interlinked through a commitment to environmental and social justice. She works with universities, government institutions and NGOs in Europe, the USA, Pakistan and internationally.

www.brunel.ac.uk/shssc/people/social-work/susan-buckingham

Juliet Davenport

Juliet Davenport is the founder and CEO of Good Energy, one of the UK's first entirely renewable electricity supplier and generator companies. Good Energy was conceived as a business which could harness consumer and business environmental concerns and be profitable. It has become a catalyst for entrepreneurship among dozens of renewable power suppliers in England. Driven by Juliet's

recognition of the importance of high standards of customer service, Good Energy has come first in three of the last four years of the *Which?* energy customer satisfaction survey. Juliet sits on the Energy UK board as a representative of smaller suppliers and in June 2015 was appointed to the Natural Environment Research Council. She has been awarded the OBE for services to renewables.
www.goodenergy.co.uk/about/juliet-davenport

Diane Elson

Diane Elson is Emeritus Professor of Sociology at the University of Essex and chair of the UK Women's Budget Group (a network of researchers and activists producing critical analysis of UK government budgets). She is the author of many publications on gender and development, and was the lead author of the first edition in 2000 of the *UNIFEM Progress of the World's Women* report. She currently serves as an adviser to UN Women and is a member of the UN Committee for Development Policy. In 2006, she was named as one of fifty key thinkers on development.
www.essex.ac.uk/sociology/staff/profile.aspx?ID=129

Sarah Fisher

Sarah Fisher is the Advocacy and Policy Manager at the Population and Sustainability Network (PSN). This is an international network bringing together development, environment and reproductive health organizations, government departments and policy research organizations to increase awareness of the importance of both population and consumption factors for sustainable development. It takes a rights-based approach to population issues, advocating universal access to reproductive health services, including voluntary family planning.
www.populationandsustainability.org

Anna Fitzpatrick

Anna Fitzpatrick works at the Centre for Sustainable Fashion at the University of the Arts in the UK. The CSF was devised to question and challenge reactionary fashion cultures, which reflect and reinforce patterns of excessive consumption and disconnection from nature and our environment, to expand fashion's ability to connect, delight and identify individual and collective values. Their work explores new perspectives, relationships and processes that balance ecology, society and culture within the artistic and business context of fashion. They examine women's roles in the production and consumption of fashion and how this can be harnessed to bring about positive change for sustainability.

www.sustainable-fashion.com

Marylyn Haines Evans

Marylyn Haines-Evans is vice-chair of the National Federation of Women's Institutes and also chair of the Public Affairs Committee. The Women's Institute (WI) was formed in the UK in 1915 to revitalize rural communities and encourage women to become more involved in producing food during the First World War. Since then the organization's aims have broadened and the WI is now the largest voluntary women's organization in the UK. The WI currently has 212,000 members in around 6,600 WIs. It celebrates its centenary in 2015.

www.thewi.org.uk

Jenny Hawley

Jenny Hawley is working as a freelance editor for Friends of the Earth, contributing the introduction to the book and managing production and marketing. Jenny has worked for human rights, environmental sustainability and wildlife conservation in British and international charities for twenty years. She has an MSc in Environment and Development from the University of East Anglia in the UK.

Nathalie Holvoet and Liesbeth Inberg

Nathalie Holvoet and Liesbeth Inberg are academics at the Institute of Development Policy and Management at the University of Antwerp in Belgium. Their piece for this book, based on their paper in the journal *Climate and Development*, investigates to what extent and in what way thirty-one sub-Saharan African National Adapta-

tion Programmes of Action (NAPAs) integrate a gender dimension in the different sectors that are especially related to climate change.
www.uantwerpen.be/en/staff/nathalie-holvoet

Emma Howard Boyd

Emma has spent her twenty-five-year career working in financial services, initially in corporate finance, and then in fund management, specializing in sustainable investment and corporate governance at Jupiter Asset Management in the UK. She is currently the chair of trustees for ShareAction, the movement for responsible investment, which harnesses the power of the investment system to protect the environment and achieve social change. She is also deputy chair of the Environment Agency and a member of the 30% Club Steering Committee.
emmahowardboyd.com/about; 30percentclub.org

Fatima Jibrell

Fatima Jibrell is the founder of the international NGO Adeso: African Development Solutions (previously known as Horn Relief), whose mission is to work with communities to create environments in which Africans can thrive. In 2014 Fatima received the Champions of Earth award from the UN Environment Programme as a Laureate for Inspiration and Action for 'building environmental and social resilience amidst war and devastation'.
adesoafrica.org; www.unep.org/champions/laureates/2014/jibrell.asp

Melissa Leach

Melissa Leach is director of the Institute of Development Studies (IDS) at the University of Sussex in the UK. She founded and directed the STEPS Centre from 2006 to 2014 and is co-chair of the Science Committee of Future Earth. As a social anthropologist and geographer, her research in Africa and beyond has addressed a variety of environmental, agricultural, health and technology issues, integrating gender and feminist political ecology perspectives. Her recent books include *Green Grabbing: A New Appropriation of*

Nature (2013); *The Politics of Green Transformations* (2015) and *Gender Equality and Sustainable Development* (2015).
www.ids.ac.uk/person/melissa-leach

Caroline Lucas

Caroline Lucas is the first Green Party MP in the UK, re-elected for a second term in 2015 with an increased majority. She joined the Green Party in 1986 and served as a county councillor on Oxfordshire County Council until 1997; she became one of the UK Green Party's first MEPs in June 1999. She is an active campaigner on a range of issues and is a vice-president of the RSPCA and a CND National Council member. She is also a UNICEF parliamentary champion and a member of the Committee of Patrons of the Stop the War Coalition.
www.carolinelucas.com

Wanjira Maathai

Wanjira Maathai is chair of the board of the Green Belt Movement, a Kenyan environmental organization that empowers communities, particularly women, to conserve the environment and improve livelihoods. Wanjira also directs the Partnership for Women's Entrepreneurship in Renewables (wPower) Hub at the Wangari Maathai Institute for Peace and Environmental Studies.

The Green Belt Movement was founded by Wanjira's mother, Professor Wangari Maathai, in 1977 to respond to the concerns of rural Kenyan women about decreasing supplies of water, food and firewood for fuel and fencing. GBM encouraged the women to work together to grow seedlings and plant trees to bind the soil, store rainwater, provide food and firewood, and receive a small monetary token for their work.
www.greenbeltmovement.org

Lyla Mehta

Lyla Mehta is a Professorial Research Fellow at the Institute for Development Studies at the University of Sussex in the UK, and a Visiting Professor at Noragric, Norwegian University of Life

Sciences. She trained as a sociologist (University of Vienna) and has a PhD in Development Studies (University of Sussex). Her work focuses on water and sanitation, forced displacement and resistance, scarcity, rights and access, resource grabbing and the politics of environment/development and sustainability.

www.ids.ac.uk/person/lyla-mehta

Kate Metcalf and colleagues from the Women's Environmental Network

The Women's Environmental Network's mission is to make the connections between women's health and well-being and environmental issues. WEN works directly with women in the UK, providing information, training and workshops on matters of local food-growing, health and climate change, to encourage and inspire women to make change in their lives, families and wider networks. WEN's vision is an environmentally sustainable world in which we have achieved gender equality. Their piece for this book was prepared by Kate Metcalf, Connie Hunter, Julia Minnear and Georgie Johnson, with contributions from Molly Alden, Heather Millen, Tabitha Kleinert and Victoria Tedder.

www.wen.org.uk

Maria Mies

Maria Mies is a sociologist and author of several books on women, economic sustainability and the environment, and co-author with Vandana Shiva of *Ecofeminism*. After working for many years in India, she became head of the Women's Studies Programme at the Institute of Social Sciences in the Hague, and subsequently Professor of Sociology at the Cologne University of Applied Sciences. Having retired from teaching in 1993, she continues to be active in a range of women's and environmental movements.

en.wikipedia.org/wiki/Maria_Mies

Esther Mwangi

Esther Mwangi is principal scientist in the Forests and Governance Programme at the Centre for International Forest Research. Her areas of research interest include the dynamics of property rights to land and natural resources, multilevel linkages in resource governance, gender, policy implementation and strategies for linking knowledge to action.

www.cifor.org/scientist-detail/2862/esthermwangi

Julie Nelson

Julie Nelson is Professor of Economics at the University of Massachusetts Boston in the USA. A leading writer on feminist economic thought, she currently conducts research on feminism and economics with special interests in ethics, methodology and implications for social and environmental policies. She was a founding board member of the International Association for Feminist Economics.

www.umb.edu/academics/cla/faculty/julie_a._nelson;
sites.google.com/site/julieanelsoneconomist/home

Cathy Newman

Cathy Newman has been a television news presenter and journalist for Channel 4 News in the UK since 2006. She also writes about politics in the *Telegraph* newspaper and in her Channel 4 News blog. She previously worked on national newspapers, including the *Financial Times* and the *Independent*, for more than a decade. Since joining Channel 4 News, she has broadcast a string of investigations and scoops, including sexual harassment allegations against the Liberal Democrat peer Lord Rennard. She has worked to expose sexism and the harassment of women in the UK Parliament, and the need for a change in culture and working practices.

www.channel4.com/news/cathy-newman

Yvonne Orengo

Yvonne Orengo is an independent development communications practitioner and the director of The Andrew Lees Trust (ALT UK). ALT UK was launched in 1995 following the tragic death of Andrew Lees in southern Madagascar while filming the imperilled Petriky forest. Lees was Campaigns Director of Friends of the Earth at the time. Yvonne lived and worked in the south of Madagascar for more than six years, developing the Trust's social and environmental education programmes. She continues to work with the Trust and mentor the counterpart Malagasy NGO, Andry Lalana Tohana (ALT Mg). www.andrewleestrust.org; www.andrylalanatohana.org; www.orengo.co.uk

Fiona Reynolds

Fiona Reynolds was director general of the National Trust in the UK from 2001 to 2012. She was previously head of the Cabinet Office Women's Unit in the UK government, director of the Council for the Protection of Rural England (now the Campaign to Protect Rural England) and Secretary to the Council for National Parks. Fiona is now Master of Emmanuel College at the University of Cambridge, Senior Independent Director of the executive board of the BBC and chair of the Green Alliance.
www.emma.cam.ac.uk/contact/fellows/?fellow=314

Sarah Richardson

Sarah Richardson is an associate professor in history specialising in political, constitutional and gender history at the University of Warwick in the UK. She is the author of *The Political Worlds of Women: Gender and Politics in Nineteenth Century Britain*, a book which discusses the diversity of female political culture in the nineteenth century.
www2.warwick.ac.uk/fac/arts/history/people/staff_index/srichardson

Vandana Shiva

Vandana Shiva is a world-renowned Indian philosopher, environmental activist and author. She is one of the leaders and board members of the International Forum on Globalization. She has authored more than twenty books, including the landmark *Ecofeminism* with Maria Mies. She is a member of the International Organization for a Participatory Society. She has received widespread recognition for her work, including the Right Livelihood Award.
vandanashiva.com

Barbara Stocking

Barbara Stocking was chief executive of Oxfam from May 2001 until February 2013. She was the first woman to lead the charity, one of the UK's most successful and best-known international development organizations, and she put poor women and gender quality at the forefront of Oxfam's work. She became the fifth president of the all-woman Murray Edwards College, University of Cambridge, in July 2013.
www.murrayedwards.cam.ac.uk/contacts/contactdetails/
personal_pages/dame_barbara_stocking

Nidhi Tandon

Nidhi Tandon is from East Africa, and is director of Networked Intelligence for Development. Nidhi works on security of livelihoods, at the nexus of food, habitat, environment and poverty in the context of globalization and increasing disparities between peoples and nations. Much of her work revolves around rural women's rights and self-determination, and in particular the relationships between women and water, energy, natural resources and the policy decisions that affect their lives.
networkedintelligence.com/wp/home

INTRODUCTION

Why Women Will Save the Planet, a collection of articles from women across the globe, demonstrates that women's empowerment is essential to securing a healthy and safe environment in which people and nature can thrive. The lesson of this for the environment movement is that it must campaign for gender equality in order to achieve environmental sustainability.

The articles also demonstrate that women are more vulnerable to environmental degradation and climate change, so the women's movement must embrace these concerns. They identify that discrimination against women and against environmental degradation have the same root causes, so addressing both together is necessary.

I'm a lifelong supporter of Friends of the Earth and Greenpeace, and I'm a feminist. I've worked in the environment and human rights movements for twenty years, but I have to admit I hadn't properly considered the relationship between environmental sustainability and gender equality. I suspect I'm not alone.

Of course, I've known that enabling women (and other marginalised groups) to reach their full potential would surely increase our chances of mitigating climate change, cutting air pollution, stopping deforestation, halting the loss of wildlife species and more.

I know that discrimination and abuse of women is still rife in societies around the world, in developed and developing countries, in rural and urban communities, in families, workplaces and public life. Yes, there has been huge progress in many countries over the last century to tackle this in law and in practice, but nowhere near enough.

Yet I've not thought of gender equality as an environmental issue – and nor has most of the environment movement, which is overwhelmingly silent on the issue.

Friends of the Earth commissioned this book as part of its 'Big Ideas' project, a three-year programme of research and dialogue to identify the major changes needed to solve the immense environmental and social challenges we face in the world today. One of the questions the project aims to answer is: 'Could women's empowerment transform the chances of achieving environmental sustainability?' The answer, provided by this book, is emphatically yes.

Thanks to the insightful articles in this book from women across the globe, I now understand the criticality of women's empowerment to environmental sustainability, and vice versa. I hope that this book spurs the environment movement into action and encourages more collaboration with the women's movement, finding common causes and pursuing common solutions.

In this introduction I draw out some emerging themes, but I cannot hope to do justice to the depth and breadth of the issues discussed, so I'd encourage you to read the articles themselves. They demonstrate the variety and complexity of interactions between women's empowerment and environmental sustainability, and how these extend to all sectors of society – politics, economics, the media, households and beyond. It is important to keep in mind that women are as diverse as humankind itself and so to be wary of generalisations: while there is some evidence of greater environmental concern among women than among men, this is not necessarily always the case, and 'women' are not a homogeneous group.[1]

The articles in this book point to a wider and substantial body of work by academics, practitioners, campaigners and others – women and men. Their work opens up a whole new world of opportunities to find solutions that simultaneously address environmental and social challenges, setting us on a faster route to well-being and sustainability.

It's clear that change is needed in four key areas:

» Recognising the importance of **women's roles in bringing about environmental change**, whether as campaigners, household managers or decision-makers;

» rooting out **gender bias** in our culture and society to ensure that everyone can play their part in progressive environmental change;

» fundamentally **transforming our economic system** to take proper account of women and the environment;

» **sharing power more equally** across society by empowering women and other marginalised groups and exploring different types of power.

Below I go into more detail on each of these.

Recognising women's role in environmental change

Women have been pioneers of the environment movement from the beginning. Much of this campaigning work has focused on people and public health: clean water and air, green spaces, controls on pesticides in food. Fiona Reynolds describes Octavia Hill's efforts to improve public health through nature in Victorian England. Caroline Lucas points to the importance of scientist Rachel Carson's 1962 book *Silent Spring*, which sparked the American environment movement. Sarah Richardson demonstrates that the work of many, many other women in securing environmental gains has been marginalised by largely male historians.

The historic tendency of much of the environment movement has been to prioritise charismatic species and nature reserves above the well-being of indigenous people. Now it is recognised that today's greatest challenges and solutions to environmental sustainability – climate change, food production, land use, consumption, population growth – are fundamentally about people (Reynolds).

Too many in the environment movement have understood the importance of women's empowerment narrowly and simply as improving sexual and reproductive health and rights in order to reduce population growth. This then also restricts the analysis of women's empowerment to those countries where women do not have these rights. Sarah Fisher argues cogently that ensuring sexual and reproductive health and rights for women is essential in its own right but also as a means of empowering women as agents of environmental change.

Put simply, women make up half of society and therefore must be part of the solution. They have a critical role in managing natural resources at household or community level, as argued by activists, practitioners and academics such as Shukri Haji Ismail Bandare, Fatima Jibrell, Vandana Shiva and Wanjira Mathai. Gender issues have been addressed in many development and conservation programmes in forestry, agriculture, water and other sectors, as discussed by Quinn Bernier and her colleagues, and Esther Mwangi. Yet this reality seems to have passed by the mainstream environment movement, at least in the Western world.

As Nidhi Tandon emphasises, women are often more immediately concerned than men with basic needs and social issues – such as food, water, shelter, fuel and healthcare – which depend directly upon a healthy natural environment. As a result, women also are often more vulnerable to the impacts of environmental degradation and climate change.

Vandana Shiva also highlights gender difference in knowledge and skills. She points out that this arises simply by virtue of women's different experiences, concerns, roles and responsibilities, and that this often extends to agriculture, natural resource management and biodiversity. Where women have the power and autonomy to exercise such skills, they deliver wider benefits. Food growing, for example, can empower women to gain control over their body and personal health, to assert land sovereignty, to connect with nature, to gain therapy for the mind, and to build friendships and communities, as noted by Celia Aldridge, Richardson, Shiva, Tandon and Metcalf et al.

Rooting out gender bias

Since the 1970s, ecofeminism philosophy and activism have asserted deep connections between women and the environment. Two of the leading voices in this movement, Maria Mies and Vandana Shiva, have contributed to this book. There are many diverging strands of ecofeminism. One of these embraces the idea of an intrinsic connection between women and the environment as a powerful, spiritual force for good; this has an ancient history in mythology and religion. It is argued that concepts such as 'Mother Earth' and 'Mother Nature' reveal the feminine as closer to nature, compassionate, communal, fertile, nurturing and emotional.

Yet others, such as Julie Nelson, argue that this is not an intrinsic relationship but a product of social norms that only reinforces unhelpful stereotypes. She suggests that, following this logic, men and the masculine are associated with control over nature, more rational, individual and logical.

Regardless of this debate, it is clear that the global economy, politics, the media, education, religion and households are all gendered to greater or lesser degrees. Many contributors argue that our whole economic and social systems, our very language, are gender biased in subconscious, deeply embedded ways. This, they argue, reinforces assumptions and prejudices, and shapes the way we think and behave about women and the environment.

As a mother of a boy and a girl, I've been surprised at how differently they are treated by many people and how children's toys and clothes are still labelled for boys and girls – gender differences that quickly turn into damaging inequalities. This extends into children's experience of their environment – getting muddy, climbing trees or collecting insects are often seen as boys' activities, influencing children's lifelong connections with nature.

Cultural assumptions about gender are powerful and often taken for granted. Interventions such as the viral #LikeAGirl campaign in 2014 help to expose how commonly used language reinforces gender bias and undermines women and girls.

Rooting out this bias in our cultures and social structures is an essential step, not only in achieving gender equality and social justice, but in environmental sustainability too.

Interestingly, Shukri Haji Ismail Bandare talks of 'gender complementarity' in Somalia because she finds that in her context the term 'gender equality' is too confrontational. I'm sure she is right and that the term has become loaded. Yet we must recognise deep and entrenched gender bias and discrimination where it exists through explicit gender analysis. This is vital to understanding current inequalities, hidden realities and the potential impacts of our decisions, wherever they are, whether in politics, organisations, professions, education, broader society or our homes.

Transforming our economic systems

As noted above, many of the articles in this book demonstrate that women's critical roles in achieving environmental change go largely unrecognised. Similarly, 'the environment' itself is often not treated as a serious political, economic or social issue, and environment ministries are the poor cousins in government.

Julie Nelson highlights the parallels between women and the environment in our economy: they are both invisible resources, not formally recognised or valued in the economy. Yet our global-ised system depends fundamentally on natural resources – the raw materials of manufacturing, agriculture and construction – and the unpaid work of bringing up children, running households and building communities, which is overwhelming done by women.

We take both women and the environment for granted; as Shiva says, both become 'commons' that are considered of little value and exposed to abuse. Celia Aldridge highlights the parallels between the violent exploitation of women, such as trafficking and pros-titution, and large-scale exploitation of the environment, such as large-scale mining, dams and intensive agriculture.

Our language frustrates us. As Nelson points out, we are often reduced to expressing ideas in binary categories: natural/man-made; social/environmental; productive/unproductive; global/local; male/female.

Yet our world is not black and white; it is complex, shifting and subjective. Progress is not linear; as Shiva notes, women's empower-ment can be increasing in one way yet decreasing in another, while sustainability similarly progresses and regresses at the same time.

This all creates exclusions and false oppositions; we talk about the economy, society and the environment as separate entities when in fact they are interdependent parts of the same system, argue Lyla Mehta and Melissa Leach. If we are to achieve environmental sustainability or gender equality, we must overcome these barriers and recognise the complexity and interdependence of our world.

This will help us to find practical, holistic and equitable solutions and to shape interventions that match the realities of people's lives. A fundamental part of this is a transformation of our economic system to take proper account of the 'externalities' of women and the environment (Nelson).

The way that we measure success is critical. 'Economic growth' and 'development' sound inherently positive and have become ends in themselves, rather than a means to an end; their social and environmental impacts, which may be extremely negative, often become side issues. Elson, Reynolds, Shiva and others argue that defining success in terms of gross domestic product (GDP) is wrong and that new definitions of progress and measures are required to achieve well-/being and sustainability.

Sharing power more equally

Susan Buckingham, Cathy Newman, Juliet Davenport, Emma Howard-Boyd, Nathalie Holvoet and Leisbeth Inberg all provide evidence of gender bias across social sectors – in education and academic research, politics, business and even in climate change adaptation plans. Women are often not considered – however consciously – as being suitable or able to perform certain roles. Even in the fashion industry – predominantly aimed at women as consumers – men dominate in senior positions as decision-makers and managers, says Anna Fitzpatrick.

The same is true also of the environment movement; as US-based journalist Suzanne Goldenberg has highlighted: 'the very top of "Big Green" is as white and male as a Tea Party meet-up'.[2] A November 2014 comment piece in the journal *Nature* points to the dominance of male voices in the conservation movement, despite the presence of senior women.[3]

Why is this? Perhaps because the environment is often seen as 'out there', as a separate category from society and the economy, even by those of us in the environment movement itself. People and socio-economic factors have been blamed for environmental degradation but we have not routinely taken a gendered approach to understanding environmental behaviours or to shaping campaigns and strategies (Holvoet and Inberg). This has to change. As Barbara Stocking shows, integration of gender throughout an organisation is essential to ensuring gender equality in its work, and this takes conscious, explicit effort and ongoing monitoring and evaluation.

In many cases, in all sectors of society, women are not only under-represented but undervalued; even where they have a place at the table, their voice is often not heard (Davenport, Elson). Working practices and decision-making processes often exclude women or prevent them from reaching senior levels – for example, when they are responsible for the care of children or other relatives, as well as household tasks (Bernier et al., Howard Boyd). It is clear that full participation for women and men can only be achieved if household and community responsibilities are shared more equitably across society.

More often than not, women have less independence, status and mobility in their personal lives and are more vulnerable to discrimination and violence, as demonstrated by Isabel Bottoms and Amena Sharaf, and Kate Metcalf and her colleagues. Nidhi Tandon rightly points out that men – particularly those from marginalised communities – also face inequality, domestic violence or other barriers to participation in society. As Holvoet and Inberg argue, the broader issue of discrimination cannot and should not be separated from women's oppression. In order to achieve diversity and equality across society, anti-discrimination measures need to be backed up with political and material support. In particular, as Buckingham says, everyone must have the chance to be represented and engaged in decision-making processes. Elson, Lucas, Leach, Mehta and Tandon suggest that this can be achieved through alternative power structures or pathways, such as collective ownership and management of resources. Yvonne Orengo shows how the media can be a powerful tool in empowering women and wider society to take an active role in bringing about change.

Conclusion

A number of clear findings stand out from this book.

First, and perhaps most obviously, ensuring gender equality through the empowerment of women is simply the right thing to do. The environment movement has a responsibility to integrate this principle throughout its policies, programmes and practices, just as any organisation, business, government and community has. This will help to ensure that environmental interventions have a positive impact on the well-being of all – women and men.

Secondly, women's empowerment is critical to achieving environmental sustainability. This doesn't mean that women have all the solutions (and men are off the hook), nor – in my view – that women have any special 'feminine' qualities that make us better environmental stewards. In other words, *Women Will Save the Planet* but not alone because, given the scale of the challenges we face, we must exploit all the available knowledge, skills, diversity and creativity that humankind can bring. If we are to achieve environmental sustainability we need gender equality in politics, business, education, religion and, yes, environmental groups and other civil society organisations.

Finally, gender inequality is both a symptom and a cause of an unequal and environmentally damaging society. We cannot separate out the need for gender equality from other struggles for a fair, equal and environmentally sustainable society. This means the environment movement, the women's movement and other movements for social justice and equality must work together. Undoubtedly this means challenging the male-dominated, growth-driven economic system that dominates our most powerful social institutions – politics, business and the media. We need to create a system based on different values, where success is measured by integrated social and environmental outcomes, not profit or GDP. We need to focus again on the kind of world in which we want to live and the kind of lives we want to lead.

How can you help?

Achieving gender equality, social justice and environmental sustainability is not possible without people like you agitating for change, whether in your workplace, in politics or more broadly in society. We all have a part to play, whatever that may be. If you are already involved, then I applaud you. Achieving the changes suggested in this book would be transformational or, in the words of Friends of the Earth, a Big Idea. So if you want to do one thing after reading this book, I'd recommend you get involved and stand up for change.

Jenny Hawley

1

DIANE ELSON

University of Essex

Women's empowerment and environmental sustainability in the context of international UN agreements

Introduction

Why should environmental activists be interested in women's empowerment? Not because women are intrinsically closer to nature than men, and better equipped to save the planet. But because neither environmental sustainability nor women's empowerment can be achieved without challenging patterns of economic growth and configurations of economic power that do not take into account non-market resources, not only climate and oceans, but also the unpaid care work that is vital to human well-being, and which is disproportionately women's work. There are important synergies between environmental sustainability and women's empowerment that need to be explored, and the social movements focused on each goal can be strengthened through collaborative efforts. These arguments are explored here in relation to UN agreements pertaining to the environment, and the struggle over what 'green economy' will signify in practice.

International UN agreements on the environment and women's empowerment

Beginning with the UN Conference on Environment and Development in Rio in 1992, a series of international agreements have linked the participation of women in activities related to the agreements as important for fulfilment of the aims of the agreements. Thus, Principle 20 of the official Rio Declaration on Environment and Development states that the full participation of women is essential to achieving sustainable development.[1] The trio of global environmental conventions that followed this conference – the United Nations Framework Convention on Climate Change (UNFCCC), the Convention on Biodiversity (CBD) and the United Nations Convention to Combat Desertification (UNCCD) – all make reference to the importance of enhancement of women's participation in relevant public bodies.[2]

A concern with women's empowerment is repeated in the outcome document of the Rio+20 United Nations Conference on Sustainable Development, *The Future We Want*:

> We recognize that gender equality and women's empowerment are important for sustainable development and our common future. We reaffirm our commitments to ensure women's equal rights, access and opportunities for participation and leadership in the economy, society and political decision-making. We underscore that women have a vital role to play in achieving sustainable development. We recognize the leadership role of women, and we resolve to promote gender equality and women's empowerment and to ensure their full and effective participation in sustainable development policies, programmes and decision-making at all levels.[3]

However, despite the lip-service paid to women's participation in decision-making, it appears that there has been little of substance, with efforts ranging from 'exclusion to nominal inclusion'.[4] The discussion on gender and climate change focused primarily on local-level vulnerabilities and adaptation; with only limited attention to gender issues in discussions involving large-scale technology, market-based initiatives and climate finance.[5] A pioneering effort to construct an environment and gender index included indicators for presence of women in Conference of Parties (CoP) delegations and policy-making positions, and inclusion of gender issues in UNFCC reports, UNCCD reports and CBD reports. It found that the global average for women was 36 per cent of those participating in intergovernmental negotiations on climate change, biodiversity and desertification.[6] The Conference of Parties in 2012 adopted a resolution to promote gender balance in bodies of and delegations to UNFCC and to include gender and climate change as a standing item on the CoP agenda. However, these negotiations are only one space among many, and there is little data on women's ability to exercise decision-making power in environmentally sensitive production and consumption processes, especially those dominated by multinational corporations.

There is indeed evidence that women's participation in environmental management can make a difference: for example, their effective involvement in community forest management bodies has yielded positive outcomes for both forest sustainability and gender equality.[7] However, a recent UN Women report argues that there has too often been a presumption that women could be harnessed as 'sustainability saviours' based on the assumption that women are especially close to nature and have time to spare:

Women–environment connections – especially in reproductive and subsistence activities such as collecting fuel wood, hauling water and cultivating food – were often presented as if natural and universal rather than as the product of particular social and cultural norms and expectations. Ensuing projects and policies often mobilized and instrumentalized women's labour, skills and knowledge, adding to their unpaid work without addressing whether they had the rights, voice and power to control project benefits.[8]

Moreover, it is vital to recognise that some measures to address environmental sustainability may have adverse impacts on some women. For instance, biofuel production could run counter to the ability of women smallholders to provide food for their families. Higher consumer prices for energy may encourage consumers to 'econo-mise' in their use of energy and not to waste it, but in the context of poverty and inequality may confront low-income women with the terrible dilemma of providing 'heating or eating' for their families.

What matters is not the simple presence or absence of women in climate change delegations or on committees to manage envi-ronmental resources. What matters is how women's empowerment and sustainable development are framed, how the determinants of gender inequality and harmful climate change and environmental degradation are understood, and what kinds of measures are intro-duced to reduce them both. Are the means of implementation profit-driven? Or are they rooted in collective social investment and regulation, recognising the importance of resources and activities that are not commercialised?

Meanings of empowerment and sustainability

Both of these terms can be understood in narrow ways, disconnected from rights and justice. For instance, women's empowerment can be understood as more women being present in the public sphere, participating in the market economy or being elected to parlia-ments and other public bodies. But this ignores the question of the quality of this participation. Do women enjoy the rights at work that are set out in human rights treaties and ILO Conventions? Are women earning a living wage? Are their jobs secure? Are they able to combine employment with caring for other people without being penalised by low wages, poor promotion prospects, lack of security, unhealthy working environments? Are the women in parliaments, and other public bodies, mere tokens, subject to sexist practices, with most women unable to exercise real decision-making power? A much broader understanding is offered by the UN Committee on the Elimination of Discrimination Against Women, which suggests that women are empowered 'by an enabling environment to achieve equality of results' in terms of enjoyment of all human rights,[9] some-thing that applies to the private sphere of the home and community, as well as to the public spheres of the market and the state. This requires transformation of existing societies and economies and not merely integration of women into the public sphere, as Articles 3 and 5 of the Convention on the Elimination of All Forms of Discrimination Against Women indicate. This has been spelled out by the UN Committee on the Elimination of Discrimination Against Women, which has said that governments must adopt measures to bring about 'a real transformation of opportunities, institutions and systems so that they are no longer grounded in historically determined male paradigms of power and life patterns'.[10]

The disproportionate responsibility that women bear for carrying out unpaid work is an important constraint on their capacity to realise their rights, as has been emphasised in a recent report by the UN Special Rapporteur on Extreme Poverty and Human Rights.[11] Thus, a key transformation is the recognition, reduction and redistribution of the unpaid work of caring for families and communities, so that unpaid work that is drudgery (such as collecting fuel and water) is reduced, and other unpaid work, such as caring for children, is redistributed, some of it to men in households and communities, and some of it to paid workers in public and private sectors. Both women and men need time to care for their families and communities, and time free from such care – something that is often discussed in Europe in terms of 'work–life balance'.

Environmental sustainability can be understood in terms of not breaching the planetary boundaries that have been identified as keeping the planet within a safe operating space for humanity.[12] But this ignores the question of inequalities between people, the distribution of the costs and benefits of actions to avoid breaching critical thresholds, and the foundational importance of respect for human rights.[13] It is important to keep in mind intergenerational issues so that we can 'meet the needs of the present without compromising the ability of future generations to meet their own needs'.[14] But in doing so, we must not ignore the fact that many people are dying today because of unmet needs – for instance, the maternal mortality of low-income women in developing countries has remained stubbornly high despite the Millennium Development Goals and many avoidable deaths are occurring. Thus we need to be not only Friends of the Earth but also Friends of the Poor, and those subject to discrimination. These considerations are perhaps addressed by the post-Rio+20 discourse about the three dimensions of sustainability: social, economic and environmental. But this can be a cover for a wish to simply maintain unequal patterns of profit-driven economic growth, hoping to avoid social disruption, economic crises and environmental disasters through piecemeal adaptation and mitigation measures, rather than transforming our economies and societies.

Both 'empowerment' and 'sustainability' as used in most UN documents are ambiguous concepts, whose meaning is revealed only in the context of specific practices. If the practices of profit-driven economic growth dominate, this will severely restrict the kinds of 'empowerment' and 'sustainability' that are possible to those that are profit-conforming, and may in fact prevent the transformations that are necessary for women to be fully empowered, and use of natural resources to be fully sustainable.

There is evidence that strongly suggests that the underlying causes and consequences of unsustainability and gender inequality are deeply intertwined and rooted in profit-driven economic processes.[15] These involve market liberalisation, productive and financial activity geared to short-term profits; unrestrained material consumption; unparalleled levels of militarism; privatisation of public goods and services and reduction of the capacities of governments to regulate and redistribute. As well as environmental degradation and harmful climate change, these processes have caused in many places crises of care, which entails the breakdown in the abilities of individuals, families, communities and societies to sustain and care for themselves and future generations, undermining people's rights and dignity.[16]

Green economy: gender equitable and environmentally sustainable?

The idea of promoting a green economy has become popular in UN agencies as a way to address environmental sustainability and create 'green' jobs.[17] There are several variants of 'green economy', though most embrace the goal of economic growth; the difference being mainly in terms of the relative roles of public and private investment. Dominant variants of green economy assume continued, even enhanced, profit-driven economic growth, through green business investments and innovations that increase energy and resource efficiency, and prevent the loss of ecosystem services. They call for financial valuation of 'natural capital', payments for ecosystem services, and schemes for trading carbon and biodiversity credits and offsets, arguing that the problem is that markets fail to price natural assets and ecosystem services, resulting in overuse of 'natural capital'. Governments must define private property rights in ecological assets and create markets to trade them.[18] However, UNEP has a broader vision, seeing a green economy as one that ends extreme poverty, improves human well-being and enhances social equity while reducing carbon dependency and ecosystem degradation, and furthering sustainable and inclusive growth.[19]

The case for 'green' public investments was much discussed and promoted as part of the (short-lived) counter-cyclical macroeconomic policies adopted in the wake of the 2008 global recession in both developed and developing countries, often framed as a 'global green new deal' (GGND) in which government spending would be directed towards technology and employment generation in ways that enhance environmental protection and raise efficiency, for instance by retro-fitting energy-inefficient buildings or infrastructure.[20] UNEP's version of GGND emphasised the principle of common but differentiated responsibilities of developed countries, emerging economies, countries with economies in transition, and least developed countries. A 'fair and just GGND, therefore, should consider including developed countries' additional support to other countries, especially least developed countries, in the areas of finance, trade, technology and capacity building in the interest of effectiveness as well as fairness'.[21]

Gender equality has been a marginal concern in most of the green economy proposals. Given the extent of gender segregation in employment, there is a risk that efforts to 'green' industry will not only bypass women, but actually marginalise them. Sectors targeted for green employment expansion, such as energy, construction and basic industry, are very male-dominated. Among 'green' jobs that already exist, women tend to have low representation and/or occupy the lower value-added rungs. For instance, in the OECD, where women hold more than half of university degrees, only 30 per cent of degrees in science and technology (key areas for green jobs) go to women.[22] In developing economies, women are highly concentrated at the low value-added end of existing green jobs, for instance as informal workers in waste collection and recycling. However, there have been efforts to organise waste pickers worldwide, and women are more likely than men to participate in waste picker organisations, perhaps because they tend to be concentrated in lower-earning waste picking activities, and are typically paid lower rates than men for equivalent work.[23] Organised waste pickers are better able to circumvent middlemen and negotiate fair prices for their materials from buyers. There are also attempts to better incorporate waste pickers into waste management and recycling activities, countering the push towards incineration and landfill technologies, and instead promoting zero waste strategies that maximise recycling and provide decent employment for the poor.[24]

UN Women[25] has called for targeting specific skill development and education for women, and efforts to break down gender stereotypes, while at the same time pointing to several examples of new 'green' jobs that have included women. For example, in the 'Working for Water' project in South Africa, where peope were trained to remove invasive alien plants to enhance water security, successful efforts were made to specifically recruit women, youth and people with disabilities to take part. In Bangladesh, as part of a larger project to extend electricity to rural areas by installing solar home systems, women were trained to install and repair solar panels and electrical outlets, serving as 'rural electricians'. In the United States, the Women Apprenticeship in Non-traditional Occupations (WANTO) programme gives grants to community-based organisations that provide openings for women into non-traditional occupations, such as pre-apprenticeship programmes, with recent rounds emphasising green jobs.

But there are other important dimensions of a green economy besides the gender-equitable creation of green jobs. A key issue is what kinds of ways of life are supported by the goods and services produced.[26] Do they support a competitive, 'privatised' way of life, built around individual consumption, in a consumerist culture in which possessing more material goods than your neighbours is always better? No matter how energy efficient the shopping mall, no matter how many jobs, both for women and men, have been created in its construction, if this becomes the emblem of the good life, and entry into it an aspiration for all those now excluded, it is hard to see how this can be socially and environmentally sustainable, and genuinely empowering for women.

An alternative would be production that is environmentally sustainable and supports a cooperative way of life, central to which is the production of public goods that are used by all – public health, education, transport, water and sanitation, energy, streets, parks etc. Some services might be free at the point of delivery, such as health services. For others, such as water, multi-part tariffs, which charge the better off more per unit than the poor, could be used. This alternative would incorporate a substantial amount of collaborative production by non-profit institutions such as cooperatives and community enterprises; and services run by the local or national state would be organised in partnership with the users of services. For-profit production would be regulated to serve the public good, rather than the shareholders.

Conclusions

A system that supports a cooperative way of life is better equipped to take into account goods and services that are not priced and paid for in money, such as the non-market realms of nature and family care. The ability to take into account resources that are not marketed and not produced for a profit, whether unpaid work caring for family and friends, or the atmosphere and oceans; not taking them for granted as 'bottomless pits', able to absorb any demands made on them; recognising both their importance and the distinctive value of not subjecting them to a commercial calculus – all this is central to the attainment of both women's empowerment and environmental sustainability. Many environmental campaigners know a lot about how to take into account environmental resources without subjecting them to the calculus of monetary profit and loss. Many campaigners for women's empowerment know a lot about how to take into account unpaid care without subjecting it to a calculus of monetary profit and loss. The two sets of campaigns can be mutually strengthened, both in the context of UN agreements, and at national and local levels, if they work together.

2
WANJIRA MAATHAI

Green Belt Movement, Kenya

Women as drivers of forest restoration to combat climate change

Wangari Maathai, the Kenyan environmentalist and 2004 Nobel Peace Laureate, was fond of recounting a children's story she'd been told on a visit to Japan. A huge fire breaks out in the forest, runs the tale. All the animals are transfixed and overwhelmed by the conflagration. All but a hummingbird, that is, who resolves to do something about it. She flies to the nearest stream, dips her beak into it, and drops a bead of water onto the flames. The elephant, the lion, the giraffe and the other animals laugh at her, as she flies back and forth over and over again. 'You're just a tiny humming-bird,' they jeer. 'What difference do you think you can make?' And the hummingbird replies: 'I'm doing the best I can.'

For many who heard Wangari tell the story, the message of maximising our abilities and passions for the greater good rather than descending into cynicism or despair was galvanising. Wangari embraced this interpretation wholeheartedly. Yet we also knew that a more challenging, even provocative message lay within it. Personal virtue and effort aside, the parable of the hummingbird makes clear that the bird's actions are futile without the assistance of the larger animals – such as the elephant, which could, of course, carry much more water – or concerted determination on the part of all the animals to do something. But even then, whatever the animals do will likely only hold back the fire's range or mitigate its ferocity.

That message had more relevance than ever in September 2014 as hundreds of thousands of people marched in the streets of New York and more than two thousand other marches took place around the world. We demanded that our leaders take urgent action to address climate change as heads of government, industry and civil society gathered at the United Nations for an unprecedented global warming summit.

One of the most far-reaching commitments at the UN Climate Summit 2014 was the New York Declaration on Forests, a global framework that identifies ten actions to improve the world's forests.[1] One such action in the Declaration aims to restore vitality to 350 million hectares of degraded forest landscapes by 2030 – a move that could reduce emissions by up to 8.8 billion tons per year by 2030, the equivalent of taking more than two-thirds of vehicles off the roads.[2]

While forest restoration holds great promise for many countries[3], this ambitious new target is especially important for Africa. As we're already seeing, if done right, restoration could boost food and water security, improve livelihoods, and curb climate change in some of the most vulnerable regions on Earth.

Through her work with the Green Belt Movement (GBM), the organisation she founded in 1977 and which has planted more than fifty million trees throughout Kenya, Wangari Maathai understood in her bones the commitment of the hummingbird. In her case, the bird represented the grassroots women's networks who nurtured the seedlings, tended the small trees after they'd been transplanted, reforested their own land and then critical watersheds – largely unsung and underfunded. This work continues today with GBM groups growing and planting 4 million new trees in Kenya each year.

What does restoration mean for Africa?

Africa is already experiencing some of the most dramatic extreme temperature events ever seen. In 2012, 70 per cent of major droughts occurred in Africa, with more than sixteen million people affected.[4] The African continent has already warmed by about 0.5°C over the last century. The Intergovernmental Panel on Climate Change predicts worse to come – without dramatic action to reduce emissions, average annual temperature on the continent is likely to rise by 3 to 4°C by the end of this century, resulting in a 30 per cent reduction in rainfall in sub-Saharan Africa.[5]

We know that restoration could be a key part of the solution to these problems.[6] Agriculture, forestry and other land use change accounts for about one quarter of greenhouse gas emissions globally.[7] Restoring degraded lands – rather than continuing to chop down pristine forests for agriculture and other purposes – can help to both rein in warming and adapt to higher temperatures.

How do we achieve the restoration target in the Declaration?

The Declaration's restoration component will be fulfilled only if it benefits those most vulnerable to the impacts of climate change, such as rural communities throughout Africa. As Declaration signatories move forward with commitments, it's important that they keep a few things in mind:

1) It's about cooperation and planning

We now have a target, but the question is: How do all the restoration stakeholders – such as landowners, farmers, national and sub-national governments, scientists, researchers, the private sector and NGOs – feed into that target? Right now everyone is running in their own direction. We need coordinated, national efforts with a common agenda that can engender a mass restoration movement. That goes against the traditional wisdom of many NGOs and government agencies. They are used to waving their flags as high as they can because they are all struggling for the same pot of money. Restoration could be so much more effective if we worked together – including engaging local communities.

For example, the Green Belt Movement (GBM) in Kenya is working in partnership with the Clinton Climate Initiative, the government of Spain and the United Nations Environment Programme (UNEP) to restore degraded land in the Enoosupukia Forest Trust Land and the Maasai Mau Forest.[8] GBM encourages local communities to work together to plant trees in degraded areas, which helps prevent soil erosion, store rainwater, and provide food and firewood. Communities receive a small monetary token of appreciation for their work, and the trees planted help mitigate climate change by sequestering carbon. To date, more than one million trees have been planted across 1,000 hectares of degraded lands – enough to sequester 200,000 tons of carbon dioxide.

Yet this is a drop in the ocean – we need urgently to scale these efforts up to create an impact on a planetary scale. The science, knowledge, capacity and commitment already exist. The missing piece is the collaboration between partners. And we need increased technology transfer and finance to facilitate the process.

2) It's about matching science with policy

Existing structures and government policies don't necessarily facilitate restoration. For example, Kenya uses the 'non-resident cultivation' method for forest plantation development. The concept is based on farmers shifting cultivation to new areas, so they do not have rights to the land they till. In theory, under this system, farmers cultivate crops in agroforestry systems for a period of three years, after which time the trees dominate the sites and cultivation is no longer possible, so farmers move to other land. In reality, farmers often restrict tree growth so they can stay in those fields longer.

This has led to land being degraded and to a massive deficit in national tree planting. Scientists and policy-makers need to work together to understand the right balance for both forestry and agriculture, society and the environment – all of which need to coexist across landscapes. Governments need to be more than experts in signing treaties; they also need to facilitate action on the ground.

3) It's about women

Women in Africa are often responsible for providing their households with the basic necessities of life – food, fuel and water. Biomass such as wood and forest products provides 80 per cent of the primary domestic energy supply in Africa.[9] This exploits forests and degrades land. It's also hard on women – GBM was founded to respond to the needs of rural Kenyan women, who reported that their streams were drying up, their food supply was less secure, and they had to walk further and further to get firewood for fuel and fencing.

Historically men own the land in the majority of Kenyan counties. Today most rural women still do not own land and are often not invited to decision-making meetings on land use. During times of drought, women must travel further and work longer to meet subsistence needs – collecting water in Samburu and Kajiado can take much of the day, as women may need to travel 20 kilometres. Thus climate change increases the already heavy burdens placed on women.

Climate change requires that women and men have access to information that enables them to deal with an uncertain environment. GBM has recognised the need to build capacity in both women and men to reduce conflict and foster greater understanding of the challenges facing women, so that they have the opportunity to start adaptation initiatives with the support of their husbands and communities.

GBM is a partner in the wPOWER initiative, launched by the US State Department, which is empowering women in seven countries to play major roles in the renewable energy value chain by producing, using and marketing more efficient cooking stoves and solar lighting products. The initiative is working with women to restore landscapes and provide fast-growing alternatives, such as bamboo, to reduce pressure on forests as a source of fuel and charcoal. Bamboo not only sequesters carbon, it also provides the raw materials for a myriad of commercial products.[10] Women can help drive the restoration movement with entrepreneurship in green energy.

So communities (rural and urban) cut down fewer trees, burn less kerosene and inhale less poisonous fumes. In this way, fewer greenhouse gases are released, forests are protected, indoor air quality is improved along with health, and women earn their own income; as a result, they and their children have more opportunities to learn and thrive. The wPOWER 'Hub' or nodal point is housed at the Wangari Maathai Institute for Peace and Environmental Studies at the University of Nairobi.

The women entrepreneurs of wPOWER, like the women tree-planters of the GBM networks, along with millions of others like them, know all too well the consequences of very non-metaphorical forest fires: drought, desertification, hunger, and water and fuel-wood scarcity. They are feeling the 'heat' of climate change right now. This heat wasn't of their own making, yet they are suffering disproportionately from it.

Women are often on the front lines of environmental challenges – not just as victims, but as a critical force for sustainably managing natural resources and increasing energy access, which helps to combat climate change, and improve livelihoods and community health. By building skills that improve women's participation in and influence on environmental governance we can build climate resilience, helping establish cultures of peace and improving community energy access.

4) It's about communication

We must ensure that legislators and media are well informed, equipped and engaged. With the right information, journalists can spread the word to the public and legislators can create policies that foster the right environment for the restoration agenda to succeed. We cannot do it without them.

From international commitment to real action

The New York Declaration on Forests provides the big picture. At the community level, we're already seeing the benefits of restoring landscapes. Now we need to scale successes across Africa – and across the world – through cooperation and good planning, matching science with policy, gender empowerment and strong communications. It's time to work together to start a restoration revolution.

We may interpret the hummingbird story as a message for us to reduce, reuse, recycle; to cut down on our car travel, switch to green energy for our homes, or eat less meat and more vegetables as our contribution to dousing the fire. These are all valid responses to the realities of global warming, but they won't be enough. The hummingbird story can be read as a parable of tragic inaction, a failure of the collective will.

Climate change will not be mitigated, let alone stopped or reversed, unless all the countries of the world become serious about systemic, total and orchestrated reorientations of their economies and our ways of living on the Earth. The historic emitters must take the lead, but the new 'climate powers' – the large current greenhouse gas producers – need to join them.

And that means recognising one of Wangari's other messages about why we are despoiling our environment and entrenching poverty: a lack of good governance. For the thirty years that she was urging us to plant trees to stop soil erosion, retain water and store carbon, Wangari was also insisting that accountable political structures that used resources (whether capital, natural or human) equitably and responsibly were essential.

The need for good governance isn't confined to Africa or the global South. Corruption, greed and faith in short-term pay-offs, Wangari insisted, knew no boundaries, weren't confined to certain industries or multinational corporations, and infected every stratum of society. Indeed she reminded us often: political leadership and good policy matter.

The hummingbird challenges us to organise, to hold our political leaders and global industries accountable and demand that they, and we, accept the potential difficulties, even sacrifices, that we'll have to make to transition from a fossil-fuel and extractive global system to one organised around genuine sustainability and responsibility. We can't assume that someone or something else will put out that fire for us at some point in the future.

The hummingbird challenges us to stanch the fire that's been created in our own patch of forest – the Earth itself – no matter the perceived futility of the action or the passivity of those standing by who could do more through collective action, but choose not to.

3

LYLA MEHTA and MELISSA LEACH

Institute of Development Studies,
University of Sussex

Why do gender equality and sustainability go hand in hand?[1]

Gender inequality and patterns of unsustainability

Dominant patterns of development have not delivered. In a world that is ever more globalised and interconnected, poverty and inequality are increasing, not decreasing. Ecological shocks such as floods, droughts, polluted land and oceans, destroyed landscapes and livelihoods are creating deep threats to the well-being and survival of future generations. These ecological changes are particularly affecting a third of the world's population directly dependent on natural resources for their livelihoods and well-being.[2] Furthermore, every day thousands of children die from waterborne diseases, more than a billion people go hungry, more than a thousand die in pregnancy and childbirth, and many lack the secure, decent jobs they need to provide dignified lives for themselves and their families. The poorest 20 per cent of the world's population control only just over 2 per cent of global income.[3] The recent multiple crises of climate, food, finance and resource scarcities also indicate that neoliberal market-driven processes have largely failed. There needs to be a refocus on the problems arising out of unfettered growth and unsustainable patterns of production and consumption on the part of the rich and the middle classes around the world, as well as the negative impacts of extractive and polluting industries and manufacturing.[4] These deeply interlocked economic, social and environmental problems point to a crisis of unsustainability. They also indicate that unsustainability and its counter, sustainability, need to be recast and reanimated as political terms that can help us recognise and tackle the drivers that have led to the current predicament, and spur vigorous debate and action towards more prosperous and just futures for all.

Since the 1992 United Nations Conference on Environment and Development (UNCED) there has been widespread acknowledgement that sustainable development is not possible without gender equality. Despite several differences in the various conceptual debates around gender and the environment (e.g. ecofeminist, Women, Environment and Development (WED), Gender, Environment and Development (GED) and feminist political ecology, FPE), there is now a wide consensus that the environment and sustainable development are not gender neutral. They are shaped by and shape gender relations which in turn determine environmental outcomes. Feminists and gender analysts have also called for a radical rethinking of capitalist modes of production and consumption as well as the social justice and equity concerning resource use. In sum, without gender justice there can be no environmental justice or sustainability.[5] Thus, it is surprising that despite much of the progress made in the 1990s on firmly placing gender on the map of sustainable development issues, current high-level debates on the green economy, planetary boundaries and the Anthropocene have been surprisingly gender blind and not adequately radically transformative.[6] This chapter highlights some of the fault lines in current global thinking, in particular from a gender and social justice perspective, before highlighting alternative pathways to sustainability that promote both social and gender justice.

Whose Anthropocene and who sets the boundaries?

Highly influential currently is the rise of scientific concepts and arguments centred on notions of the *Anthropocene and 'planetary boundaries'*. These concepts are grounded in an emerging set of earth system sciences suggesting that we have entered a new geological epoch, the Anthropocene, in which human activities have become the dominant driver of many earth system processes, including climate, bio-geochemical cycles, ecosystems and biodiversity. The extent of human influence, driven by intensifying material production and consumption, has grown rapidly since the Industrial Revolution and has accelerated dramatically since the 1950s (see the following section). A series of nine planetary boundaries has been identified, referring to the biophysical processes in the Earth's systems on which human life depends.[7] Together, these serve to keep the planet within Holocene-like conditions and thus define a safe operating space for humanity. Potentially catastrophic thresholds are in prospect, it is argued, which will compromise development both globally and locally. It is thus urgent that development pathways reconnect with the biosphere's capacity to sustain them.[8]

While the science is still developing, the concept of planetary boundaries has been rapidly taken up within policy debates, including those around Rio+20. Yet many actors, including developing country governments, have contested the concept, interpreting it as anti-growth and anti-development. Some suggest that planetary boundaries bring a return to 'limits to growth' thinking and a privileging of global environmental over local concerns, justifying top-down interventions that protect the environment at the expense of people and their livelihoods. It is also worth asking: who defines which boundaries and for whom? Boundaries at local and regional scales will be different from global ones; women and men and rich and poor people will define boundaries differently. That steering development within planetary boundaries should not compromise inclusive development that respects human rights has been proposed by Raworth,[9] whose 'doughnut' concept takes the circle of planetary boundaries and adds an inner circle, representing a 'social foundation'. In between these is a 'safe and just operating space' for humanity, within which development must take place. Yet even this fails to address the possible divergences and trade-offs between some people's notions of a good life and visions for the future, and scientifically defined environmental limits. Meanwhile, the new, neo-Malthusian narratives of impending scarcity and catastrophe implied by some interpretations of planetary boundaries arguments risk justifying a return to draconian policies and unjust responses that limit people's rights and freedoms. To date, and with the exception of Raworth,[10] who introduces 'gender equality' as one dimension of the 'social foundation' of humanity's safe and just operating space, discussion and advocacy arising from the planetary boundaries concept has been gender blind.

Green economies: business as usual?

The idea of '*green economies*' is capturing the attention of governments, businesses and NGOs alike. According to UNEP, which launched its Green Economy Initiative in 2008, a green economy is 'one that results in improved human well-being and social equity, while significantly reducing environmental risks and ecological scarcities. In its simplest expression, a green economy can be thought of as one which is low carbon, resource efficient and socially inclusive'.[11] Although this would appear to demand an integration of environment, economy and social development no different from other conceptualisations of sustainable development, in policy and practice green economy thinking has come to drive a particular range of approaches. These include a focus on business and private sector action, albeit motivated and regulated by the public sector, in investments, technologies and innovations that enhance energy and resource efficiency, and prevent the loss of ecosystem services. There are opportunities to deliver profit, employment and environmental sustainability at the same time in forms of 'green growth', it is claimed, provided investments are correctly targeted. Indeed, it is argued that the emerging green tech economy – in areas such as renewable energy – will be worth $4.2 trillion annually by the year 2020.[12]

While these approaches assume that continued economic growth can be reshaped in green directions, others argue that environmental constraints will require much-reduced rates of growth – or even no growth – as well as different types of growth. Thus

Jackson[13] argues for a shift in economic thinking and strategy to emphasise the pursuit not of growth, but of prosperity and well-being. Investments in services and care, as well as in 'green' action in the areas of sustainable food production and marketing and clean energy, are seen as key. These arguments link with growing debate around alternative economies and solidarity economies,[14] drawing on evidence from mostly local-scale modes of organising, and social movement activism, around the world. Green economy thinking also calls for a focus on maintaining and enhancing natural capital, supported by valuation and accounting measures that build on, but extend, the environmental economics work of the 1990s,[15] and on market-based approaches to environmental protection. The latter include an array of schemes to value and trade aspects of ecosystems now (re)defined as commodities to include schemes for trading carbon credits and offsetting emissions, such as those associated with clean energy, forests and agriculture under the CDM, UN-REDD and voluntary schemes. While livelihood benefits to local people are often claimed, it is highly variable whether these are realised in practice. Critics point to mounting evidence of such financialisation and commoditisation of ecosystems being linked with forms of land and resource dispossession, or land, water and green grabs.[16] Little wonder, then, that many women's organisations from around the world have resolutely rejected this concept.

While green investments and technologies are important areas, questions of justice and social values are often missing in the debate. Thus narrow forms of financial value – on ecosystems and resources – overlook social and cultural values, including those that have emerged from the long coexistence of people and ecosystems. And attention to the differentiated social – and gender – implications of 'decoupled' and green economies – and even prosperity-focused care economies – is often lacking. Not addressed is whose priorities count, and who may gain or lose from the resulting policies and interventions. Also, even though there is some mention of MDG3 on gender equality, the Green Economy Report makes no mention of the differentiated impacts of the green economy on men and men and what exactly the transition to the new economic model will mean for different groups of women and men.[17]

Critics see the green economy concept as one that continues with the business-as-usual gobal economic model which is the root cause of global environmental destruction, social exploitation and inequality.[18] It has also been criticised for being a market-based approach that justifies the commodification and enclosure of resources, and carbon schemes such as REDD that undermine local livelihoods, justify land grabs and also displace local people, especially women subsistence farmers who comprise most of the food producers in developing countries.[19] In all the recent approaches outlined above, we find an overly technocentric and economistic focus; in different ways, each opens the way for either a techno-regulatory, top-down style of development, or a neoliberal market-led one. At the same time, new and problematic narratives of environmental catastrophe and crisis are afoot. Underplayed are questions of power, and of social values, distribution and justice – including gender – both in how problems of sustainability emerge and how they, and responses to them, are experienced.

By contrast a gender-equitable sustainable development framework would combine care economy and green economy approaches to address the exploitation of women's largely unpaid care work and also question the use of natural resources and the environment as an inexhaustible source of productive inputs. There has also been new work from feminist economists and analysts reinvigorating earlier critiques of the separation between production and social reproduction and the power relations that uphold these.[20] There are also calls to replace efficiency with sufficiency,[21] with sharing, redistribution and 'commoning' as the guiding principles. By a so-called 'caring economy' feminists are calling for a redistribution of labour and value creation that goes beyond the market, efficiency and remuneration[22] and for a new conception of what constitutes 'the good'. All these different strands are calling for a new transformatory politics that will lead to different pathways across different scales, like those being advocated by 'green economy' and planetary boundary specialists.

Pathways to gender equality and sustainability

If one thing is clear from this account of recent thinking, policy and practice, it is that sustainability and sustainable development are political. Dimensions regarding what to prioritise, and what actions are undertaken (or not), are all subject to diverse interests and perspectives, and are thus contested. Sometimes contestation is across spatial scales, as when global and local priorities conflict; sometimes across timescales, as when governments struggle to reconcile long-term environmental agendas with short-term domestic interests and political cycles; and sometimes between social groups with diverse positions and values. Even if not explicit at the outset, such contestations have often proved to undermine even the best-conceived sustainable development policies and programmes. This means that sustainable development policy and practice cannot simply proceed as a technical and managerial exercise, but must embrace a more normative, politicised approach.

There are also gender-related problems around different approaches to sustainable development and gender that need to be avoided. In the name of environmental protection, local women and men have sometimes been dispossessed from their lands, forests and water resources; problematic linkages between women and nature have led to the essentialisation of the roles of women as so-called 'carers' of nature, and they have been made responsible for environmental chores that have drawn on their voluntary labour. Such past mistakes and pitfalls must definitely be avoided in future.

Linking gender equality and sustainable development is therefore vital for several reasons. First, this is a moral and ethical imperative: building more equitable gender relations that support the human rights, dignity and capabilities of women, intersected by differences of class, race, sexuality, age, ability and circumstances, is a central requirement of an ethical world order. Secondly, to avoid women becoming victims, the all-too-common pattern whereby women suffer most from environmental, climatic and economic shocks and stresses, undermining their vital roles in sustaining their families and communities, must be redressed. But thirdly, and most significantly, it is vital to build on women's agency. Attention to gender offers routes to improving resource productivity and efficiency, to enhancing ecosystem conservation and sustainable use, and to building more sustainable, low-carbon food, energy, water and health systems. Not just victims, women have been and can be central actors in pathways to sustainability and green transformation. Yet crucially, this must not mean adding 'environment' to women's caring roles, or instrumentalising women as the new 'sustainability saviours'. It means recognition of and respect for their knowledge, rights, capabilities and bodily integrity, and ensuring that roles are matched with rights and control over resources and decision-making power. Here we respond to a growing consensus that gender equality and sustainable development can thus reinforce each other, in powerful ways.[23] Also, attending to gender differences and relations provides a vital lens on and way to address the social and political, as well as economic and environmental, challenges and opportunities that must be core to pursuing sustainable development, and highlights ways that women can be powerful agents of green transformation. Finally, gender-focused and feminist analysts and movements have long provided strong and radical alternatives to patterns of unsustainability that promote gender inequalities, as well as other forms of injustice. They call for a reimagining of sustainability in which gender equality is a key element, and provide powerful tools to enable such alternative imaginaries and transformations.

The concept of pathways helps to capture this. Pathways are the alternative directions in which social, technological, economic and environmental systems might co-evolve.[24] Pathways are shaped by values, by selective kinds of knowledge, and by power. They can encompass particular policies, projects and interventions. It is clear that dominant pathways of change – the motorways, to extend the analogy, of global development – are moving in directions that are thoroughly unsustainable and not enhancing gender or social justice. Challenging such current unsustainable pathways, and identifying and building alternative pathways to sustainability that embrace gender equality, is the challenge of our age.

The pathways approach helps in conceptualising how institutions, power and knowledge can interact to create and sustain
pathways that are either unsustainable or – alternatively – offer
routes to sustainable development. Thus a local example might be
the interactions of water and food, gender divisions of labour and
responsibility, and different water management systems (including
irrigation) that provide water for productive users. Nationally,
we might be concerned with the interactions of state policies and
markets involved in food systems. And a global example might be
the interactions of dynamic climate processes with international
regulation, carbon market schemes and finance aimed at curbing
greenhouse gas emissions and impacts. Yet most sustainability
challenges involve interactions across scales. Thus we might be
concerned with the impacts of global climate processes on local
land ecologies and uses, or with the ways that household, state
and market institutions interact to shape the dynamics of food and
water access. For gender equality to flourish, pathways therefore
need to generate multiple capabilities and freedoms that go beyond
basic material needs and rights. They also need to include opportunity and process freedoms that allow people to convert resources
to multiple capabilities.[25] The hope is that these then feed back to
sustain ongoing processes of pathway generation and maintenance
that further reinforce sustainable development and gender justice.
But this will often not be a linear process; there will be unexpected
events, opportunities and setbacks, to which people, institutions
and ecologies will need to adapt and respond. Also, pathways, by
virtue of their dynamic nature, have unintended social, technological and environmental consequences which also affect outcomes in
terms of gender (in)equality. Thus, it is important to build inclusive
learning and deliberation processes and ways to monitor exclusion,
trade-offs and emerging opportunities.

Fortunately, this is a time of opportunities. Alternative concepts
such as 'Buen Vivir' and 'Sufficiency Economy' are being proposed
in different parts of the global South. There are many alternative pathways to sustainability and gender equality but these are
currently unrecognised. They exist in urban and rural spaces where

women and men make and sustain their livelihoods, in women's cooperatives and movements, in the writings of feminist scholars and in the margins of bureaucracies and global institutions. We need to seek out these champions and create conceptual and policy space for their ideas and practices that can powerfully challenge the logic of '*Homo economicus*' and dominant patterns of consumption and production that are promoting structural inequalities and unsustainability. These alternatives need ultimately to merge care and dominant economy approaches to create a green transformation that is gender and socially equitable. To do this, challenging power relations in both formal and informal realms and transforming institutions in the process through a nimble insider–outsider positioning and politics of gender-progressive alliance-building will be essential. After all, feminists have always been the ones to provide the most trenchant critiques of dominant thinking and ways of life, usually from the margins. It is now time to reclaim those margins and promote new ways of being.

4

CAROLINE LUCAS
UK Green Party MP

Is there a specific role for women in helping to achieve environmental sustainability through politics?

> We are not meek and we are not weak. We are angry – on our own behalf, for our sisters and children who suffer, and for the entire planet – and we are determined to protect life on Earth.
>
> Petra Kelly, German Green MP (1947–1992)

It was a potent image.

Just a woman in jeans, arms laden with sunflowers, a beaming smile.

But to me, it encapsulated a great deal. The woman's name was Petra Kelly, a founder of the German Green Party. The image captured her entry into parliament on her first day as a Green MP.

It represented to me a new kind of politics, politics as something personal – as everything we do from the moment we awake, as all the choices we make, as people-centred.

Certainly Petra was the greatest inspiration of my political life, and a person you might say summed up the Green movement. She embodied feminism, peace, activism, and inspiration – an amazing politician. She had a formidable intellect, spoke passionately of the Green Party as the 'anti-Party Party' – a party that went beyond the usual party politics, embracing grassroots democracy and non-violent direct action.

And here she was, a woman, a Green – an elected MP.

It gave me tremendous hope. It made me feel bolder – and Westminster somehow closer.

I've taken great inspiration from the pioneers like Petra, who, when faced with fierce opposition, even ridicule, persevered and pushed for change regardless. When finally I found myself within Westminster's halls – a Green MP in the heart of the British Parliament – their wisdom impressed itself upon me more than ever.

It's often been said that it's not easy being a woman in politics. I think perhaps it's harder still when your work centres on a passion for people and planet. But I firmly believe that women do have a specific role in helping to achieve environmental sustainability. And I believe we can do so through politics.

But Parliament's priorities are thoroughly back-to-front. We have £500 billion to bail out the banks in the financial crisis, £100 billion for a new nuclear deterrent system. But when it comes to protecting our most precious assets, to preventing catastrophic climate change – to talking sustainability, renewables, emissions reduction targets and eliminating fuel poverty – political will (and resourcing) swiftly diminishes. We only have one planet and, according to the latest Intergovernmental Panel on Climate Change report, a limited time frame to prevent the irreversible impacts of climate change upon it.

The mandate is clear and urgent, and successive governments have gone to great lengths to be seen as Green. But when it comes to driving through substantive change, the appetite evaporates.

Prime Minister David Cameron dubbed climate change 'the biggest threat facing Britain and the world' during the 2013 winter floods – yet it's been unapologetically disregarded as the domain of anti-business types, madcap revolutionaries, idealists – and feminists.

I think of the wonderful marine biologist Rachel Carson, whose groundbreaking book *Silent Spring* was one of the most influential ever written on the environment and ecology. Which inevitably incited the wrath of the major chemical corps it challenged. Carson was publicly ridiculed, threatened with legal action and labelled 'a spinster' and 'hysterical'.

But the undeniable quality of her peer-reviewed research withstood the predictably gendered smear campaigns and it's hard to overstate the book's legacy.

Part fairy story and part meticulous study, *Silent Spring* breathed life into science, making academia not only accessible but *unputdownable*. Its message went viral (or the 1960s equivalent of), tangibly shifting the public (and eventually political) perception of environmental concerns.

In the UK alone, it helped spark the creation of PEOPLE, which, in the 1970s, developed into the Ecology Party, which grew into the Green Party. It has informed much of my own work – as an activist, an MEP in Brussels and an MP in my Brighton constituency and Westminster.

In the male-dominated fields of politics and science, Petra Kelly and Rachel Carson influenced – even shifted – entrenched patterns of thought. They didn't 'step outside the box': they re-formed it from within.

In her narrative Carson irrevocably altered our understanding of the fundamental yet fragile connection between person and planet. Kelly, with incredible passion, connected planet and person with politics. Their ideas and uncompromising courage of conviction challenged the status quo and, in time, altered minds and hearts globally.

They were creative, innovative, dynamic forces to be reckoned with. But they had to be – their gender compelled it – as women in their fields, they had to work harder, and their work had to be flawless. They were human, humble, passionate about people and planet – qualities which, I believe, helped capture public imagination, ensuring their theories took flight and their legacy endured: and environmental sustainability took a determined step forward.

Both were unique talents. But one might argue that gender played a role in their success – that their very experiences as women contributed to their worldview and thus their work. Were they simply brilliant women, or did their brilliance stem in part from being women?

And if it's the case that the hand we're dealt as women – our unique experiences – can be a tool to our advantage, can we do more to harness that, develop it, as politicians and activists for the environmental cause, to stand on equal footing in our so very patriarchal halls of power and further our cause?

Women and leadership

Kelly's thoughts on women and power have deeply influenced the way I approach my work in Westminster. I love this quote from her, connecting feminism, activism and leadership:

Feminism seeks to redefine our very modes of existence and to transform non-violently the structures of male dominance. I am not saying that women are inherently better than men. Overturning patriarchy doesn't mean replacing men's dominance with women's dominance. That would merely maintain the patriarchal pattern of dominance. We need to transform the patriarchal pattern itself.

The work of feminist women and pro-feminist men is to liberate everyone from a system that is oppressive to women and restrictive to men, and to restore balance and harmony between women and men, and between masculine and feminine values in society and within each of us. Feminists working in the peace and ecology movements are sometimes viewed as kind, nurturing Earth mothers, but that is too comfortable a stereotype. We are not meek and we are not weak. We are angry – on our own behalf, for our sisters and children who suffer, and for the entire planet – and we are determined to protect life on Earth.

There is a saying: Where power is, women are not. Women must be willing to be powerful. Because we bear scars from the way men have used their power over us, women often want no part of power.

But playing an active part in society, on an equal footing with men, does not mean adopting the old thought patterns and strategies of the patriarchal world. It means putting our own ideas of an emancipatory society into practice. Rather

> than emulating Margaret Thatcher and others who loyally
> adapt themselves to male values of hierarchy we must find
> our own definitions of power that reflects women's values
> and women's experience [...] This is not power over others,
> but power with others, the kind of shared power that has to
> replace patriarchal power.

I think that applies across the board – from Parliament to grassroots
environmental campaigns.

It's undeniable that women have to work harder to get heard.
And we cannot hope to be heard, to change climate policy, if we are
unable or willing to embrace power. And I don't mean mimicking
the old structures designed to oppress rather than liberate, much
less empower, us – but embracing that which sets us apart, those
uniquely female experiences which contribute to our view of the
world and our place in it.

Our political power structures are patriarchal. Just watch Prime
Minister's Questions (it's even worse in person); saturated with
sexism, with audible comments about the way women look.

What it if were more gender balanced?

More female MPs wouldn't necessarily make for a more
compassionate, friendly Parliament. But it would diversify politics
and (as any ecologist will tell you) diversity is the key to strength,
and survival. And such a change is long overdue.

I don't necessarily think women are better at selfless giving, but
perhaps there really is something born of our unique experience
which is advantageous in using power well and in furthering the
environmental cause.

Perhaps the extent to which women have had less power – or,
as Kelly says, because we 'bear scars from the way men have used
their power over us' – we're more aware of the sensitivities in using
it over others, over nature. Furthermore, perhaps the female experience of fighting for the right to be heard in politics – national,
local, grassroots – makes us naturally better equipped to fight for a
cause that has also traditionally been neglected, ridiculed even, in
politics. I don't suggest that we are innately or inevitably (or always

– think Margaret Thatcher) programmed this way, but that as a result of our experience in a patriarchal world, we can empathise with a neglected cause – and, one might argue, will more naturally be drawn to it in the first instance.

I'm reminded of a conference I attended, on the subject of climate change. It'd been organised by a woman and every speaker was female. She said to me at the time, 'I got so fed up with going to meetings where the best person to speak on merit would have been a particular woman who, often, would be sat in the audience.'

Speaking at that conference was great. It felt less competitive, more honest – with people saying much more about what they felt about the subjects, not just what they thought – and as a result it felt more balanced. None of those things are intrinsically tied to the fact the event was dominated by women but, given our culture, it's more likely that a high proportion of women will shift the nature of any dialogue or debate.

Women were not being favoured as speakers simply because of their gender – they were given a platform because they were the most capable, most compelling and probably the most overlooked too.

Perhaps a more gender-equal Parliament would make politics more like a public service, less self-serving and elitist. Perhaps one of the reasons more women don't stand for election to Parliament is because politics has become something all too many people consider as a career – rather than a way to make a difference.

Collaboration

In the European Parliament, where a third of MEPs are women, I virtually forgot about gender. The work culture was far more conducive for a woman – far less grandstanding, more cooperation. Compromise wasn't a dirty word but a noble pursuit of common ground. In Westminster, you're in a noticeable minority in every committee, in every debate. We have some fantastic female voices there, but they're woefully under-represented.

We won the right to sit in the House in 1918 but since that time just 369 women MPs have done so – yet in Parliament right now, there are over five hundred male MPs. Ours is supposed to be the mother of all parliaments: yet just 28 per cent of MPs are women. Afghanistan tops us in that poll.

Green politics sets store by gender balance and advocates a different ethos of leadership and power that, I think, sits far more comfortably with the European Parliament than our own patriarchal version – and I think Westminster can learn a great deal from it.

It stresses collaboration over competition. It's about making a difference, not climbing ladders. It emphasises balance.

To be alone and in conflict with all would be hopelessly ineffective. I collaborate across parties very well, and perhaps that's down to a number of things – my politics, my own ethos, my experience in the European Parliament, a sense of urgency in the face of climate change, my gender.

But the culture, vested interests and workaday rules of Westminster are rigged against women – against anyone, in fact, trying to do things a bit differently.

Politically independent community leaders are disadvantaged because we don't have a proportional voting system.

And without state funding for political parties the 'old boys' networks continue to thrive along with every other bloated symbol of the status quo – a status quo that has been built by men and, I'd argue, depends upon the continued disenfranchisement of women.

Changes are creeping in – prior to 1987 women had never made up more than 5 per cent of MPs.

But Westminster has always dragged its feet. We need to keep fighting for reform, challenge the establishment and make the system fairer, more balanced.

And politics isn't confined to Parliament. It's everything we do, and something we are. Grassroots activism in the UK is blooming: creative, dynamic, resilient, resourceful, passionate – and highly influential.

Like Petra, my own involvement in party politics was sparked by activism, particularly around the Campaign for Nuclear Disarmament (CND) in the 1980s, and I was involved in the CND protests at Molesworth and at Greenham Common. I supported other causes too, but it was reading *Seeing Green* by Jonathan Porritt in 1986 that suddenly made clear to me how all these issues were underpinned by the political process. The Green Party offered a political solution which recognised the connections and stood for real and necessary change.

But one of the things I love most about the Green Party is that it has never broken from its activist origins. It embraces grassroots and established political systems as complementary – their collaboration as necessary to achieving real change.

Parliament can learn much from that; from the best examples of grassroots democracy and non-violent direct action, historic and contemporary.

Deeds not words

Were the suffragettes a group of unusually brilliant, creative women – or did their experiences as women influence the movement and make them brilliant?

They knew all about being ignored and excluded – and all about fighting back. True experts of direct action, on one occasion two women posted themselves as human letters to Downing Street; on another, they boarded a boat and unfurled banners opposite the terrace of Parliament. They boycotted the census, on the grounds that 'if women don't count, neither shall they be counted'.

They taught us how to find our voice, and use it. To constantly speak up and speak out.

To be courageous.

But perhaps, more than anything, we can take from them a passionate commitment to never give up.

The fantastic Tamsin Omond, a founding member of activist group Climate Rush, has been heavily inspired in her work by the suffragette movement. What a great example of an exciting and influential political independent trying to do things a bit differently. And she's not alone – just skimming the landscape of grassroots campaigning shows the influence women have – from Anita Roddick, founder of the Body Shop, to the EveryDay Sexism and No More Page 3 campaigns.

The suffragettes won us the vote. We can sit in the House. The Commons belongs to us – but still it's controlled by a privileged male elite and their vested whims. We need to change that. To make it easier for voices like Tamsin's – and others – to be counted, and make Parliament truly representative and accountable to the people.

A hundred years ago, Emmeline Pankhurst said, 'to be able to be militant is a privilege'. She was right, and now is the time to use our voices, collectively, to speak out to prevent our government from sleepwalking into climate catastrophe.

Too often our efforts are disjointed, and we're the weaker for it. We must collaborate much more.

Canadian author and social activist Naomi Klein – a bona fide rabble-rouser for change – consistently and convincingly connects the dots: between politics and people, financial chaos and climate chaos – and advocates a joined-up strategy for change. Campaigners should unite, she says, because the root of our problem is the same: unrestrained corporate greed. There's an urgency to this fight and it's a battle we must win. To do so, we must recognise and respond as one, 'weaving' our fights into 'a common narrative'.

Her fuss-free, commonsense take on people, planet and politics captures imaginations and wins debates hands down.

Feeling as a catalyst

And – simple though it may sound – I believe a great deal of what we're seeking boils down to something so simple, it's almost counter-intuitive: feeling.

Why is it that we're so squeamish about discussing how we *feel* about the climate crisis?

Perhaps it's that such a traditionally female attribute is equated with weakness; and emotion as an absence of reason – another legacy of a patriarchal power structure.

But only by talking through how we feel will we manage to dig deep enough to find the creativity and innovation that are needed to respond effectively to what many now recognise is the biggest threat facing humankind.

We need to find the courage to look the crisis in the face and genuinely connect with it on an emotional basis, without flinching.

I remember how, when I first heard that there had been a record loss of summer sea ice, and that greenhouse gas concentrations in the atmosphere were at their highest point for possibly 800,000 years, it felt like a physical kick in the stomach. I felt literally winded, short of breath – and very tearful.

There is such a thing as too late, and the idea haunts me.

But if facing the true horror of what we are doing to our climate is a prerequisite to generating the political will to act – to move from the elegiac to the practical – how do we equip ourselves to do so?

Not without hope.

Hope is a potent catalyst, far more so, I'd argue, than fear. And while our failure to adequately appreciate and guard against ecological destruction fills me with frustration – and sometimes despair – my hope, as Petra Kelly might say, is not meek or weak. It is urgent and raging, and I think that's helped, rather than hindered, me in getting heard as an MP and campaigner.

It's a hope that believes a better world – away from cyclical war, the annihilation of the earth's treasures and the grinding down of the poor and marginal – is possible.

And in my book, that's a worth a fight.

We need to actively choose a better future – and make it happen. Martin Luther King had a dream, not a nightmare, and we need that same vision today. We need to harness the transformative power of hope, so it can be turned into creative and innovative solutions.

Nature is full of inspirations, and not for nothing did sunflowers fill Petra Kelly's arms as she entered the German parliament. The most powerful ideas grow in strength with the right energy, motivation. Heads turned to the sun, these flowers reach sturdily up, improbably high, towards a promise of something better.

It's a simple idea, but remains a deeply radical one: that if we decide we want a different kind of future, we can reach it. That just making the commitment can be the catalyst we need.

But every voice counts. We must reclaim politics as everything we do. And – lobbyist, activist, international NGO or MP – cooperation between us is crucial. Being powerful *with* one another – living out the wonderful words of Robert F. Kennedy:

> Each time someone stands up for an ideal, or acts to improve the lot of others, or strikes out against injustice, she sends forth a tiny ripple of hope, and crossing each other from a million different centres of energy and daring, those ripples build a current which can sweep down the mightiest walls of oppression and resistance.

Or, to quote the wisdom of Dr Seuss, in his excellent book *The Lorax*:

> Unless someone like you cares a whole awful lot, nothing is going to get better. It's not.

5

SUSAN BUCKINGHAM

Feminist geographer, Brunel University

The institutionalisation and masculinisation of environmental knowledge

This chapter considers how universities and the knowledge produced within them are gendered, and the likely impacts of this on environmental decision-making. I review how masculinism dominates higher education, particularly in subjects which are most environmentally influential, and suggest that this matters for a number of reasons. Women experience disproportionate negative environmental impacts compared with men, are more likely to express greater concern for environmental problems, and more inclined to mitigate those problems at the domestic and community scales, where they have some decision-making power. However, because women are poorly represented in larger-scale decision-making, the nature of decisions taken at the national and global scales are constrained and unrepresentative. Of course, whether or not having gender balanced decision-making makes a difference to all this, there is still a gender justice case for women to take their fair share, though, as this chapter will argue, representative decision-making needs to include women (and men) with different backgrounds and life experiences.

I write as an academic who has followed a broadly (though not entirely) conventional career path: studying and lecturing on geography and researching and writing about environmental issues. Before achieving my professorship, I was relatively unencumbered with caring responsibilities. Since then, caring for an increasing frail parent gave me some insights into the lives of (mostly, though not exclusively, women) colleagues who have made compromises in their promising careers so that they could spend time with their children and adult relatives for whom they care. I have combined my academic responsibilities with environmental activism in the Women's Environmental Network, which, as an erstwhile trustee and chair, I represented from time to time in national fora. This impressed on me just how masculinist the mainstream environmental movement is, not to mention politics and environmental businesses more generally. The arguments in this chapter emanate from these experiences, as well as the research I have conducted and supervised over the years. As I will discuss, I am both cautiously optimistic about the potential for change, as well as daunted by the scope of work to be done to achieve this.

Institutions of education

The eco-feminist writer Carolyn Merchant observed how, since the Enlightenment, knowledge has increasingly become the preserve of experts, and experts (predominantly men) have become increasingly specialised. In the UK we specialise early: those who stay on beyond compulsory education are limited to studying three or four subjects at advanced (A) level, and if they apply to university, these will determine what courses they will be able to follow. This is particularly so in subjects which have an explicitly environmental bias, such as environmental management, engineering (in which transport, energy, waste management and water expertise mostly lie), ecology and so on. These undergraduate degrees mostly demand A-levels in maths and sciences, and these subjects are heavily dominated by male students, biology being the exception (8 per cent of all female A-level students taking this compared with 6.9 per cent of all male students). Almost twice as many males as females take maths, and more than four times as many males as females take physics. The gap is narrower in chemistry with 5.4 per cent of all female students taking the A-level compared to 6.9 per cent of all male students.[1]

The so called 'STEM' subjects (science, technology, engineering and mathematics) are the most lucrative, earning universities higher government financial contributions per student; and securing more PhD and research funding.[2] It is often these subjects, through their financial advantage, which dominate the character of universities. And they dominate the decision-making which shapes our environment.

Through seniority, the university becomes still more male dominated. While the proportion of all female university researchers in the European Union (EU-27) is 40 per cent,[3] the number is substantially lower in science, maths and engineering, disciplines which produce the highest number of graduates overall. Table 5.1 indicates the distribution of researchers by seniority, and it is clear that the proportion of women never exceeds that of men, and that gender inequalities are greatest in science and engineering (S&E). European Commission data also shows that the subjects with the lowest proportion of appointments of women at Grade A (professor or equivalent) are engineering and technology (7.9 per cent of which are women). The EC reports that the gap between men and women appointments at each level closed between 2 and 4 percentage points during an eight-year period. If we split the difference, this means that it will take over one hundred years to close the gap between men and women in all subjects, but in the region of 275 years between men and women in science and engineering. Some of us might consider this too long to wait.

Table 5.1 Percentage distribution of men and women in academic research posts in the EU, 2010[4]

	Male all	Female all	Male S&E	Female S&E
PhD students	51	49	62	38
PhD graduates	54	46	65	35
Grade C	56	44	67	33
Grade B	63	37	77	23
Grade A	80	20	89	11

But some, in higher education, business and environmental organisations, also wonder why this matters, and argue that they, and their organisational practices, are gender neutral, whereas in their gender blindness they systematically work against gender justice. Feminist work on organisational structures demonstrates how the criteria for recruitment and progression are frequently weighted against female candidates (this could range from an insistence on maths A-level at university entrance, to a requirement for regular travel away from home or an inflexibility in working practices, for employees).

Environmental research

Research has demonstrated that women experience both direct and indirect impacts of environmental problems differently to, and often more intensely than, men. For example, Denton[5] reported women's significantly higher death rate in the 1991 Bangladeshi floods and attributed this to a number of culturally related factors; while the disproportionately high mortality of women in the 2003 European heat wave has been noted by Fouillet et al.[6] as an incidental finding of their research for which they were unable to identify any clear explanation. Indirect gender-related violence tends to increase at times of environmental crisis.[7] Women are also more likely to be involved in the immediate consequences of environmental disasters, and Maureen Fordham's research[8] in the UK has shown how women's additional care burden (both practical and emotional) substantially increases after severe flooding. However, this research tends to be the exception, and mainstream research on both catastrophic and chronic environmental problems regularly neglects gender, with the result that we are missing opportunities to develop a better understanding of how gender relations and environmental problems affect each other.

Research which has the capacity to create or resolve environmental problems has been resolutely dominated by masculinised concerns. For decades, transportation planning has been predicated on the commuting habits of the male 'householder' and has failed to adequately plan for those with multiple caring responsibilities requiring complex trip chaining. How much better to plan for a 'mobility of care', as proposed by Spanish researcher Ines Sánchez de Madariaga.[9] Or take the lack of attention to gender in studies of the potential effects of environmental chemicals on human reproductive health. Studies here have mainly focused on the reproductive health of men.[10] There is some indication that this may be about to change as the US National Institutes of Health and the European Union (through its research programme 'Horizon2020') have both recently created requirements for research proposals it considers to include a statement on how they will be more inclusive of women (in terms of research staff), and/or sensitive to gender (in terms of research content). Success, of course, will depend on how rigorously this criterion will be judged against myriad others, and also what the arrangements will be for monitoring the gender awareness that is promised in the proposal. At the time of writing, this was not clear. There is also a recent move among science journals, including *Nature* and *The Lancet*, to insist that every article they publish identify the ways in which gender and sex differences have been accounted for.[11]

Institutional working practices and decision-making

Women consistently report greater concern about environmental problems, as well as a stronger tendency to take proactive measures to prevent them.[12] And yet women are nowhere near equally represented in the decision-making which affects our environment. There are two strands to calls to make decision-making gender balanced: under equal opportunities and rights in which women should not be discriminated against (and this requires a consideration of current expectations about what are the appropriate qualifications for jobs as well as the conditions of working); and because it is likely that, given enough women in decision-making positions, those decisions are likely to be more sound, and environmentally sensitive.[13] Both these imperatives have underpinned calls for the inclusion of more women in the United Nations Framework Convention on Climate

Change (UNFCCC), the principle of which was eventually agreed in 2011, although at the time of writing the final shape of this had not been determined.

Nowhere is decision-making more male dominated than in the industries which crucially affect our environment: architecture, transport, energy, water and waste management.[14] In my own research into gender in municipal waste management, there was a clear trend of senior decision-makers progressing through engineering careers who envisaged waste management as a problem of waste disposal, requiring engineering solutions, rather than one of behaviour, which considers how we consume and discard. From a large number of questionnaire returns, which revealed this engineering tendency, the research team identified case studies from which we could explore how different kinds of management might yield different approaches. In two municipalities, waste management was led by staff with unusual career trajectories. In Dublin (the city which had pioneered charging for plastic bags, and making illegal the disposal of cigarette butts on the street), the waste team was driven by women who had come from careers in education; while in West Sussex, the team was led by a male economist, with a women deputy with a background in marketing. This municipality had been an early advocate of reusable nappies and nappy laundering services, and also had a higher than national average recycling rate.[15] These beacons aside, the waste management industry is not seen by the women working there as hospitable.

The marginalisation of part-time work and the expectation that career progression depends on availability, being 'present' and working long and unsocial hours pervades higher education (which generally assumes that students have no caring responsibilities and live on or close to campus) as well as paid work. Rakibe Kulcur's work on environmental non-governmental organisations (ENGOs) has shown how much they depend on staff working evenings and weekends, and how flexible working is discouraged and available only to selected high-status staff. In a revealing interview, the chief executive of one ENGO asked Rakibe if she had children, and when she admitted to having a daughter, the response was that she could bid farewell to a career in the environmental sector.[16] Even more worrying was the number of her respondents (women as well as men) who could not see the reason for their organisation to take a gender perspective, consigning this 'specialist' area to women's and development organisations (on the basis that while women's relationship with the environment is clear in the global South, gender differences are not an issue in the global North). In the waste management research referred to earlier, an environmental organisation in Portugal opined (in one of those gems of translation) that thinking of gender in regard to their conservation work was 'extra terrestrial for our kind'.

The combined effect of these working practices, and the focus on a particular kind of credentialised expertise, disadvantages people (mostly, but not exclusively, women) who do not fit the conventional mode of worker with a linear education and career, and no caring responsibilities. Indeed, working long hours, with frequent trips away from home, has been found to suit best the worker who has a partner at home fulfilling the majority of household maintenance tasks, as Doreen Massey found when researching the male-dominated high-technology industry in Cambridge.[17] Where women are able to win places at this well-established table, they are likely to emulate this masculinist model, and have no children (or to achieve promotion later than their male colleagues, once their children are older), to live on their own, or to live with a partner who has more flexible work arrangements. Kulcur found this in the senior women she interviewed in environmental organisations, including women whose husbands had retired, while Magnusdottir and Kronsell[18] identified that the majority of women working in environmental decision-making in Scandinavia (and this is, unusually, around one half of the total) had not led to changes in decision-making, partly, they surmise, owing to their adherence to the traditional decision-maker model. It is, then, important to recognise that masculinity does not evenly map onto being male, nor does femininity equate to being female.

The failure with the scope of how gender has been considered to date, both in research and in practice, is that gender has been considered as synonymous with 'women's issues', and this has to be broadened to consider gender relations, deeply embedded in societies and structuring some of the ways in which power is exercised. To this end, an interesting review of gendered work practices suggests that where men are likely to take up paternity leave, where it is offered, women are more likely to be represented in senior decision-making positions.[19] If we are to draw women (and men) with a diversity of experience into environment decision-making, then the workforce itself needs to welcome and accommodate those with caring responsibilities, those from a wide age range, and those from different ethnic and cultural groups (ostensibly missing from environmental fields at present).

There is another avenue by which environmental decision-making can take place beyond the ingrained masculinist institutionalised framework critiqued above: the involvement of 'lay knowledge' through various forms of public participation. Contributors to this book argue that indigenous peoples, often women because of their responsibilities to provide food and other household necessities, possess important knowledge about nature and natural processes (Vandana Shiva; the Green Belt Movement of Kenya). Reported elsewhere, women's caring responsibilities have exposed them to particular environmental problems which affect family members' health, and this has spurred them to understand these in detailed and sophisticated ways. Lois Gibbs and her campaigning against the chemical pollution of her neighbourhood is a good example of 'citizen science' which challenges local authorities and companies to take responsibility for damage to people and their environments.[20] (See also, for example, Hilda Kurtz, Julie Sze and, on 'citizen science', Allan Irwin). Challenging institutions to incorporate these different kinds of expertise into environment decision-making is important, and would help to answer the call that there aren't enough sufficiently (institutionally) qualified and experienced women to fill the decision-making posts.

And so to return to higher education and why gender balance matters. The kind of research we all do is influenced by our own experiences and our own priorities. No matter how much we strive to be 'objective', we are subjective human beings with particular socio-economic and educational backgrounds, personal responsibilities and everyday life experiences, which influence our research choices. If research is to truly respond to and embrace the society in which live, then those designing that research need to reflect that society, in all its variety.

If higher education follows its current neoliberal path, women making careers in environmentally related research will continue to be pressured to mimic their male colleagues' work practices and behaviours. Without a restructuring which allows for flexible working, does not insist on travel (which EU research frequently demands in order to foster cross-country knowledge exchange) and facilitates both men and women to incorporate their caring roles with their paid work, there is a danger that the women who make it to those decision-making positions (and this will be true in business, NGOs and government also) will be those who have no caring responsibilities, or have the resources to buy effective care – not something that is automatically available on a PhD stipend or an early career researcher salary.

Key intervention

Demasculinising environment research, policy-making and campaigning, such that gender relations are seen as being at the core of and embedded in environmental problems, and current research, work and decision-making practices, rather than as one of the problems contributing to environmental degradation. Institutional practices need to be designed so that social (including gender) and environmental justice are core considerations, rather than afterthoughts.

6

YVONNE ORENGO

Andrew Lees Trust

Media empowering women in southern Madagascar

'I don't want to get married,' says Charlotte, 'it's just like being a slave.'

Charlotte is in the Andry Lalana Tohana[1] (ALT Mg) production studio in Ambovombe, capital of Androy, southern Madagascar. She is editing a radio programme about women's rights as part of ALT's 'Village Voices for Development' (VVD) project.

ALT Mg is the local partner of the Andrew Lees Trust (ALT UK), a social and environmental education charity set up in memory of former Friends of the Earth campaigns director Andrew Lees, who died in 1994 while investigating the development of a Rio Tinto mine in southern Madagascar. ALT Mg is the embodiment of Andrew's and the Trust's belief in local empowerment and testimony to a vision of sustainable development through local ownership. For eighteen years ALT teams have worked with media – especially radio – to engage and empower local people, particularly women, to take an active role in managing their natural environment more sustainably and in bringing about social change.

'I too am against marriage, I cannot accept so many things that come with it!' says Hanitra, a single mother and Director of ALT Mg, as she works with Charlotte to prepare another phone-in programme at the local radio station.

Cattle are more important than women

Antandroy[2] society is male dominated, deeply hierarchical and full of complex *fady* (taboos). Gender relations are dictated by strict cultural norms, as well as certain spiritual beliefs that hold women inferior to men.

Antandroy men regard women as a 'resource', second only in importance to their cattle. Indeed, women spend a great deal of their time collecting domestic firewood and water – both of which are in short supply, taking them many kilometres from home each day. They are also expected to cook and take care of children and elderly family members.

Traditionally excluded from decision-making processes, Antandroy women are not allowed to speak in public. During a VVD focus group, a villager explains to Charlotte her feeling of exclusion: 'If I was elected mayor I could speak publicly; but following Antandroy tradition I am not allowed to lead a debate or launch a discussion.'

Frequently deprived of education to become teenage mothers, and living in a polygamous society, a woman can find herself embroiled in fraught family dynamics and politics. The women tell Charlotte that often they cannot even speak within the family setting or talk about day-to-day problems with their husbands. 'Men decide our lives for us,' one woman explains.

Life in the Androy

Known as the 'People of the Thorns' owing to the unique spiny forest indigenous to this southern region of Madagascar, the Antandroy are an extremely hardy people. They inhabit a drought-ridden, isolated environment with poor infrastructure, living without electricity, running water or sanitation; literacy rates are low and families in eighteen communes or more face three months of food shortages annually.[3]

The acquisition of Zebu cattle dominates the pastoralist lifestyle of the Antandroy. A wealthy man may have 600 head of cattle, the poor man a few goats. They both live in a wooden hut and wear simple clothes. The only way to tell them apart is by their head of cattle: the bank account.

However, cattle are rarely sold except in times of extreme hardship or for a funeral. Cows are linked to the spirit world, the interlocutor between the physical dimension and the ancestors. You rely on the ancestors for prosperity and the well-being of your family. Taking your place among the ancestral spirits is a serious business.

When a man dies, all his cattle are slaughtered and the horns placed on his tomb. The more cattle slaughtered, the better his life after death. What meat is sold provides for a small concrete house on the tomb for his spirit to live in, because the afterlife is longer than this one. His wooden hut is burned down, the living left with nothing.

When asked why the Antandroy abide by these harsh traditional funeral practices, the men respond: 'This is a hard environment, it's no good being born with a silver spoon in your mouth.'

Speaking of spoons, in Antandroy custom, when her husband dies, a woman may not inherit his house or lands. She may inherit spoons; possibly even a kitchen stool.

This is the subject of the radio programme that Charlotte is busy preparing.

Talking about inequality

Charlotte has been with a group of village women, recording perspectives about their lives and questions about their rights to inherit land. The Village Voices radio project has catalysed dialogue on the subject and is hosting phone-in programmes to widen local debate. The most recent has involved a panel of specialists – an expert in local Antandroy customs and a similarly well-versed professional in Malagasy national law.

In Malagasy law, women have the right to inherit land but this is not recognised or respected in the Androy. On live radio, the panel has answered questions called in by the general public and by members of the project's Radio Listening Groups. There has been shock in the community at the dissonance between local custom and constitutional, legal rights of women. Men are asking questions. Women are debating what to do.

Charlotte has recorded the testimony of a local woman, Feteline, whose father heard the VVD radio programme and decided to give his land to his daughters immediately – while he is still alive. Now Feteline is about to receive a resource that will sustain her and her family for generations to come.

'I'm really surprised by my father's decision,' says Feteline, 'I get my part of the heritage which is a piece of land; my brothers can't oppose his decision after his death. This land is for my descendants, for my children and my children's children. If I am in difficulty, it is only land I have bought myself that I will have the right to sell.'[4]

Charlotte listens and nods approval as she edits the tape. Asserting opinion via a public radio broadcast is something new for women in this region.

When the VVD project began, the ALT team discovered that local understanding of human rights was low; awareness of and respect for women's rights was almost non-existent. The project has addressed this through community video showings, training and radio programmes.[5] Yet raising awareness is just the first step; enabling people to act on those rights is a very different challenge.

Barriers to speaking out

ALT teams are highly experienced at using the media as a tool to empower communities[6] and give voice to citizens[7] in southern Madagascar. Project VVD evolved from these experiences in order to respond to the need for improved governance during the prolonged political crisis of 2009–14.

In 2008, when ALT assisted the UNDP to study communications in Madagascar,[8] it found there were limited channels for citizens to voice their opinions in public; even less opportunity to express themselves through the media. However, 90 per cent of respondents believed the media could help improve their lives and almost half would be willing to speak through media if the opportunity arose.

The lack of public debate has a negative effect on governance – specifically transparency and accountability – but to create open dialogue is to face multiple social, political and cultural challenges, including extreme poverty,[9] low education and literacy rates, geographic isolation and poorly resourced local media.

Despite being the most popular and accessible media on the island, radio stations are highly vulnerable to closure if they broadcast content considered antagonistic to government interests. The UNDP study identified just one local phone-in programme being broadcast; it was soon closed down, deemed too controversial. Later UN studies reported freedom of expression restrictions still prevalent in 2011.[10]

There is no ratified freedom of information law in Madagascar and the media is largely self-censoring for fear of reprimand or reprisals. This fear permeates all levels of society.

The strict hierarchical systems and social taboos, *fady*, dictate who speaks, about what, for whom and when. In the south, breaking the *fady* can carry grave penalties – *tody* and *tsiny*[11] – whereby a person believes they can fall sick or suffer death for having disrupted the balance or harmony in the predominant social order.

Being poor, young and especially being a woman presents additional barriers to freedom of expression.

Village Voices: opening up debate

The Village Voices project has been designed to circumnavigate these barriers to communication and open up dialogue by providing a neutral and anonymous space via local radio where people of any age, gender, social status or education level can talk directly to leaders.

Village Radio Listening Groups which participate in the project are provided with solar-powered telephones and wind-up radios. In focus groups facilitated by ALT they identify key problems and formulate questions to ask the local leader/decision-maker responsible.

Women meet in focus groups separately so they can discuss their opinions freely. All questions are recorded anonymously and then played to the relevant local decision-maker, whose answers or commitment to action are recorded. These are then edited together as if in a live debate between the villagers and decision-maker – something that would rarely occur in normal life in Androy.

During the broadcast, the desired information is exchanged together with wider, key messages: it is acceptable to demand transparency from your leaders; decision-makers are accountable to their constituents; both men and women have a right to know and speak out.

This is a bottom-up initiative and the local community is determining the agenda. The listening groups discuss the answers provided, then follow up with more specific questions. The interactive, participative process enables them to reframe their questions and re-engage with decision-makers until they are satisfied with the final outcome.

Women find their voice

An evaluation of the VVD project after just six months of broadcasting demonstrated that awareness of women's rights had increased significantly[12] – more than 60 per cent of respondents recognised that women and men had equal rights. More than 55 per cent of citizens participating in the phone-ins were women. They were able to speak in public on a range of issues and have a voice in the debate – a significant change for women in this remote area of the south.

Many women reported changes to their relationships as a result of this new-found freedom of expression: 'I proposed a way to resolve a family tension about money. I felt I had my rights respected because my husband accepted my ideas'; and greater social cohesion: 'I chose to share my husband's salary with his second wife, though I did not have to'; they also found the confidence to address men in authority: 'I liberated my husband from the police when he was falsely accused; it's the first time I spoke out and put my opinion forward to protect my rights.' Men also shifted in their perspective: 'before I did not listen to my wife, but we speak freely now'.

Living in this region, Charlotte remarks on changes she has observed in the community: '[…] since VVD began in 2012 I see that women now understand they have rights to express themselves and this brings some changes in relations with their husbands – they take more risk to speak their ideas. I have calls from women all the time asking for more programmes on the subject of women's rights. Many people like these programmes – even the men are curious to understand more!'

This is powerful testimony to the tangible impact of media on the lives of women. In 2007, after nine years of educational broadcasts across the south by ALT's 'Project Radio', an evaluation demonstrated that simply having access to a radio in the village brought significant change for women.[13] Project Radio gave women direct access to news and information, rather than their relying on male elders as their primary source. Women reported all manner of benefits from this direct access: 'Now I understand where all the family money is going!' one woman exclaimed, after learning via radio about the cost of cattle passports. Her husband had not seen the necessity to tell her.

ALT positioned women to lead Radio Listening Groups in 3,000 villages across the south. Placing the wind-up radio with women was a calculated strategy to diffuse social barriers to access and enable village groups to listen to the radio; also to avoid capture of the resource by powerful male elites. Women have successfully facilitated more than 68 per cent of Radio Listening Groups since 1999 as a result of ALT's positive gender approach.

Empowering women in managing natural resources and sexual health

The radio programmes about women's rights to inherit land reflect a key area of concern for most southerners, indeed for most Malagasy.[14] Land is the primary source of food and livelihoods. In the south, approximately 82 per cent of the population are rural producers living in poverty.[15] Access to agricultural land is the basis of life and also carries the sacred significance of ancestral lineage.

For women to own and work land efficiently is part of a wider challenge about how Africa will meet its food security needs. For women such as Feteline, just the one small step of listening to a radio programme with her family has transformed her life, bringing an unprecedented inheritance of farmland and the prospect of future food security for her and her children. The FAO estimates that women farmers producing the same yields as men would increase agricultural output in developing countries between 2.5 and 4 per cent: 'Increasing production by this amount could reduce the number of undernourished people in the world in the order of 12–17 percent.'[16]

ALT has ensured that women have participated in and influenced this agenda in southern Madagascar. Over three hundred women were trained in the nutritional benefits of reintroducing drought-resistant sorghum, an ancestral crop of the Antandroy. Employing radio, video, TV and press in urban areas, women team leaders successfully promoted sorghum production to farmers and families. This change in agricultural production delivered a 53 per cent increase in families' nutritional intake during the annual hunger gap.[17]

Similarly, women have promoted and led changes in natural resource management with the help of media. Radio broadcasts about fuel efficiency helped women access ALT's stove training project and the benefits of the Toko Mitsisty (TM stove); almost 65 per cent more efficient than the traditional Toko V stove,[18] it reduces the time that women spend collecting wood and allows them to develop small enterprises such as weaving and baking.

As a result, the project was able to train and mobilise 120 local women to train other women to build over thirty thousand fuel-efficient stoves across the south. In villages with radios, 28 per cent more women maintained and continued to use the TM stove.[19]

ALT has effectively produced hundreds of radio programmes in response to the information needs of women, including on vital health issues such as vaccination of children, postnatal care and birth spacing; over two-thirds of women in villages with radio could name at least one birth control method compared to 27 per cent of women in villages without radios.[20] For sexual health issues too ALT's radio programmes have catalysed shifts in attitude and behaviour:

> Encouragingly, as well as understanding the HIV prevention messages heard, women in Andranokinaly [village] recognised that HIV prevention messages need to be adopted by men as well as women to be effective, and felt that it was acceptable to talk to men about the risks of HIV and unprotected sex. The impression received was that the radio broadcasts are opening up space for women to discuss issues among themselves, and possibly could be contributing to greater communication between men and women on issues of fidelity and sex.[21]

Last word

In the remote lands of southern Madagascar, both traditional (radio) and new media (telephony) have made a powerful contribution to how women effect social, economic and environmental change.

Charlotte has been editing radio programmes with ALT for almost ten years. As a young woman in Androy, and like many young women in Africa, she finds that radio has offered her more life opportunities and provided a creative livelihood.

'Being single gives me freedom,' explains Charlotte. 'Since I worked with ALT to produce radio programmes it changed many things for me: I have learnt and heard things I never knew before … functions of justice and human rights, for example. All this was new to me and it improves my abilities and my ideas to take steps towards what I want.'

Can there be real sustainability without local ownership and good governance? Charlotte and Hanitra witness daily how the media plays a significant role in answering this question – engaging citizens to understand and act on their rights, and empowering communities to take an active role in their development and in managing the natural environment.

Hanitra feels strongly on this subject: 'It is not easy to work in the field as a woman. But I feel free because working with the media is a way I can express myself. Before I did not really understand the role of communications, but through my experiences working with ALT I am convinced that communications is the pillar for all activity in development, without it there is nothing.'

7

JULIE A. NELSON

Economist, University of Massachusetts Boston

Empowering a balanced and useful economics of sustainability: the role of gender[1]

A more subtle relation between gender and sustainability

The issue of gender and sustainability does not end with the issue of the empowerment of women, although that is certainly important. Feminists have sometimes made a crude but useful distinction between 'sex' and 'gender'. Biological distinctions among male, female and intersex persons are referred to as 'sex'. So, for example, gathering and analysing information about women is an analysis at the level of sex. 'Gender', on the other hand, is used to refer to the cultural expectations, biases, beliefs and practices that are created on top of these distinctions. The discussion of societal *gender* norms – for example, whether it is considered appropriate for women to take leadership positions – is also important in efforts towards sustainability.

This chapter, however, takes gender analysis to a different, more subtle but yet more permeating, level. Human thinking – across the sexes, and apparently also across many cultures – has a tendency to be *cognitively gendered*: that is, as humans with limited brainpower, we have a well-documented tendency to simplify the world by splitting it, in our minds, into simple binary categories such as 'masculine' versus 'feminine'.[2] We find it very easy to think in dualistic terms. We even create beliefs about transcendent 'essences' based on this handy (and largely unconscious) organisational strategy.

Meanwhile, discussions of sustainability – and, in particular, of climate change – have increasingly focused around economic questions. Should we have carbon taxes? Can we 'afford' mitigation? Can economic growth continue? Who should bear the costs of adaptation? Do we need to invent an entire 'new economy' to achieve sustainability? This chapter explains how these discussions have been distorted and limited by unexamined – and deeply cognitively gendered – assumptions, and how a re-examination of these assumptions opens new doors.

The mainstream discipline of economics is, as I will describe below, strongly *cognitively gendered* as masculine. As a result, it takes only the most partial and incomplete view of economic realities. Although economists have a strong voice in current national and international policy-making, contemporary mainstream economics makes a very bad guide.

Furthermore – and here I depart from many other critiques – much of the distorted view preached by the mainstream is also uncritically accepted by many who propose 'alternative' or 'new' economies. As a result, these visions also offer unnecessarily limited and biased guidelines for action. Understanding the role of gender is therefore crucial to the project of improving analyses and motivating more effective action, no matter what your starting point.

The state of mainstream economics

My own training in academic economics (I hold a PhD) was of the thoroughly mainstream (also referred to as 'neoclassical') sort. Teaching at European and North American universities, and in many other parts of the world as well, is dominated by this approach.[3]

'Production' is a major focus of mainstream economics. This is true at the micro level, where models of production choices made by profit-maximising businesses are central. At the macro level, economists are fixated on gross domestic product (GDP) and its growth rate. But the definition of 'production' is narrow. The core models look only at the production of goods and services destined for sale in markets. And production is assumed to require two (and only two) factors: 'capital' (variously, machinery or finance) and 'labour' (the time and skills of adult – traditionally male – workers).

While micro-theories of production focus on business, micro-theories of consumption focus on households. Households, like businesses, are considered to be unitary, rational, autonomous, self-interested decision-making economic agents. Households, in mainstream theory, have three (and only three) roles: they consume goods and services purchased on markets, supply adult workers to labour markets, and enjoy leisure.

I noticed, over time, that women and nature share similar treatment in mainstream economics. They are largely invisible. Women's traditional, non-marketed, production of provisioning and care in homes and communities is completely ignored. Similarly, the productivity of nature is pushed into the background. When considered at all, women and nature are treated as passive 'resources' for the satisfaction of male or human desires, and treated as totally subject to male or human control. Explicit attention to, or appreciation of, them and their activities is deemed unnecessary, as they are assumed to possess an infinite capacity for self-maintenance and self-regeneration.

One would search in vain in the core models of economics for any inkling of where the materials used in production came from, or where the waste from the production process goes. Similarly, one would search in vain in most descriptions of economic agents for a discussion of where people come from, or where they go when they are broken or used up. The bearing and raising of children, and the care of the aged and sick – traditionally women's responsibilities – are, like nature, considered too unimportant to mention.

Another odd bias that became obvious to me had to do with the methods of analysis preferred in mainstream economics. As an undergraduate student, I was exposed to some discussion of real-world issues, as well as simple mathematical models meant to represent the behaviour of economic agents. Business firms were modelled as though each consisted of only *one* decision maker, who had only *one* goal (profits), and produced only *one* good, for *one* market. This was convenient, since 'maximising profits' could then be easily expressed in graphical and calculus terms – one just solved for the high point on the mathematical 'profit function'. I expected that in graduate school we would study more real-world issues by, for example, doing some hands-on investigating of how business boards and managers actually make decisions about their goals and their products and locations, and how they manage to get their decisions implemented by motivating workers and negotiating with suppliers and communities.

Instead, I was surprised to find, we started with the same extremely simple models, and merely went deeper and deeper into elaboration of mathematical fine points. I discovered that prestige in the profession came with being as abstract, technical and quantitative as possible, while disavowing hands-on research, concreteness, engagement, discussion of ethical issues, and anything else that smacked of softness or messiness.

This biased approach is reflected, for example, in the way the economics of climate change tends to be analyzed in US academic and policy contexts[4] and (although with *slightly* greater attempts at nuance) in the reports of the Intergovernmental Panel on Climate Change.[5] These assume that human well-being can be numerically measured, and that well-being is based purely on consumption (GDP). Furthermore, the changes in well-being related to climate change are assumed to be of a small, marginal nature suited to evaluation by standard calculus tools. People are assumed to think about future generations in the same way we think about short-term financial investments. Consideration of the ethical issues related to global inequalities is often eliminated through assumptions that are disguised as being merely technical.[6] Technology and machinery are generally assumed to be so easily substituted for natural resources that economic growth can continue unfettered for ever.[7] In this way, consideration of the foundation of economic life in society and nature, as well as consideration of moral responsibility and the possibility of uncontrollable change, are assiduously avoided.[8]

My two musings – about the content of economics, and about its methods – came together for me in the 1980s when I discovered feminist scholarship on the history and philosophy of science.

Feminist critiques of (social) science

In the 1980s, a number of feminist historians and philosophers, including Evelyn Fox Keller[9] and Sandra Harding,[10] brought to light the strong binary *gendering* that underlay the historical development of science. They pointed out how imagined binary oppositions between 'man' and nature, mind and body, order and chaos, and males and females strongly influenced the Western conception of where people fit into the order of the world. From Plato and Aristotle, through Descartes and Bacon, the image of scientific knowledge as the masculine means to firmly control a dangerous feminine Nature emerged.

In the early 1990s, feminist economists began to notice that the definition, models and methods of mainstream economics followed just such a cognitively gendered pattern.[11] The choice of economists to one-sidedly favour, for example, the analysis of production for markets over production for own use, mental decision-making over bodily needs, control over interdependence, and reason over emotion follows point by point the typical cultural associations of masculinity with high status, 'hardness' and power, and femininity with low status, 'softness' and weakness.

The elevation of quantitative and technical work in the profession, to the neglect of more engaged methods and consideration of normative (that is, ethical) concerns, likewise reflects gender bias. A look back at the history of the discipline reveals that the methods were chosen not because they portrayed the world most accurately, but precisely because they gave the discipline of economics the aura of being a 'hard' science.[12]

The myth of the machine

This 'physics envy' demonstrated by the economics profession has led to a very odd result, but one that has permeated contemporary

society: people have come to believe that market-using economies are machine-like 'engines', 'driven' by self-interest, blindly
following 'market logic' and 'imperatives of growth'. We have come
to believe that economies somehow operate in a realm set apart
from dependency on the natural world. (Economists left those
considerations to the natural sciences.) We have come to believe
that they somehow operate in a realm set apart from human soci-
ality, interdependence and moral consideration. (These were left to
sociology and philosophy.) How bizarre.

This problem has been accentuated by the recent ascendance
of neoliberal thought, which takes the core assumptions of mainstream economics to an ideological extreme. Neoliberalism suggests
that market-using economies (should) have only one possible kind
of institution – unregulated businesses – and one norm – 'greed is
good'. Not only does neoliberal thought suggest that such a 'pure
market' economy is possible, neoliberalism presents this view as a true
understanding of the deep underlying essential nature of capitalism.

In fact, as a number of (dissident) economists, business theorists, legal theorists, economic sociologists and business leaders are
increasingly pointing out, real economies – even capitalist ones –
are actually *part of* nature and society.[13] Economies are actually
deeply entwined and co-constituted with the natural environment,
public regulation, cultural beliefs, real human emotional motivations, social practices and complex ethical norms. A 'pure market'
has never, and can never, exist: markets and business are thoroughly
shaped by norms and institutions.

Mainstream economists' claim that firms *should* 'maximise
profit', for example, is dangerous not only for humans and the environment, but for businesses themselves and the system in which
they function.[14] Real businesses find long-term success by balancing
multiple goals, and organising cooperation among shareholders,
customers, suppliers and workers to achieve them. A single-minded
focus on short-term financial outcomes is, in contrast, behind many
of the corporate and financial scandals and crises of recent decades.[15]
The idea that firms (not only 'should' but) *do* aim to 'maximise
profit' has likewise been exposed as a myth from commentators

within the corporate sector itself. While short-sighted firms may adopt only financial goals, these days such goals tend more towards ridiculous compensation of top-level executives than towards profits for shareholders.[16]

Unfortunately, many 'alternative' economic views put forth in the literature on sustainability suffer from a failure to distinguish between (1) how market-using ('capitalist') economies *actually* operate and (2) how the masculine-biased core models of mainstream economics have *told us* they operate ('neoliberalism'). Accepting that mainstream dogma about markets and businesses being mechanical, inhuman and separate from 'society,' they suggest alternatives that are merely reactive instead of transformative. This is a tragic error.

If advocates of capitalist economic systems believe profits and markets to be 'engines of growth', these opponents adopt the same mechanical image to characterise them as destructive juggernauts, intent on destroying more socially oriented values.[17] If the conventional approach is pro-globalisation and large-scale, then these critics are diametrically pro-local and small-scale; if current elites are pro-technology, these critics are diametrically Luddite and anti-technology; if policy debates focus on humans in industrialised societies, these critics diametrically venerate the untouched wilderness, indigenous cultures and non-human species; if those in control praise profits and private property, these critics advocate a complete disavowal of both.

Such critics' strong voices have often served an extremely useful role in bringing attention to processes of environmental destruction and the need to dramatically change course. But such analysis is insufficient radical. 'Radical' means 'going to the root', while such prescriptions leave the root assumption about the nature of economies unexamined.

A necessary intervention: reinventing economics

The widespread belief that 'the economy' and 'society' are somehow separate and opposed realms was invented by mainstream economics. Letting cultural biases about the relative values of things culturally coded as masculine or feminine hold sway, mainstream economists ended up by 'playing with half a deck'. The result is economic advice that contributes to the neglect of the environment by fixating on markets and economic growth. When not informed by a gender analysis, however, 'alternative' analyses too often merely switch to the other half of the deck. By blindly rejecting capitalism and large-scale activity, they also become inadequate for guiding us in the direction of sustainability.

A balanced view of market-using economic life, on the other hand, recognises that real-world economies are social creations. They run on both competition and cooperation, both reasonable self-interest and socially oriented norms, both innovation and conservation. We recognise that we create our economies through our individual expectations, beliefs and actions. We create them in our homes, communities, civic activities and workplaces. We create them through our collective actions, whether through 'outside' action such as boycotts or demonstrations, or 'inside' action such as shareholder resolutions or effective organisational leadership. We create them through lobbying, legislation and regulation. A 'provisioning' approach to economics frames it as the study of how societies organise themselves to provide for the survival and flourishing of life.

Or, unfortunately, about how they *fail* to do so.[18]

Such a realistic and pragmatic view opens the door to a wide range of action. The image of an inescapable mainstream 'market logic' stifles any initiative towards sustainability. An idealised vision of a purely cooperative, non-monetised, local economy of sharing motivates action, but does not seem to appeal to more than a smallish cadre of true believers. The pragmatic view, in contrast, suggests actions that can be taken here and now – not only by inventing new institutions, but by dedicating ourselves to making the economic institutions we already have, and in which the vast majority of us already function, respond to the realities of social and environmental needs.

One need not, for example, dogmatically limit oneself to, nor dogmatically oppose, market-based environmental policies such as carbon taxes or licences to pollute. We will obviously need far more than just a carbon tax to ameliorate the problems arising from climate change – especially among the most vulnerable populations. But if a well-designed, sufficiently large carbon tax could encourage conservation and conversion to more sustainable energy sources, can we really afford to miss this opportunity? Likewise, one need not have blind faith in, nor entertain blind opposition to, technological innovations or global-scale economic activity. A pragmatic and balanced economics approach goes with what can work, not with what is ideologically pure. It requires far more non-dogmatic, hands-on research and experimentation, and far less armchair theorising.

One more note on gender

Is this 'ecofeminism'? While I work on both feminist and ecological issues, I reject the close association of women with carefulness, community and connection with nature that can be found in some of the ecofeminist literature. I see that as simply the flip-side of the image of the association of men with agency, individualism and control of nature that got us into all this trouble in the first place.

It may be that, owing to positions in the power structure and common experiences, women and men may sometimes, on average, have different views or behaviours. But women *and* men (and anyone else) are fundamentally and equally embodied. Women *and* men (and anyone else) are individual; are connected; are rational; are emotional; are moral beings. An essentialist view that identifies women with nature and morality has the dangerous side effect of letting men morally 'off the hook' for action on sustainability. Yet, given the urgency of the environmental crises facing us, we all need to pull together.

Last words

Our habitual dividing up of the world into 'masculine' and 'feminine' camps has contributed to the creation of a belief that market-using economies are 'economic machines'. Moving us past that fundamental trap, a gender-balanced way of thinking opens new vistas. It avoids the trap of seeking a non-existent 'man versus nature' state of security, control and infinite economic growth. And it avoids the merely reactionary trap of retreating from commerce into a romanticised vision of a strictly local, cooperative, Earth Mother, no-growth society.

Of course, such an intervention will not be easy. We have centuries of deep-seated old habits of thinking about (and thinking *using*) gender, and thinking about economies, that need to be overcome. Ideological neoliberalism and ideological anti-globalisation make much simpler bumper stickers and rallying flags than does a pragmatic and nuanced 'provisioning' approach. Empowered people need an empowered economics, however, if we are to move in the direction of sustainability.

8

ANNA FITZPATRICK

Centre for Sustainable Fashion, University of
the Arts London

The role of fashion in bringing about social and ecological change

The Centre for Sustainable Fashion (CSF) is a University of the Arts London research centre based at the London College of Fashion. Created in 2008 by Professor Dilys Williams, the centre's design for sustainability research is applied across three central areas: developing curriculum and education for sustainable development, setting agendas in government and the public arena, and working with industry to challenge those in design and business to rethink structures and systems. Our work therefore explores new perspectives, relationships and processes that balance ecology, society and culture within the artistic and business context of fashion.

Through engaging with fashion in a more holistic manner we can begin to explore ways in which fashion can contribute to sustainability for all involved, and recognition can be given to understanding and appreciating value, building in resilience, the need for economic stability and viability, and the importance of respecting nature. These are some of the core values that contribute to our thinking about sustainability and shape our approach, in which empowerment, care and understanding are also nurtured. For CSF design is a crucial element in moving the fashion system away from a mechanical one and has the potential to be utilised as the vehicle to nurture elements that create stronger human relationships and a deeper connectedness between humans and nature.

This chapter will explore CSF's approach to fashion and sustainability through our guiding themes and examples of our work. Inherent in this holistic approach and methodologies are principles of empowerment, empathy and critical practice. First a brief outline of the importance of fashion as part of our culture, a tool of communication and as a global industry with significant economic leverage.

Why fashion?

Fashion is about more than the clothes we cover our bodies with; it is fascinating precisely because it brings together deeply private, personal and political expressions of ourselves, while opening a space for debate around the production and consumption practices that shape this particular historical moment. It is an industry, a means to a livelihood and a form of expression that surpasses the individual self. This form of non-verbal and embodied communication provides a mirror, in which, if we look closely enough, we can see a reflection of the society in which we live. More often than not, our gaze into this mirror is rather two-dimensional and a deeper look would discover new worlds of possibilities. Around the world millions of women buy fashion as a move towards distinction and independence and across the world millions of women are engaged in its making and production. In some cases, this too is a means to independence; in others, quite the opposite. To discuss fashion and the potential it has to bring about positive change in the lives of all involved in its production, consumption and use means acknowledging the value contributed by all involved. Those involved are, for the most part, women.

Despite the importance of the fashion industry both culturally and economically (fashion contributes £26 billion annually to the UK economy[1]), it has not always been given the consideration or recognition that architecture and food industries, for example, receive in terms of the indisputable human dependence on such industries. Fashion's complicated relationship with the media and the proximity of engendered industrial relations add interesting layers to the analysis. Femininities and feminisms are also central to the equation and to an area seen mostly as trivial: Bruzzi and

Church-Gibson[2] highlight the difficultly in theorising fashion as all too often it is seen as 'too trivial to theorise, too serious to ignore'. This leaves fashion in a difficult space where the cultural strength and power of fashion to engage, express and communicate are ignored and fashion is dismissed as wasteful, narcissistic, superficial and trivial. Lipovetsky[3] also recognises this neglect: 'it turns up everywhere on the street, in industry, and in the media, but it has virtually no place in the theoretical inquiries of our thinkers [… It is] seen as a superficial issue'. The challenge then is twofold – a recognition of the importance of fashion but also an approach within fashion to place value, resilience and relationships centrally.

It is through placing relationships at the heart of fashion that we can use it as a positive force to engage and empower all involved. Through what better lens can we view questions of women's empowerment and sustainability than through fashion? As the Director of the Centre for Sustainable Fashion, Dilys Williams, states: 'Engaged, as I am, in exploring what fashion can offer to sustainability, I witness around me incredible examples of women's great work, from the communities that I am part of at the Centre for Sustainable Fashion to wider communities across the world. This is no coincidence, as what sustainability needs has synchronicity with what women engage in every day: holism, compassion, reflection, imagination, collaboration, humility and quiet boldness.'[4]

For once, gender imbalance is not a key concern of the fashion industry per se. Women are not under-represented within fashion but rather undervalued. However, it is crucial to note, when it comes to the balance within the industry, that men, in factories, hold the senior roles, in many fashion businesses the owners and managers are predominantly men, and there is a gender power imbalance within the industry from production through to advertising that needs to be addressed. It is an industry in which the majority of makers are women, who in turn are making things for other women. In Bangladesh, for example, 80 per cent of the workforces are women, making garments largely for export, and the importance of the industry is recognised as significant in countries striving to reach UN development goals. As the OECD recognises, 'sustainable development can only be achieved through long-term investments in economic, human and environmental capital. At present, the female half of the world's human capital is undervalued and underutilised the world over.'[5] Through our approach and work at CSF we hope to shift the focus, redress the balance and shine light on the gender blindness in the undervaluing of human capital involved in fashion.

Our call to action is that a socially and environmentally foregrounded approach to guide the examination of the fashion system is in order. We need to step back and approach problems with a wider lens, giving room to the complications, contradictions and nuances inherent in the system. Fashion must be recognised as a viable tool of empowerment on multiple layers. A greater understanding of design is needed too, placing it more centrally while recognising, as Yuniya Kawamura does, that 'fashion is not created by a single individual but by everyone involved in the production of fashion, and thus fashion is a collective activity'.[6] As Williams states, 'fashion is derived from the bringing together of people through the crafting of form with beauty and value. At the heart of humanity lies the ability to cherish and to be cherished, so processes of creation, enjoyment and caring should imbue the relationships that fashion makes real.'[7]

To recognise fashion as a collective activity is part of our approach to sustainability, since it is through the lens of fashion that we look for solutions to make connections, empower and connect. To echo Kate Fletcher, CSF's Professor of Fashion, Design, Sustainability, 'the whole is the problem – the cumulative values, discernments, habits of mind, industrial practises, business models, economic logic, deep societal forces and aggregated individual practises that make up the fashion and textile sector [...] and it is the whole we must understand before we consider the functions and needs of its elements. Sustainability is dependent on how the parts work together, not on how the parts work in isolation'.[8] As well as embracing this holistic approach, our work identifies that sustainability is a moving concept. Domenski et al. remark that 'sustainability may be defined as a dynamic balance among three mutually interdependent elements: (1) protection and enhancement of natural ecosystems and resources; (2) economic productivity; and (3) provision of social infrastructure such as jobs, housing, education, medical care and cultural opportunities'.[9] Our work seeks to be considerate of the processes of the system within which people work, not solely focused on the product. A product cannot possess sustainability, but it can be designed to respond to its makers and users in a sustainable way. Sustainability is not singularly about minimising negative impact, but also about maximising positive impact, allowing individuals, communities and economic systems to flourish.

If sustainability requires a consideration of the system as a whole, design then has a larger part to play than might at first appear. Decisions made in concept creation ripple and expand across the whole production, wearing, caring and ultimate exhaustion of a piece – as Alastair Fuad-Luke says, 'design is manifest in all facets of contemporary life',[10] and design can be about drawing people into the system rather than having them passively watching from the periphery, and in doing so dynamic and empowered relationships are enacted that are intra-active and reflexive. Design has the potential to connect and empower all involved, and putting design at the heart of the fashion system means situating relationships centrally, which in turn has radical knock-on effects. Rather than protectionism and competition being central tenets of the system, cooperation and sharing will be moved into the limelight. The skills needed in a contingent world require a new type of education, one that learns and teaches 'through' sustainability practices rather than learning 'about' sustainability information.

Our work is shaped by five guiding themes: engage citizen participation, dream with eyes open, radicalise design practice, challenge conventional aesthetics, and be a voice for change. These themes inform the different aspects of our work. With fashion as our context and a dynamic 'definition' of sustainability that is about more than product, we utilise our themes to nurture and strengthen relationships and maximise the positive impact fashion does and can have. In this section we will highlight how these themes influence our work and projects.

Figure 8.1 The Centre for Sustainable Fashion's guiding themes

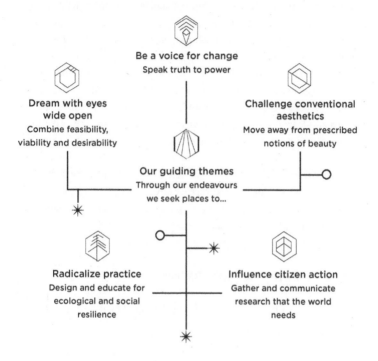

Be a voice for change
Speak truth to power

Dream with eyes
wide open
Combine feasibility,
viability and desirability

Challenge conventional
aesthetics
Move away from prescribed
notions of beauty

Our guiding themes
Through our endeavours
we seek places to...

Radicalize practice
Design and educate for
ecological and social
resilience

Influence citizen action
Gather and communicate
research that the world
needs

Influence citizen action (empathy)

> A person with Ubuntu is open and available to others, affirming of others, does not feel threatened that others are able and good, for he or she has a proper self-assurance that comes from knowing that he or she belongs in a greater whole and is diminished when others are humiliated or diminished, when others are tortured or oppressed.
>
> Desmond Tutu

All our work exemplifies these themes but some encapsulates certain aspects very clearly. In 2007 CSF's Director, Dilys Williams, devised Shared Talent in order to explore the relationships that are crucial to the creation of fashion. Challenging the typical hierarchical approach to traditional fashion production, the emphasis is on honouring the value of each person's contribution to both the processes and products of production – creating a more heterarchical approach to traditional design methodologies. Shared Talent's first iterations were applied in communities in South Africa, West Africa and India, challenging geographic, cultural and economic assumptions and learning through shared perspectives. Through providing a sense of mutuality to nurture collaboration, emergent properties of the relationships developed included distinction beyond price and construction technique. A central tenet of the project was fostering empathy, to cultivate trust, directly between people, and to visualise interdependence between people and nature. We seek to encourage this through play and the exchange of ideas – by thinking big and making connections between people, things and places.

Dream with eyes wide open (define)

> All human beings are also dream beings. Dreaming ties all mankind together.
>
> Jack Kerouac

An element of fashion is about imagination, pleasure, fantasy and joy. Dreaming is part of that, but our world is always anchored in the possible. For deeper empowerment and sustainability there is a need to combine feasibility and viability with big thinking and hope – there is scope for different systems, alternative outcomes for different problems – there is no one-size-fits-all solution, yet to find solutions we must recognise context and clarify what we are trying to do. Despite all that fashion can offer in the creative realms, it also offers the possibility of employment, economic stability and opportunity. Many issues within the current system result from the complexity of the supply chain as it weaves across the globe from textile producers to makers to retailers and consumers, so of course we need to engage with industry to impact positively in this sphere.

As well working with the big players in the industry – the high street and the high-end brands – there is still an important and lively, creative space for smaller producers that needs to be sustained and supported. Two CSF projects – FIRE Up and Creative Hub – offer support networks and mentoring for small and medium-size enterprises (SMEs). FIRE Up is a space for collaboration between designer fashion businesses and academic researchers to catalyse innovation, bringing research closer to industry, and to stimulate sustainability for the sector, while Creative Hub offers support to SMEs working in this area – in our current intake 80 per cent of the businesses are run by and provide employment for women. These build on CSF's London Style project, which culminated in a year-long collaboration with *i-D* magazine called 'i-sustain', to project new messages about fashion that question the way we think about design, the purchase and wear of fashion, and stress the connection between products, people, place and time.

Be a voice for change (agency)

> I truly believe that individuals can make a difference in society [...] Since periods of change such as the present one come so rarely in human history, it is up to each of us to make the best use of our time to help create a happier world.
>
> The Dalai Lama

Fashion is a powerful tool of communication and can be harnessed for the communication of important messages and to involve people in a more active, rather than passive, system. There are many challenges in building a sustainable fashion system that present endless opportunities and possibilities. Professor Helen Storey, in her work *Catalytic Clothing*, introduced the notion that clothing and textiles can play a vital role in improving the urban environment and the health of those living within it. In a cross-discipline collaboration with University of Sheffield chemist Professor Tony Ryan, the project explores the use of technology by applying an air-purifying photo catalyst to clothing, which essentially means that as we go about our daily lives wearing catalysed clothing we can actively contribute to improving the quality of the air around us, the air we breathe, the air others breathe and the air that sustains the natural world around us. This project highlights how fashion can be used as a tool for communication, containing a message that can encourage change. The project has been used as a campaigning tool in China and in an educational setting in London, resulting in the work *Field of Jeans* – an installation highlighting the innovation and a tool for public engagement and debate.

Figure 8.2 Helen Storey's *Field of Jeans*

Radicalise practice (ideate)

> You must see design as a large and unifying concept – quite literally the remaking of the human presence on Earth.
>
> David W. Orr[11]

Though the Local Wisdom project Professor Kate Fletcher explores the 'Craft of Use' – that is, how we use and engage with our clothes.

Through moving away from a discourse about consumption and production fashion can then address creativity, resourcefulness, ingenuity and skill. We can learn to recognise and appreciate value while at the same time examining more deeply the system within which fashion currently operates and where there is room for resistance and change. The focus on use draws on the knowledge and skills that are vital in fashion and in life: 'use presents fashion opportunities and experience differently, as grounded in people's actions and approaches, as part of an iterative on-going engagement with garments that thread through and mark our lives'.[12] The implications for design and emphasis on fashion as a place of action are crucial to empowerment and hope.

Challenge conventional aesthetics (prototype)

> Be daring, be different, be impractical, be anything that will assert integrity of purpose and imaginative vision against the play-it-safers, the creatures of the commonplace, the slaves of the ordinary.
>
> Cecil Beaton[13]

In 2008 CSF established 'Fashioning the Future' to inspire curiosity, encourage the testing of ideas and create a platform for emerging thinkers, doers, designers and innovators. Starting out by offering open-source resources to students across the world, it has been developed into a more experiential immersive summer school, engaging students and tutors from across Europe. The exploration is based on Habit(AT), a research project led by CSF's Dilys Williams that explores the possibilities for fashion to contribute to resilience as the world becomes increasingly more urbanised. There is the opportunity here to work on engaging and developing a design methodology that encourages designers to actively participate, mediate public and other collaborators and to facilitate 'fashion-making as community and place-making', and the educational setting of 'Fashioning the Future' underpins CSF's commitment to change through an active and experimental education process.

As the world becomes more urbanised, communication more global and consumerism more ubiquitous, fashion becomes more and more important as a tool of engagement and empowerment. To harness the energy and potential fashion presents is to embrace the contradictions and opportunities inherent within the industry in both hard economic terms and the softer cultural ones. CSF recognises the latent possibility of addressing the pressing challenges of climate change and issues of social justice and inequality, and of anticipating the changes that the future and the Anthropocene will bring. With 75–80 per cent of the world's population expected to be living in cities by 2015, their contribution to or draining from nature and humanity will be affected by what we as individuals and collectively can do. Human ingenuity and collaboration between people and groups will create a space for positive and active solutions, and education and new approaches can create empathy and compassion, which are vital to the empowerment of those vulnerable within our current systems.

This brief snapshot of some of our work highlights the importance of a holistic approach and the recognition of the significance of design. To utilise the potential of fashion for positive change and solutions requires a more universal approach, one that mirrors the approach to sustainability in general, where the solutions are more than the sum of their parts. To borrow from Deleuze, the fashion industry without sustainability is a body without organs.

9

CELIA ALLDRIDGE
Activist with the World March of Women

How the defence of the commons and territories has become a core part of feminist, anti-capitalist struggles

Women on the march for autonomy over our bodies and self-determination of our territories ... until we are all free!

The World March of Women (WMW) is an international, feminist, anti-capitalist movement bringing together organised grassroots women – as individuals or as part of groups, collectives, trade unions, social movements, etc. – in the struggle against all forms of inequality and discrimination against women. WMW actions are founded on anti-systemic analyses of the patriarchal, racist, lesbo/homophobic, capitalist system, with the aim of transforming women's lives through international solidarity, the strengthening of women's resistances and the construction of feminist alternatives. We carry out our struggles in our communities, workplaces, families, public spaces, and in alliance with other progressive social movements.

This essay looks at how the defence of the 'common good' and of our territories has become an organic part of WMW analyses and actions. It begins with a brief look at key WMW documents in order to illustrate the evolution of internal debates, beginning with the idea of environmental protection, and followed by the collective construction of the WMW Action Area 'The common good and public services' (from 2006 onwards). It ends with a look ahead to the 4th WMW International Action in 2015 and the formulation of a working concept of women's territories.

During this period, at both the local and international levels,[1] the WMW has highlighted the relationship between the exploitation and commodification of nature and of women's work and bodies as infinite resources within the current phase of capitalist accumulation. As the 4th International Action approaches, this essay will show how the WMW continues to defend and strengthen feminist alternatives towards the building of societies in which the harmonious relationships between women and their bodies, between peoples and between people and the environment, lie at the heart of the production–reproduction model.

Women reflecting on and strengthening their relationship with nature and the environment

The first key WMW document was collectively written in 2000 to accompany the 1st WMW International Action, and comprises seventeen demands for the elimination of the causes at the root of poverty and violence against women, one of which mentions the need for food security for women. In 2003, the WMW Declaration of Values was adopted during the 4th WMW International Meeting (IM), and includes a more explicit reference to women building 'a world in which the environment is protected'.

The content of the 'Women's Global Charter for Humanity' was collectively discussed and constructed by WMW activists around the world – including a significant and growing number of rural women's groups – throughout 2004 and officially adopted at the end of the year. It describes the world women want to build, based on five values – equality, freedom, solidarity, justice and peace – and includes references to equal and fair access to natural resources, environmental preservation and sustainability and food sovereignty. This charter was physically and politically taken around the world during the 2nd WMW International Action in 2005, inspiring and strengthening grassroots women and their groups in urban and rural areas!

However, it was in 2006 that WMW activists really began to engage with the environmental debate, following the lead of the WMW–Philippines in relation to the concept of biodiversity, and from allied movement La Vía Campesina in relation to the struggle for food sovereignty. At the 6th WMW International Meeting in Peru in the same year, four WMW Action Areas were proposed, with a strong debate taking place around environmental issues that was the first step towards the definition of the 'The common good and public services' Action Area. Delegates discussed women's role in the protection of biodiversity, seed diversity and cultivation, the use of medicinal plants, and the struggle for continued access to land and water, among other issues.

It was during this same IM that delegates revised the 'Goals of the WMW' and incorporated a specific environmental objective to the list of objectives and values, thus reflecting the debate outlined above. Objective #7 was written as follows: 'Develop and implement feminist actions and proposals that denounce the economic and financial institutions that promote the exploitation and degradation of our resources, climate change and the loss of our biodiversity. Struggle for the self-management of our environmental resources based on a development model that respects the basic needs of present and future generations.'[2]

WMW international actions and activities are shaped by local struggles and therefore it is the IM host country activists that set the tone for feminist training sessions and public activities that are included in the programme. At the 7th IM in Galicia in 2008 local WMW activists organised two days of food sovereignty activities – a local produce market, a public conference and cultural activities – and environmental issues were a prominent part of political debates. Delegates also progressed significantly with the final versions of the four WMW Action Areas, including 'The common good and public services', which affirms the principles of food and energy sovereignty, the struggle against the privatisation of nature and the highly polluting capitalist production–consumption model and our commitment to strengthening the bonds of exchange and knowledge between rural and urban women.[3]

Ariel Salleh acknowledged the evolution of the feminist-environmental debate as an organic part of WMW struggles in the preface to her 2009 anthology *Eco-Sufficiency and Global Justice: Women Write Political Ecology*, where she names the WMW as one of the social movements with whom the book's aim to rethink human–nature relations will resonate.

In 2010, 144 WMW activists from forty countries concretely demonstrated their solidarity with women from the DR Congo, during a five-day programme of public debates and actions in Bukavu, South Kivu, including a women's march with 20,000 women (and men) on 17 October. We supported the protagonism of our DRC sisters as they lifted their voices and expressed their demands and solutions for long-lasting peace, and we suffered together with them as they shared their horrendous stories of an armed conflict provoked by the fight for control of mining and forest resources that has devastating consequences for women and their communities. The control of women's bodies through mass rape, sexual and physical violence continues to be used as a weapon of war in the struggle for the control of South and North Kivu territories and the rich mineral resources they contain.

The People's Summit 2012: feminist resistance against the green economy and false market solutions

Women and men around the world are resisting the fact that nature is considered as a resource at the service of corporate profit, that is unlimited or just another product, and that becomes increasingly expensive as it becomes more and more scarce due to improper use. We women, in particular, are very active in these struggles. Our experience of being made invisible and with the devaluation of the work we do to care for others is very similar to the invisibility and devaluation of nature.[4]

Hundreds of WMW activists joined thousands of other civil society activists for the People's Summit in June 2012 to denounce the market solutions to climate change, the 'green' economy and the commodification of nature. For seven days, the streets of Rio de Janeiro, Brazil, were occupied by banners, slogans and the WMW feminist *batucada*[5] that accompanied cries of 'No to patriarchy and green economy. Yes to feminist, solidarity economy!', 'Climate justice with equality for women!' and 'Eco-capitalism does not resonate with feminism!'

As part of the Summit programme, 700 national WMW grass-roots activists as well as a small international delegation took part in several demonstrations (including a People's March with 80,000 participants), and also in plenary sessions, self-organised workshops/conferences and people's assemblies. From within these spaces we affirmed our feminist struggle for social and environmental justice and against the commodification of nature, life and our bodies. Although the WMW did not take part in the official conference, our strong physical and analytical presence at the People's Summit contributed to the weakening of other, institutional, feminist discourses that, for example, promoted the REDD++ mechanism without debating its impacts on women and their communities.

The WMW is constructing its feminist critique of the green economy and of false solutions to the current environmental, food and climate crises from the grassroots upwards. Women know from personal experience that the market 'solutions' offered by trans-national corporations and governments are causing these crises in the first place. These market mechanisms exclude indigenous and local communities and intensify environmental destruction and climate change, and include: unlimited consumption and growth; monoculture agricultural production for export; the production of agrofuels; genetically modified seeds; industrial fishing and livestock breeding; and the enclosure of communal land for 'environmental preservation' (for the carbon market, for example).

Owing to their socially constructed responsibility for sustaining their families and communities, it is women who feel the main effects of the corporate exploitation of their land and the 'common good' (water, seeds, knowledge, etc.) and whose work and bodies are controlled through commodification, economic dependence on husbands and families, violence and excess medicalisation. From a young age, girls and women are prepared for their 'natural' tasks as non-remunerated caregivers and wives primarily in the private sphere – the home and family – and low-paid employees in the public sphere – in the services, as health or education professionals, as domestic workers, etc. In this way, women are considered responsible for the reproduction of the labour force both in terms of household chores (cleaning, cooking and washing, etc.) and emotional care of family and community members (showing love, affection and commitment).

Women's time, energy and re(production) capacities are considered infinite resources and are thus at the same time invisible (considered outside the sphere of the market) and appropriated by the capitalist patriarchal system. Faced with the current crises mentioned above, the system relies on women's work to 'make up for' the destruction and privatisation of the common good and increasing precariousness of paid employment. Women take on multiple exploitative jobs or intensify their agricultural labour in order to continue feeding their families in the face of rising food prices. Women walk further and further to collect firewood or water, and they pick up the emotional and physical pieces of their homes and communities when they are destroyed by 'natural' disasters provoked by climate change.

On the other hand, it is also women who – from within their communities – are constructing concrete alternatives as part of the struggle for a radical transformation of the production, reproduction and consumption model. We struggle for the deconstruction of the sexual division of labour – which considers women uniquely responsible for care work, as seen above – and demand the reorganisation of domestic and care work with shared responsibility between men and women and state support. Initiatives in the areas of solidarity economy, food sovereignty and agroecology are challenging the dominant economy, as is the priority given to building solidarity between women at local and international levels and between rural and urban women. To confront the multiple crises faced by women and our communities, it is essential that these bottom-up alternatives incorporate women's contributions and anti-patriarchal, anti-racist and anti-capitalist analyses and actions.

WMW activists are guided in this struggle by feminist economy and ecofeminism analyses, particularly where they converge around social and material relations. Ecofeminism analyses strengthen our understanding of exploitation within the system, such as Salleh's explanation of capitalism as 'built on a social debt to exploited workers; an embodied debt to unpaid women for their reproductive labor; and an ecological debt to peasants and indigenes for appropriating their land and livelihood'.[6] In dialogue with ecofeminists who have developed a radical critique of the hegemonic development model – such as Maria Mies, Ariel Salleh and Vandana Shiva – feminist economy analyses affirm the need to establish a model that prioritises the 'sustainability of human life'. This model is envisaged as based on 'a harmonious relationship between humanity and nature and between human beings'[7] and the relocation of collective well-being at the centre of economic and territorial organisation.

World March of Women 4th International Action: a year of feminist struggle for bodily autonomy and territorial self-determination

We are indigenous women,
We are peasant women,
Daughters of the land and of life,
Struggling for our territories and sovereignty.[8]

As part of the preparation process for the 4th WMW International Action in 2015, activists have dedicated time at the local and international levels to analysing the current phase of capitalist accumulation known as 'accumulation by dispossession'.[9] This process is dependent on the 'same violent mechanisms of accumulation that were at the system's origin', including 'the appropriation of nature', and 'control over women's bodies and lives'.[10] During debates at the 9th IM in Brazil in August 2013 delegates and allied group guests from forty-two countries debated the current context of multiple crises and exchanged experiences of 'accumulation by dispossession' in their communities. Many of them shared very similar stories of struggles related to the defence of their land (rural and urban spaces) and for bodily autonomy; however, they had different understandings of the concept of 'territory', depending on their local realities.

In the Europe region, there are countries (for example, France and Switzerland) in which nationalist and/or right wing groups have co-opted progressive discourse and thus the idea of territory has become a concept associated with the defence of 'our' borders from outsiders, xenophobia, anti-immigrant violence, exclusion, sexism and hate politics. In the Asia-Oceania and Arab regions, we have heard the experiences of sisters from New Caledonia and Palestine, for example, for whom 'territory' is a colonial term representing the 'possession' of their country by another.

On the other hand, in the Americas region, WMW activists relate strongly to the 'defence of territory' as defined by our Guatemalan sisters, who have spent the last three years collectively discussing this concept. We have learnt that territory is 'where we live, we dream, we decide, we do, we define belonging, symbolism, spirituality, culture' (unpublished WMW Guatemala document, 2014) and that there are four defining features: our body (our primary territory), our land, nature that gives us life, our collective history. In the Americas, as in other regions, women personally and collectively experience a direct relationship between the violent exploitation of our land and the 'common good' – through large-scale mining, hydroelectric dams, monoculture agricultural production, etc. – and the violent exploitation of our bodies – through prostitution, sexual violence, trafficking – and the appropriation of our labour.

In Cajamarca, northern Peru, corporate mining megaprojects are destroying women's relationships with their territories (land, water, bodies), as expressed in the destruction of their means of subsistence (family farming, rearing of livestock) and a marked increase in sexual violence. Prostitution and trafficking have become much more widespread – as women's bodies are made available to male mining workers – and HIV and sexually transmitted diseases are on the rise. Women and their communities are attacked by sickness owing to contaminated water and by the state, which uses extreme physical violence to protect the interests of the transnational mining corporations.

In Altamira, the town closest to the Belo Monte hydroelectric dam construction site in northern Brazil, the impact on women's lives is very similar. Women's work is exploited through very low wages (for example, as cleaners in offices and workers' accommodation), while prices have risen significantly in accordance with the wages of Belo Monte educated technical staff. Women are no longer able to afford to pay for collective childcare (which used to be organised among themselves). Sexual violence, prostitution and trafficking have risen significantly, particularly among vulnerable teenagers. 'Women's bodies, through prostitution, are used as a mechanism to pacify tensions between [male] workers'[11] and as part of their right to leisure time, with whiter-skinned women reserved for better-paid workers, and the 'cheaper' bodies of local women of colour swapped for drugs.

In Paraguay, where indigenous and peasant women are also experiencing commodification of their work and bodies parallel to the strengthening of the agro-business model of land privatisations, monoculture and export production, the current pro-business president publicly recognised and stimulated this abusive relationship when he proclaimed that 'Paraguay is easy. Paraguay is like a beautiful woman'[12] at a meeting with Uruguayan entrepreneurs in October 2013. At the beginning of 2014, the president once again referred to the violent exploitation of both women and the Paraguayan territory when he encouraged Brazilian entrepreneurs to 'use and abuse Paraguay'.[13]

Although she does not use the expression 'territory', Federici[14] describes an identical appropriation process in relation to 'the commons'. She explains how, through the process of capitalist accumulation – in its original, primitive form and now in its 'accumulation by dispossession' phase – the commons have been fenced off, expropriated, privatised and over-exploited for market profit. As part of these enclosure processes, women not only lose access to the commons, but '*women themselves become the commons*'[15], as we have seen in the examples above. Women's bodies become the commons of men and the market for sexual exploitation. Parts of women's bodies become the commons for reproduction of the workforce – wombs and vaginas for giving birth, hearts and hands for care work. Women's labour becomes 'a communal good [...], a natural resource'[16] available for unpaid domestic and care work, for unpaid professional 'help' to families and communities.

For Federici[17], feminism is fundamental to defining the commons as sites not only of collective production and consumption but also of the social reproduction of life. Efforts to collectivise domestic and care work are led by women for whom community relations promote the valorisation of their labour and the survival of their families and territories. WMW and other activists around the world are demonstrating that it is we women who 'are the main social force standing in the way of a complete commercialisation of nature', and who have 'joined hands to chase away the loggers, made blockades against mining operations and the construction of dams, and led the revolt against the privatisation of water'[18]. Women are resisting the violent attempts to destroy their relationship with their territories and actively constructing the alternatives and elements that they and their communities need in order to live well within their territories.

Popular feminism is constantly being (re-)created as 'a tool that gives us visibility and allows us to be protagonists of our histories and of our country'[19]built on the unity between rural and urban women. Women are self-organising as experienced workers in their own right, and not just 'helpers' for their male community members, in order to give visibility and value to their labour. Women working in the fisheries and artisanal fishing sector in the Azores, for example, have created their own associations and networks across the different islands and now have a growing role in the fisheries sector and are taking part in fishing industry events that were once considered men-only.

Women are (re)claiming the streets and urban spaces and creating feminist alternatives to the xenophobic, nationalist discourse, as was the case in Switzerland in November 2014 when WMW activists took to the streets to say no to the 'Ecopop' initiative that aimed to drastically reduce immigration levels on the basis of 'protecting the Swiss environment and natural resources'. We are (re)occupying territories that were once under the control of armed forces or groups and (re)constructing territories that allow the free movement of people and knowledge without frontiers or restrictions based on race, colour or sexuality.

Women are struggling against the capitalist appropriation of our territories, such as in Mozambique's northern region where women are protagonists in the campaign against the mega-agribusiness project ProSavana. In a similar way, in India and Brazil, two countries that have hosted international sporting events in the last few years, women are saying no to the commodification of their bodies for sex-tourism profit and resisting forced evictions from their urban territories. In Cajamarca, Peru, and countless other places and spaces, women are self-organising in the face of intense state violence to defend their commons and reconstruct their harmonious relationship with nature and its rhythms.

During the 4th WMW International Action, from 8 March to 17 October 2015, we, World March of Women activists, continue to march for autonomy over our bodies and the self-determination of our territories under the slogan 'Women on the march until we are all free!'

WMW key documents

» 'The common good and public services' (2009), www.marche mondiale.org/actions/2010action/text/biencomun/en
» Goals (revised in 2006), www.marchemondiale.org/qui_nous_ sommes/objectifs/en
» Declaration of values (2003), www.marchemondiale.org/qui_ nous_sommes/valeurs/en
» Demands (1998, 2001), www.marchemondiale.org/revendi cations/cmicfolder.2006-01-13.7149178479/cmicarticle. 2006-01-13.8582817191/en

» Rules and By-laws (revised in 2011), www.marchemondiale. org/qui_nous_sommes/statuts/en/base_view
» Women's Global Charter for Humanity (2004), www.marche mondiale.org/qui_nous_sommes/charte/en/base_view

10

VANDANA SHIVA

Philosopher, activist and co-author of *Ecofeminism*

Hand in hand: women's empowerment and sustainability

What would you say to those people who say 'save the planet first and talk about equality later'?

I would say that you can't save the planet without equality. I started my own journey in activism forty years ago and in the last half-century of ecological movements, it is women who have been leading at the grass roots. Women have knowledge from their experience of being the providers for societies, the custodians of biodiversity, and that experience is vital for us to understand why the planet is being so rapaciously destroyed, as well as to understand how to save the planet.

Ten years ago, as you travelled on a train from the Punjab, you wrote an article about empowering women. Can you remind us of the main issues that you were trying to raise at that time?

This was about Punjab – where I did my physics honours and which I saw as prosperous country. I saw it erupt into deep violence, killing 30,000 people in extremism, six times the scale of 9/11. I saw that women had disappeared from the farms of Punjab; they had been replaced by chemicals and tractors. In a society where women are made disposable in the economy, they are then made disposable in their lives. In the early days I saw billboards talking about sex-selective abortion, which then became the epidemic of female foeticide. States like Punjab lead in it – 50 million girls haven't been allowed to be born in India. My sister, a medical doctor, helped to draft the law to stop female foeticide. She had a map of areas where the disappearance of girls was highest and these were the same areas where the green revolution and chemical agriculture have spread most.

What do you think, if anything, has changed over the last ten years, since you wrote that article – for better or for worse?
We are living in times where in everything there are two trends. There are two trends in terms of the destruction of the planet and the protection of the planet. There are two trends in terms of increasing violence against women – and India has become an epicentre of violence against women – but there are also trends of the empowerment of women; and it is not linear phenomena, it is very much pluralistic trends; and quite clearly the trends that protect the Earth and protect women's rights are the trends that create a decent society, a liveable society, a sustainable society.

Do you see anywhere that progress on gender equality is moving steadily forward, rather than one step forward and two steps backwards? Do you see a general trend in progress, or do you think it's circular?
I think that where gender equality is directly addressed, wherever there are bodies created to empower women directly, in law and in policy, we are doing very effective work. For example, in India we have the National Commission of Women – a statutory body for gender equality. That's the commission for which I was travelling across the country – in Punjab, in Bengal, in Tamil Nadu – to assess the impact of globalisation on women. But because globalisation, like so much else in the economy, is based on a blinkered and frag-mented vision that really has been shaped by capitalist patriarchy, it defines things in a very narrow way: GDP being one of them. If you produce what you consume, you don't produce. But most women produce for the family and the community, and what they produce is consumed there, so they don't contribute to the GDP.

The increasing violence against women we are witnessing is because of the way the economy has excluded women, marginalised women, but most importantly created a world in which everyone is made to believe that everything is for sale. Your biodiversity is for sale, your water is for sale, your land is for sale – everything can be grabbed, and into that commodification fall women's bodies. All these crazy advertisements, whether selling a car or a phone, are all about the commodification of women's bodies.

So when an economy starts to touch on the devaluation of women's role and status, it brings an increasing problem of violence against women. We must redefine economic arrangements to include social externalities, like the impacts on women and ecological externalities. We're just finishing a report on the true cost of industrial farming which concludes that it is an unaffordable enterprise if you really count the costs of soil degradation, pollinator extinction, the death of our farmers. We need new economics informed by the larger picture, an economy that puts women and the Earth at the centre.

You've written and spoken about how male dominance in power relations and male-dominated viewpoints can translate into female deaths, into violence against women, into poverty for women, and into environmental degradation – especially, but not just, in agriculture. Do you see this dominance being eroded anywhere in the world, in developing or developed countries?

We see both an intensification of patriarchal signs, blinkered by the visions of men with economic and politics power, and a patriarchal economics. And the two are converging, in terms of globalisation and corporate rule, where corporate rights have higher status than the rights of people (especially women). But we are also seeing a shift, a major shift, because the crisis has become so deep that ecosystems are collapsing, economies are collapsing – not just in poor countries but in Europe; look at southern Europe, where half of the young don't have work. When you look at the big picture, people are realising that the system is only working for very few people: as the Occupy movement put it, it's a 1 per cent model. Shifting to the 99 per cent, it is the experience of women, their knowledge and wisdom, the alternatives they have in terms of what defines an economy, of what is knowledge and science – those trends, I believe, are growing very, very fast.

As a female international activist yourself, do you hold out much hope from the myriad of international negotiations on climate change, on sustainable development goals, on biodiversity? Or is there a better way to get agreements?

Those of us who were working, especially on the Convention on Biological Diversity, and also on issues of free trade and the WTO, organised very much as women. We created a movement called Diverse Women for Diversity, which was launched in Bratislava at a Convention on Biological Diversity Conference of Parties. We created this movement for two reasons: firstly, we realised that it was only women who were left to fight the long fight, because we are not part of privileged clubs, we are excluded; but when we've crossed the boundaries, the boundaries don't matter beyond a point. Secondly, we knew that we were bringing something different into play, and I remember at Seattle we had the raging grannies, we had amazing women chefs, and we made the slogan 'WTO means Women Take On, Women Take Over'.

The work we did with the Convention on Biological Diversity, the fact that we even have a Biosafety Protocol, is because I stuck to my ground there with Article 19.3, I was appointed to the expert group to shape the protocol – it wasn't an easy job, but I don't ever give up because jobs aren't easy. At the convention negotiations in Madrid, the US government stood up, as they stand up everywhere today, and said they're bringing us into the Transatlantic Trade and Investment Partnership (TTIP), saying there is no proof of harm in GMOs, it's all safe. Then a women scientist called Elaine Ingham stood up and said 'no, my government's lying to you. I've just finished research for the Europeans.' It was research on GM organisms that were meant to convert biomass into ethanol, and her research showed that all the wheat plants died with this genetically engineered Klebsiella even though the normal Klebsiella is fine in the soil.

So at the international level, when we were organised, we had a major impact. Women's presence wasn't big in the early days of the climate negotiations but now the women's ecology movement is becoming very active on the climate issue, both internationally as well as locally.

Your work also takes you to the grass roots, where you see immense hardship and poverty. But also I'm sure you see many inspiring cases and stories of women making real progress against the odds. Can you give us some examples of what has inspired you in recent times?

Most of my work is actually at the grass roots, especially through building the movement Navdanya, for creating seed sovereignty and food sovereignty. When it comes to seed and food, women are the primary actors; they are the main savers of seeds, they have the knowledge on seeds. We've created a very large network of women's food sovereignty. I've been so inspired by the fact that women have been able to take knowledge that is theirs, adapt and evolve it to the new context. They've organised and created producer crops and, through saving their traditional seeds and doing ecological agriculture, and shaping fair-trade markets, determining the price, they are earning ten times more than farmers chasing cash crops. We have the experience of the Bt cotton in India and the dependence on seed. That dependence, a death trap, has pushed 300,000 farmers to suicide.

I can give you particular examples: women growing millets are then making products from them. The millets see them through a bad drought year, they don't need irrigation, they're good nutrition for their own family, and they're good income for when they sell it. Compared to the soya bean, the round-up ready soya – in the Himalaya, where I come from, we have a very beautiful ancient kidney bean, whose taste is so good that it sells for much more – farmers who save the [kidney bean] seeds are now using that seed to grow the crop, to use locally themselves. We work on the principle of 'first for the soil, then for the family, then for the local market, then for the national market' (then tiny bits can be exported, but authentic surpluses). So the real economy, the true economy, benefits the Earth, the women and the children, and creates well-being for all throughout the food chain.

Does the seed ownership issue influence the Fairtrade schemes? Is it a requirement of some Fairtrade schemes that the self-seeding issue comes in there?

No, all of the Navdanya programmes are based on open-pollinated, open-sourced seeds, from community seed banks, seed as a commons. It is redefining the patriarchal construction, which Monsanto put into the WTO, of seed as intellectual property. Monsanto admitted that they wrote that agreement and they were the patient, diagnostician and physician all in one. In contrast to that, seed is a commons for the women's groups. Knowledge of how to do agriculture does not lie with five biotech companies – who actually don't know anything about farming, they just know how to shoot genes with a gene-gun. It lies with the women, particularly the elder women. One of the really inspiring aspects of my work at the grass roots is we realise that the older women have more knowledge. We run a grandmothers' university to transmit that knowledge from older women to younger women as well as children.

How does that actually work in practice? Does that have to be very localised, face to face, or can people learn from a distance?

It's both. A large part is to build community biodiversity registers, through which the young who know how to write but have lost the knowledge of biodiversity get it from the grandmothers, who have all the knowledge but don't know how to read and write. If their knowledge is not documented it will be lost for ever. This transfer of knowledge happens very locally, very intimately. But the wider reach has been a very important aspect of climate adaptation.

For example, Orissa on the Bay of Bengal has always had cyclones, but the cyclones are becoming more frequent with high velocities, reaching further inland. The seeds of the climate-resilient crops, like salt-tolerant rices, have been saved by the women and are used to grow in these coastal areas. These have not just allowed agriculture to continue in spite of the cyclones, but farmers of Orissa gifted two truckloads of seeds to Tamil Nadu after the tsunami. So the open-source seed means both that the seed can become seed and is open-pollinated, but it also means that the seed gets exchanged across farming communities.

How transferable are the lessons that you're producing through your grassroots project, either in specific detail or in terms of general lessons, to other countries and other cultures?
In terms of principles they are totally transferable, because they are the principles of biodiversity intensification. To intensify biodiversity you have to turn to women. When I started to do seed collections I'd go to the village and I'd ask the men 'do you have the seeds of this, this, this?' and they'd say 'no, we only grow soya' or 'we only grow potato'. Then I'd go into the kitchen and talk to the women and they'd say 'of course we grow it', back in the kitchen you see this and this and this and this, because women have to take care of the children's health, and they are growing those crops that in the marketplace have disappeared. So the principles of biodiversity intensification, intensification of women's knowledge in agriculture, which is what then leads to the broader frameworks of agro-ecology, of the links between biodiversity and climate resilience, these work across the world. The varieties of particular crops might be different, and therefore the particular knowledge might be different, but the principles are the same around the convergence between sustainability, protecting the planet and women's empowerment, especially through the knowledge of the land, of biodiversity, of agriculture, of health. That convergence, I think, is common everywhere in the world if we look for it.

How does this dynamic play out in the cities – globally we're urbanising very quickly. What's the role of this kind of knowledge in a massively urban culture?
We are in such a deep food crisis, even though we don't realise it, as well as a deep planetary crisis, and, I would say, a political crisis of a handful of corporations trying to control the planet, its resources,

our food supply and our seeds. We've been given a model of agriculture that grows about eight globally traded commodities. In these multiple crises the city must, quite clearly, begin to look more like a village in the sense that it must conserve its water, it can't just be a consumer of water; cities must stop dumping their waste into rivers; cities must become food producers – in very little space, you can produce a lot of food. In some parts of the world – the Midwest of the USA, the Punjab in India – every part of the earth is fertile and you can make your balcony fertile.

We started a very inspiring programme called Gardens of Hope. These Gardens of Hope are for those who lost their land and their husbands, in the areas where the farmer suicides have become very intense like Maharashtra, Bihar or Punjab. But these Gardens of Hope are also spreading in schools and in urban areas, and we are encouraging people in the cities to use every bit of space to work with the soil, work with the seed, grow your own food. This works as a solution to climate change, because if we can get rid of industrial agriculture and long-distance transport, which accounts for 40 per cent of the greenhouse gases, in your little balcony with five pots you've already made a contribution. We need a mind-shift because people are feeling so helpless, that climate change is too big a phenomenon and we can do nothing about it, but when you look at 40 per cent damage and that you can have a role in reducing that, then you suddenly have power. Every citizen – women, children, everyone – needs to participate in turning the city into a producer of food. Let's not forget that in other emergencies this has been done – during the war, most food eaten in England, most food eaten in Germany, most food eaten in the USA, came from gardens.

You've campaigned personally on the issue of women's empowerment and sustainability for many years, and there's no sign you're about to hang up your boots, as they say in football. So, what keeps you going? Is it anger, is it hope, or is it something else?
It's the experience of the inner power of women and the inner power of the Earth, to produce abundance on the one hand and burst back with resilience on the other. It's that inner resilience,

that inner power, for which we have a beautiful Sanskrit word which is called *Shakti*, the power from within. It's both the power from within that I witness in women and the power from within that I experience as a women.

Who are your heroes? Do you have any role models?

Most of my role models are from the grass roots; women of Chipko, they were such an amazing inspiration for me. Peasant women who teach me so much today; I keep learning more and more from them. Most importantly, they can go through the worst of hardships and yet women don't give up, such as in the terrible climate disaster in our region last year – we've had more intense rain than we've ever had, a glacier lake burst, the hydroelectric dams aggravated the damage, and 20,000 people died. Yet women don't give up.

Do you think there's any chance of achieving a healthy planet, environmental sustainability, without gender equality? If not, why do you think gender equality is largely absent from the narrative? Not just governments and corporations, but not many environmental groups actually major on gender equality. Why do you think that is?

I don't think true sustainability is possible without gender equality. The two go hand in hand. Because the same paradigm, the same mind-set, the same worldview, that has allowed humanity to destroy the planet, is the mind-set that treats women as the second sex. One defines nature as dead matter to be exploited, the other defines women as passive, as non-creative and non-productive.

The entire challenge of protecting and defending the planet is about recognising that in the final analysis, it's the Earth that has creativity, not capital; capital is a dead construct. We have created an amazing illusion to fool ourselves that capital creates and nature is dead. When we have that switch, in that same switch is the shift that women are, actually, amazing in terms of their productivity and creativity, if their productivity was counted. So, you can't have protection of the planet without the recognition of women's contributions and women's rights.

Why is it that this has been so neglected? One, most of the grassroots movements are women-led, but by the time you get to higher levels, including in environmental organisations, they become male-led. That's in the nature of dominant power in today's world. The second reason why the issue of gender equality gets forgotten is many of those people live in very distant places, they live in their heads, in constructions, in imagination, they don't have experience. In the absence of experience, they continue to reproduce the exclusions and biases against women that those on the destruction side enjoy, and that's why there is a common agenda of patriarchal domination.

So, when you travel to Europe and talk with environmental groups here, are you aware that it's a very male-dominated milieu? The difference between my going anywhere and others going anywhere is the minute I come I get farmers attending, I get lots of women, lots of babies howling in the back; the nature of the mobilisation changes.

If you could change one thing in what remains, hopefully, a very long career, what would it be?
In my life? No, I wouldn't change anything, because even the nasty experiences have been lessons of learning. I'm going through this amazing focus by the PR industry of the GMOs, who, of all the 7 billion people on the planet, can only find me to attack. But, you know, every time they attack I learn a little more. I've responded with my deepest consciousness, with the highest of intellectual integrity and very deep compassion, in everything I've done. Whichever turn my life has gone, that's the turn I took, and I have no regrets.

Looking forward, if there's one thing you could make happen, what would that be?
I'd change patriarchal science, its reductionist, mechanistic assumptions; the whole GMO assault is based on this idea of master molecules commanding the rest of life how to behave. The world

doesn't function like that, the world is a democracy of life. Second is GDP, which was created during the Depression and for the war to mobilise resources. It's time to give up GDP, it's time to give up mechanistic science, and shift to ecological economics and to ecological science – and that is where women lead.

11

QUINN BERNIER, CHIARA KOVARIK, RUTH MEINZEN-DICK and AGNES QUISUMBING

International Food Policy Research Institute

Women's empowerment in sustainable agriculture

Civil society organisations, advocacy groups and development organisations often implicitly (or explicitly) assume that women are more likely to practise environmentally sustainable and natural resource-conserving practices, driven by a greater sense of altruism and a closer connection to nature. These claims have been echoed and picked up by other actors and project implementers for various reasons, including effectiveness and efficiency. But is there evidence to support these claims? A recent review by Meinzen-Dick, Kovarik and Quisumbing[1] analyses the various assertions that have been made regarding gender and sustainability. They conclude that the empirical evidence does not support the claim that women are 'inherently more resource conserving' and argue that any understanding of how gender relates to sustainability requires 'tak[ing] account of both women and men, their intangible and intrinsic motivations, and their material conditions and means'[2]. The theme of gender and sustainable agricultural practices, however, has been underexplored; the analyses that do exist are often limited to comparing 'male-headed' and 'female-headed' households[3]. This chapter draws heavily upon the article by Meinzen-Dick et al.[4] and extends it to suggest that the Women's

Empowerment in Agriculture Index, a recent methodological innovation designed to measure gender empowerment in agricultural development, may be a useful tool/framework for thinking about and understanding the relationship between gender and sustainability.

Gender and sustainability

Sustainability refers to the ability to manage natural resources over time, 'meet[ing] the needs of the present without compromising the ability of future generations to meet their own needs.'[5] Sustainability focuses on intergenerational decisions, over a long time period spanning multiple scales, from sustainably managing household resources to larger and more global-level implications. Inequalities at the individual, household, community and national levels contribute to different incentives, motivations and resources upon which to draw and frame decisions about sustainability. Thus, sustainable outcomes are a product of both the motives and the means and opportunities of actors – both men and women.

This chapter focuses specifically on sustainability as it relates to agricultural decisions. Agriculture is both a key contributor to and at risk from global climate changes. Agricultural practices are connected with land degradation, water pollution and over-extraction, deforestation and a loss of habitat and biodiversity, among other environmental problems. At the same time, a host of agricultural practices, from agroecology and conservation agriculture to the new emphasis on sustainable intensification and climate-smart agriculture, promise to reduce environmental impact while achieving productivity gains. Yet the gendered impacts and aspects of such practices are often under-explored or ignored.

Gendered norms concerning access to resources and behaviours thus contribute to shaping both the opportunities and the context in which men and women make decisions about sustainable agricultural practices. Male and female motivations and preferences in terms of engaging (or not) in sustainable agricultural practices are complex, enmeshed in a web of historical interactions, disputes over crucial resources, social norms and motivations, which may prevent individuals from enjoying true agency in this regard.

The WEAI and sustainability

The Women's Empowerment in Agriculture Index (WEAI) was developed in 2012 by the International Food Policy Research Institute, the Oxford Poverty and Human Development Initiative, and the United States Agency for International Development to monitor women's participation in inclusive agricultural growth within the US Feed the Future Initiative. It attempts to measure empowerment in agriculture, specifically trying to capture agency in key domains where access to and control over resources, the ability to make choices, and participation in decision-making (both at the household and the community levels) contribute to overall empowerment. It is the first standardised and comprehensive measure to capture women's empowerment in agriculture. The WEAI is composed of two sub-indexes. The first sub-index, the Five Domains of Empowerment (5DE), measures the empowerment of both men and women in five domains: (1) Production; (2) Resources; (3) Income; (4) Leadership; and (5) Time. Each of these five domains can also be considered individually and can be deconstructed to explore in greater detail the specific areas in which individuals are disempowered and not able to fully exercise their choices and motivations in terms of agricultural development (or, in our case, sustainable agriculture practices). The second sub-index is the Gender Parity Index (GPI), which compares relative levels of empowerment between men and women in the same household. In this chapter we look only at the 5DE, but the GPI could also have implications for sustainability, as an individual's extent of empowerment relative to other household members potentially has impacts on ability to act sustainably.

Early studies done using the WEAI have suggested that in many communities both men and women fall below the threshold for empowerment in various domains, though the domains in which men and women are disempowered differ, as do the relative levels of disempowerment. This chapter explores how empowerment in agriculture, as measured by the WEAI, matters for sustainable agriculture – for both men and women. We discuss each domain below, drawing upon evidence on its relationship to sustainability.

1) Production

The production domain concerns decisions about agricultural production and refers to sole or joint decision-making about food and cash crop farming, livestock and fisheries, and autonomy in agricultural production. The indicators in this domain capture a person's input into productive decisions and his or her ability to act based upon what he or she values, rather than through coercion or fear of disapproval. This indicator enables us to capture the possibility that women may make production decisions by themselves, but still might feel constrained by social norms or force of circumstance. It also reflects the situation in joint households, where a 'joint' decision may be more or less autonomous, depending on circumstances. If some types of crops or cultivation techniques are viewed as gender-specific, or if women are precluded from certain activities because they are not socially acceptable, then their autonomy to undertake sustainable agricultural practices may also be affected.

Empowerment in the production domain matters to agricultural and environmental sustainability because the choice of crops grown (or livestock reared) and the techniques used in these activities have implications for resource use (or conservation) and environmental outcomes. Such choices are also influenced by access to information, which may be more freely available to men than women, owing to the tendency of many agricultural extension systems to target their messages to men. Villamor and colleagues,[6] in their research in Sumatra, found that, contrary to expectations, women are more likely than men to accept hypothetical offers of conversion of forests to oil palm and monoculture rubber plantations, which would result in both forest degradation and emissions from deforestation. Male players from the upland area of the sample showed stronger conservation beliefs, owing to their long history of interaction with conservation and research organisations.

Research among mixed-sex groups in Tanzania by German and Taye[7] finds that women and men have different priorities as a result of their gendered responsibilities for water and trees. While women value drinking water and nurseries (owing to their lack of land and tree rights), men prioritise irrigation water and trees to mark farm boundaries. Men and women may also have different preferences for trees and plants; some research finds that while women may prefer trees with more domestic use value, potential for fuelwood, bark that can be used for medicinal purposes, or branches that provide shade for children and grazing animals, men may prefer trees that have cash value[8]. Thus, the sustainable agricultural practices that men and women adopt may be constrained by their gendered roles in production, as well as interaction with outside organisations.

2) Resources

This domain captures information on (1) ownership of land and assets; (2) decisions regarding the purchase, sale or transfer of land and assets; and (3) access to and decisions about credit. The first indicator examines whether an individual reports having sole or joint ownership of land and assets (including agricultural land, large and small livestock, fish ponds, farm equipment, a house, household durables, a cell phone, non-agricultural land, and means of transportation). Although some might argue that sole ownership is more indicative of empowerment than is joint ownership, women can be more empowered if they have joint ownership of a valuable asset (such as land) than if they have sole ownership of a minor asset. The second indicator, defined with similar assets, identifies the person who can make decisions regarding the purchase, sale or transfer of land and assets. In many societies, full ownership of assets may not apply, but holding other bundles of rights – especially rights of control over purchase and disposal of assets – can also be empowering. The third indicator examines decision-making about whether to obtain credit and how to use the proceeds from credit from various sources.

Use, control and ownership rights to land, in particular, are very important determinants of men's and women's differential ability to adopt sustainable natural resource management techniques. To have complete ownership of the resource, an individual must have the ability to alienate the resource – to rent out, sell or give away the rights to the resource. It has been hypothesised that such alienation rights provide incentives for long-term investment in the resource[9]. Two examples from Ghana illustrate this point: one study in matrilineal areas found that women were more likely to plant cocoa trees on land on which they had secure, private property rights[10] and another study[11] found that individuals with less secure land rights are less likely to leave their land fallow to allow regeneration because if they are not actively farming their land they risk losing it. Our review of evidence on gender and long-term incentives for sustainability, especially for women, found that tenure security, rather than 'ownership' as perceived in Western societies, is paramount.[12] The critical factor is that no one else has the right to alienate women from their land or other natural resources. A study in Zimbabwe by Fortmann and colleagues[13] found that the potential for loss of land and trees following widowhood or divorce was an important source of insecurity for women that limited tree planting on household land; women and men were equally likely to plant trees on community wood lots because rights over those trees derived from community membership and investment, not marital status, and hence there were fewer gender differences in tenure security.

Efforts to strengthen women's land rights have been associated with higher adoption of sustainable farming techniques. For example, land certification programmes, though not considered formal titling programmes, do convey alienation rights to certificate recipients. Deininger et al.[14] found that the more aware households were of their land rights as defined by the 1998 Uganda Land Act, which strengthened tenure security and legal protection of customary owners and women, the greater their propensity to undertake soil conservation measures. Ali et al.'s study of a pilot land tenure regularisation programme in Rwanda[15] found that female-headed households exhibited a roughly 19 percentage point increase in their likelihood to construct or maintain soil conservation structures, double the impact on male-headed households. Similarly, work in Ethiopia by Deininger et al.[16] found that community-based land registration resulted in more households undertaking new land-related investments, specifically tree planting and soil conservation techniques. A follow-up survey[17] six years after the land registration found that households with more registered land were more likely to plant trees, and that trees were more likely to be planted on *women-managed* plots with more secure rights, a finding consistent with earlier studies.

Ability to obtain credit might also enable adoption of sustainable farming techniques that require upfront investments, which may deter cash-constrained farmers. For example, building terraces or planting tree crops with long gestation periods may be impossible for women who have responsibilities to feed their families today, unless there is credit to enable them to pay for current expenses. Finally, having control over or access to resources may allow farmers' discount rates to change, making them more willing to invest in sustainable practices now for benefits in the future.

3) Income
The single indicator for this dimension measures the degree of input into decisions about the use of income generated from the productive/income-generating activities mentioned above, as well as the extent to which the individual feels he or she can make his or her own personal decisions regarding wage or salary employment.

This aspect of empowerment is important, for it would allow individuals to direct resources towards sustainable agricultural investments, including tree planting or soil and water conservation structures. Similarly, it suggests a greater degree of bargaining power over household expenditures and decisions, which include whether or not to invest in sustainable agriculture. Moreover, this would allow individuals the ability to more directly realise their motivations and preferences for sustainable agricultural practices. However, we should not assume that this necessarily correlates to greater investment in sustainable agricultural practices. Choices of investment options are likely influenced by risk and preferences, which may vary between men and women.

Without access to and control of income, individuals may similarly be forced to rely on natural resources or common property to meet family and household needs, which might increase degradation of natural resources. In some countries like India, women must provide the fuel to cook the evening meal and may do something unsustainable to guarantee short-term subsistence[18]. They may also be less inclined to participate in the sustainable management of such resources, if the proceeds or benefits of these actions fall only to men (see, for example, some of the early intra-household literature by Dey, von Braun and Webb, and Jones[19]).

4) Leadership

The fourth domain concerns leadership in the community, here measured by: (1) membership in at least one economic or social group and (2) comfort speaking in public. Group membership can contribute to sustainability by facilitating access to information, technologies, credit, building assets, and importantly in regulating access to, use and maintenance of common pool resources[20]. Certain agricultural practices, such as integrated pest management or community soil and water conservation, extend beyond farm boundaries and require coordination, which groups can facilitate. But the types of groups men and women belong to also matter: men are more likely to belong to producers' organisations, which are often a major channel for information and technology dissemination.[21] Using religious or microfinance groups may be more effective in reaching women with information about sustainable practices.

Decentralisation programmes often transfer management of both natural resources and the public finances to maintain those resources to local governments or user groups. In such cases, membership in these groups is important for influencing the investment in and use of these natural resources, and it is important to consider whether women as well as men have an effective voice. For example, are women's needs for firewood considered when forest user groups make rules for forest management, or domestic water needs considered along with irrigation in water user groups? If decentralisation programmes empower 'communities', it is important to consider *who* within the communities will be empowered.

Mere membership is not always enough. Confidence in speaking in public makes it easier for people to participate in decision-making about natural resource use and conservation at community levels. Agarwal[22] finds that the proportion of women in leadership of forest groups is important for effective participation. But when women are empowered to speak in public it does not necessarily mean they will sustain the resource base: that depends on men's and women's identification of their short- and long-term preferences and interests. As noted in the Indonesian example above, women are not necessarily always more resource-conserving, especially when they need water or fuel to meet their domestic responsibilities.

5) Time

The WEAI time domain has two indicators: (1) an individual's workload, both in productive and domestic tasks, measured over the previous twenty-four hours; and (2) satisfaction with leisure time.

In many societies, men and women undertake different tasks, as prescribed by socially relevant gender norms in that area. Women often undertake both domestic and productive roles, though this differs greatly between societies. WEAI findings from thirteen Feed the Future baseline surveys show that both men and women display high levels of time poverty across countries, though these levels are generally higher for women.[23]

The links between gendered time constraints and sustainability are complex and multidimensional. There is often an assumption that women will be affected more than men by environmental degradation, particularly as natural resources like wood and water are depleted and women must spend more time gathering them.[24] Some research does support this theory; for example, research in Nepal by Kumar and Hotchkiss[25] finds that as deforestation increases, so too does women's time burden, along with household income, food consumption and nutrition. However, evidence also points to an increase in men's time due to environmental degradation, though in different ways. Research in Ghana's Volta region shows that in times of drought men's and women's time are both affected, with women's workloads increasing and men moving to cities in search of work.[26] Research in Malaysia finds that commercial logging resulted in higher time burdens for both men and women, though over time, as men migrated, women's time burdens increased more.[27]

Time is also required to undertake many sustainable practices or engage in groups and meetings that discuss these issues. In cases where adopting a sustainable technique is time-consuming, men may have an advantage. Quisumbing and Kumar's study in Ethiopia[28] finds that while male- and female-headed households are equally likely to adopt time-intensive soil conservation techniques, adoption rates are higher in larger households with higher labour resources. Men are often more able than women to mobilise labour or hire outside labour, making it possible that women may be less able to undertake these time-intensive practices. However, even if higher levels of time are required for a particular activity, an individual may view the trade-offs as worthwhile. A study in Senegal finds that women support their husbands' adopting livestock stabling practices, even though stabling increases women's workloads, because it positively impacts their lives and the lives of their children.[29]

Conclusions

Empowerment does matter for environmental sustainability – both for men and for women. Empowerment is about the expansion of choices and the ability and agency to act on motivations and preferences for adopting (in this case) sustainable agricultural practices. Critically, many men and women around the world are disempowered in many of the domains that circumscribe their ability to act on their desires and motivations. However, we cannot assert that women's empowerment necessarily leads to greater sustainable outcomes, for as Meinzen-Dick et al.[30] found, there is little empirical evidence that women are inherently more sustainable or resource-conserving than men.

However, there are still important gender differences to address. Men are more likely to have access to key resources that enable them to adopt sustainable practices or have ownership over assets necessary for sustainable agricultural practices. Moreover, access to information about sustainable agricultural practices is critical – and often more available to men than to women. Certainly more education, awareness and behaviour change around agricultural and environmental sustainability is needed. These behaviour-change interventions will be more effective, though, when complemented with efforts to ensure that both men and women attain sufficient levels of empowerment in the five domains covered here (production, resources, income, leadership and time) to have the agency to act on their desires and motivations for sustainability.

While engaging women in sustainable initiatives is important, and can have multiple benefits for the individual and her household, assuming that women will be able to participate is problematic because it places the burden solely upon them, and this is often a burden they have no time to bear. Engaging both men and women in sustainable initiatives, and encouraging them to share the necessary time burden for involvement, is key.

12

ISABEL BOTTOMS
and AMENA SHARAF

Egyptian Centre for Economic and Social Rights

The impacts of environmental mismanagement on Egypt's poor

Many of the major sustainability challenges facing Egypt today are a result of endemic mismanagement of resources, namely: the current energy crisis; the pollution of the country's main water source, the Nile; overuse of non-renewable water aquifers; increasing air pollution in urban areas; and exploding bad-quality urbanisation. None of the Millennium Development Goals such as agricultural productivity and access to water and health services can be met without major changes to energy, water and land management and policies in Egypt. With roughly 40 per cent of Egyptians living below the poverty line of $2 a day,[1] unemployment reaching over 13 per cent, low rates of economic growth and continuous political turmoil, continuing down the path of the past sixty years will have disastrous results, particularly for the lowest-income quintiles of the population and for the bottom section of the middle class, who could easily slip into the lower quintiles.

Egypt's people inhabit and operate within lumbering inefficient systems that also offer the key to rolling out sustainable development policies across the country. The most influential of these include the distribution of land and resources for housing: while the government provides free or low-priced land for expensive and elite housing and profit-making projects, the lowest quintiles most in need of affordable housing have worked to meet their own needs, creating a huge informal housing sector that is not officially recognised by the state

– rejecting the state system of housing provision altogether. Egypt's famous bureaucracy, which holds the key to gaining access to smart cards for welfare, pensions, licences and other permissions, is notoriously old fashioned, slow and liable to petty corruption. The education system for those unable to afford the private schools of the middle and upper classes is very bad quality, and many children subsist outside the educational system their whole lives. Provision of free health services is highly geographically dependent – the urban areas have the most access, but the health service is nearing collapse with the increasing burdens of an unhealthy and growing population, and with a budget that has not increased in line with inflation over the last ten years. Distribution of pollution (air and water) is clearly in favour of the middle and upper classes, with the workers and their families placed in the immediate vicinity of industrial facilities, or whole industrial areas built up in spite of the close low-income residential population. The state's law enforcement is biased, prone to corruption and in some legal cases politically motivated; therefore police forces target the most precariously placed in society, living and working in the informal sector, for example, while failing to enforce industry's flouting of pollution regulations. Finally, governance on the local, governorate and national levels has been in huge flux in the last three years, with the military consolidating its economic and political might and now crushing dissent more robustly than ever before.

These systemic biases, which work against the low-income quintiles, are creating vast inequalities of opportunity from the day a child is born.[2] These inequalities are perpetuated as their life goes on, in an influential mix of constraining but failing systems and Egypt's Islamic culture, which has been increasingly affected by the return migration of Egyptians from the more Islamically conservative Kingdom of Saudi Arabia. Egypt's future sustainable development therefore relies on participation, ideas, policies and local action within these current constraints.

If we consider the place and status of women within the context just outlined, we find further constraining factors in daily life. In Egypt a woman's status centres around her marriage status: single, engaged, married, divorced or widowed. Generally her boundaries and freedoms are dictated thus, the effect increasing the less wealthy a woman or her family is. The secondary determinants of status are children, then employment, then health and then education. Research has shown that education is not a determining factor in marriage, but employment is; especially when one notes that employment is not an adverse factor in terms of whether women marry or not; in fact it is often seen as facilitative,[3] and studies of women of all ages show marriage does not take them out of the workplace, it only adds on time spent doing domestic work (childcare, cooking, cleaning);[4] 52.49 per cent of women working in the labour market in Egypt are married with children.[5] Furthermore, given a choice between education and marriage, young women are predominantly choosing marriage.[6]

While education might come last in the list of life priorities for the lowest-income quintiles, studies are showing that:

'The median age at first marriage among women with a secondary education or higher was 22.9 years, more than three years higher than the median age among women who have completed the primary but not the secondary level (19.3 years) and about five years higher than among women who never attended school (18.0 years). The median age at first marriage also rises with the wealthiest quintile.'[7]

Given the finality of marriage for Egyptian young women – within a year it is normal that she 'prove her fertility',[8] she is unlikely to divorce, her social status depends on a good and successful marriage – we find this to be an important timeline to consider when offering sustainable women's empowerment solutions in Egypt. We do not aim to change the centrality of marriage, but rather to suggest methods of giving young women greater choice over the direction of their lives, whether it be domestic, academic or labour related, before marriage. The final consideration for the importance of investing in young women's self-management and independence is that polls show that women who make their own financial contribution to their household have total or an equal say over aspects of how the household is run and how money is spent;

furthermore, greater financial and social independence (e.g. basic reading and maths skills) seems to reduce the likelihood of them experiencing domestic violence. We will go on to show how these issues, which are seemingly unrelated to issues of sustainability, are in the fact key factors affecting women's agency in Egypt today.

Just under half of the female population live in urban situations. In the lowest social quintiles of urban areas, it is clear that women are experiencing a web of interconnected health, housing and environmental issues that compromise their ability to be active members of the community, participate in local governance or provide for their families.

The following is a summary of the responses of women living in three different unofficial settlements in Cairo, recorded as part of a baseline study in 2013/14 by G.I.Z.'s participatory development programme.[9] They told us some of the pressures they experience daily.

> Meet **Om Islam**, she lives in a house without a roof, she has four kids and is pregnant with a fifth. Like most of the residents in Ezbet El Nasr – one of Cairo's settlements in the direst of circumstances – her family doesn't own the house they live in yet she's been living in the same apartment in the settlement for seventeen years. Om Islam lives with her four kids, her husband and her brother in law in a two-bedroom house, and like a lot of the women in the settlement, she's unaware of the reality beyond the walls of her house. Climate change is a foreign concept to her but her house is extremely vulnerable, and her family has the diseases to prove it. Om Islam suffers from a stomach ulcer and a clogged urinary tract, she admits the extreme heat makes her medical condition – and pregnancy – a lot harder. Less exposure to the elements with the construction of a roof and a building with better insulation and therefore thermal regulation would of course help.
>
> **Om Sabreen** is another Ezbet El Nasr resident, she's been living there for as long as Om Islam. Om Sabreen lives with her seven children, her husband, her son in law, her

daughter's kids and her mother. Om Sabreen has to take care of her mother who has allergies and her daughter since she had her artery replaced. And just like Om Islam, her weight burdens her and her health.

Om Doaa's been living in Ezbet El Nasr for eleven years, she hasn't left her damp, unventilated two-bedroom apartment for years. Om Doaa suffers from a medical condition in her bones. She can't afford diagnosis or treatment, so she stays inside the apartment indefinitely, when asked about the neighbourhood, her daughters and herself have no answers, they are completely oblivious to the conditions of the neighbourhood, the weather and the streets.

Om Abanoub, over 80 years old, has been living in Ezbet El Nasr for 25 years. She has diabetes, hypertension and doctors told her she has an issue with her liver but she can't afford to get it checked out. Since her husband died of a heart attack, she has not been to their room; she sleeps in the hallway, she doesn't leave the house and she hasn't been to church.

The settlement of Masaken Geziret El Dahab/Saqiet Mekki is located in Giza, Cairo. Although the social and economic circumstances in Saqiet Mekki are better than those of Ezbet El Nasr, the neighbourhood is still an unofficial settlement under legal threat of demolition at any time.

Om Torky has been living here for forty years; she suffers from allergies and digestive issues. Om Torky mentioned repeatedly how she's excited about the thought of an activity occupying her time, but she says she's never had the chance for that. Another resident who refused to reveal her name talked about how her mother suffers from a medical condition that means she spends most of her time taking care of her; she loves the idea of an extra activity just for herself but she's also never had the chance.

These are just a few of the women who live in unofficial settlements, which constitute 60 per cent of the residential areas in Cairo yet are under-represented in every system Egypt has to offer.

It was clear from this baseline study that these issues (namely quality of housing and health) imposed a heavy burden on the women. They are dominant daily refrains that are in some cases debilitating. If Egypt's governance systems were entirely open and participatory, if Egypt's labour market did promote equality of opportunity, if Egypt's private sector better facilitated small start-ups, etc., women would be required to overcome the daily challenges described above before even beginning to tackle the constraints of the systems they wish to participate in for a more sustainable Egypt.

Although these voices mostly go unheard, their health issues are not exceptions, they are the norm in Egypt, and the government is well aware of the increasing epidemic of cardiovascular disease and related issues, but the public health system is badly equipped to diagnose and treat it. In Egypt being overweight is more common in males (38.2 per cent are overweight) than in females, but there is a higher incidence of obesity in females (39 per cent) than in males.[10] These obese women are four times more likely to be hypertensive than those with a normal body mass index (BMI);[11] of the women with hypertension, 50.3 per cent were obese.[12] Hypertension is a known contributing factor to heart disease and kidney failure. Egypt has an increasing burden of cases in both areas.

Hypertension in Egyptian women is predominantly caused by a diet high in oils, fats and carbohydrates, but, most importantly, inactivity. Inactivity is of course a result of lack of mobility either from health issues, societal expectations or lack of appropriate spaces (either to exercise or to simply get out of the house). Hypertension continues to be the highest contributing factor to chronic renal (kidney) failure in Egypt.[13]

The head of the Nephrology Department at the International Medical Centre in Cairo confirms this but also identifies one cause of kidney failure as water pollution, with a build-up of heavy metals found in untreated waste water which enters the Nile and is then used as the primary source of drinking water. Public health researchers based in Minya (a rural governorate) identified drinking unsafe water and exposure to pesticides as the cause of renal diseases for an estimated 72 per cent of their patients. In general the renal disease hot spots tend to correlate with areas of unsafe drinking water, and investment in safe drinking water infrastructure is centred on the most populated and affluent residential areas in Egypt.

Water pollution negatively affects the poorest's ability to live more healthily and develop their communities, but it also makes being poor more expensive. While the rich can place themselves as far away from the sources of pollution as they please, the poor have the water and air pollution imposed upon them and must pay the treatment costs resulting from the diseases brought on by the pollution, or in some cases pay the ultimate price: death. If it is the death of the working man or woman in the family, this further grinds down their ability to lift themselves out of poverty and raise their standard of life. Additionally the government treats the drinking water of the richer urban areas so inhabitants here don't suffer the same diseases, which gives them a head start in moving up the economic ladder unhindered by the medical costs that burden the poor, and business interests are able to avoid treating their waste water because their business is too important to the government for it to enforce its own standards. This is a vicious and continual cycle that serves the few at the expense of the many, which can by no means be the basis of a sustainable society.

The effect of such local environmental and housing issues must be considered in light of poor women's lack of mobility. Their routines remain fairly static; they do not have as wide a scope of movement as their husband or male counterparts. This in turn ensures that environmental factors that affect health, whether it be damp apartments, open roofs or proximity to pollution sources, are affecting women much more than males, who tend to be working away from the home every day. Given their direct experience of 'weather', a collect-all term for their collective observations as to their vulnerability to the extremes of hot, cold, damp and dust, women's greater exposure to bad building design is a big concern.

Some of the women interviewed commented on their frustration at their lack of mobility, as only tuk-tuks (small three-wheeled rickshaws with an engine) can access the interior roads of a settlement, but often they don't penetrate the settlement very far, forcing women to walk long distances in the heat, in black abayas (body coverings), and often with health problems, small children or elderly family members. Increased spread and consistency of affordable public transport options are essential to women's mobility, which they most often need for employment, domestic shopping, healthcare or educational opportunities.

Thus our Egypt-specific recommendations for action are firmly practical in nature, and would contribute to an immediate improvement in the lives of women in Egypt, who are so vulnerable amid Egypt's plethora of failing systems. We feel that the interconnections between factors affecting women's lives must be faced and tackled in their complex totality, just as Egypt's issues of governance, economy and environment must be.

1) Better living conditions

» On-the-ground, localised spatial planning and building design workshops to help inform the informal building sector of the popular areas.

» Improved transportation within popular areas: e.g. agreed tuk-tuk stations and routes with set prices, akin to the microbus system already in place.

2) Health

» Free mobile check-up clinics working regularly in one area at a time to deal with:
  – Sexual health concerns
  – Vaccinations
  – Hypertension, weight issues and diabetes
  Mobile blood donation units are regularly deployed around Cairo, some owned by NGOs and some by the Ministry of Health

» Creation of safe spaces indoors and outdoors, for women to go with their children, to attend exercise classes and/or a gym, receive nutritional advice, walk and play with their children and friends

3) Education

» Localised adult education opportunities, advertised directly to the local women who might not feel confident about attending. The formation of street working groups so they can work together and support each other throughout the programme.

13

NATHALIE HOLVOET and LIESBETH INBERG

University of Antwerp

How gender-sensitive are National Adaptation Programmes of Action? Selected findings from a desk review of thirty-one sub-Saharan African countries[1]

Introduction

There is nowadays a growing acknowledgement of the fact that policies to address climate change are influenced not only by technological development but also by the local institutional factors and norms which generally shape human behaviour.[2] The sociocultural construct 'gender' is such a set of norms which influences how men and women are affected by and respond to climate change. In addition to factors such as income, class and caste, gender relations determine the degree of access to and control that individuals have over different types of resources, their division of labour within productive, reproductive and community activities, as well as their level of involvement in decision-making at household, community and (inter)national levels. This differential positioning in society affects individuals' vulnerability to climate change, their capacities to adapt to climate change as well as their needs and potential contributions with regard to adaptation and mitigation. The growing realisation that ignoring the mediating influence of gender relations may put into perspective the effectiveness of adaptation and mitigation policies has gradually brought gender issues onto the agenda of national and international fora.

The 2010 Cancún agreements adopted during the 16th Conference of the United Nations Framework Convention on Climate Change (UNFCC), as well as the more recent 2012 Doha Conference, are a case in point. While the original 1992 UNFCC was totally gender blind and even disregarded one of the principles of the Rio Declaration on Environment and Development,[3] the 2010 Cancún Agreements refer for the first time to the importance of gender,[4] and recognise that 'gender equality and the effective participation of women and indigenous people are important for effective action on all aspects of climate change'.[5] In line with this, the Declaration of the recent Doha Conference explicitly highlights that women continue to be under-represented and recognises that a more balanced representation of women from developed and developing countries in the UNFCCC process is important in order to create climate policies that respond to the different needs of men and women in national and local contexts.[6]

Prior to the Cancún agreements, the importance of integrating a gender dimension in adaption programmes was already acknowledged in the 2002 list of principles that guides the preparation of National Adaptation Programmes of Action (NAPAs). NAPAs are country-owned policy documents in which countries that are most vulnerable to climate change diagnose the (likely) effects of climate change and identify priority adaptation projects to address their most urgent needs.[7] One of several stipulations of the NAPA guidelines,[8] developed by the Least Developed Countries Expert Group, states that NAPA teams should include gender expertise and that processes should be participatory and involve both men and women at grassroots level as they have knowledge of existing adaptation practices, while at the same time being among the most affected by climate changes.[9]

Confronting discourse with praxis, however, demonstrates that the locally grounded knowledge of rural women and men has thus far largely been disregarded when designing national adaption policies[10] while, in addition, gender issues have hardly been taken on board when elaborating NAPAs.[11] A 2009 internal review of thirty-nine NAPAs conducted by the Gender Advisory Team of the

United Nations Office for the Coordination of Humanitarian Affairs (OCHA) points out that several of the NAPAs mention gender equality and women's empowerment as principles, though very few demonstrate a clear commitment to these principles by mainstreaming gender throughout the document. About half of the NAPAs identify gender-differentiated impacts from climate change without, however, translating this observation into project selection and/or design.[12]

Our study connects with this research agenda and complements the internal reviews with a more comprehensive gender analysis of the thirty-one sub-Saharan African NAPAs[13] that have been elaborated between 2004 and 2011. First, it examines and compares the integration of a gender dimension into the different phases of the NAPA cycle. Next, it assesses whether the different sectors that are most directly related to climate change, such as agriculture, energy, forestry, water and sanitation and health, score differently on gender sensitivity. In addition to this more quantitative assessment we also analyse in more detail the way in which women and gender issues are conceptualised in the NAPAs as well as the gender sensitivity of the underlying processes.

Our mapping of the gender sensitivity of sub-Saharan African NAPAs' contents and processes aims to feed into the work of the Gender Office of the International Union for Conservation of Nature (IUCN)[14] to render future NAPAs and National Adaptation Plans (NAPs)[15] more gender sensitive. In doing this, we aim to avoid another case of 'gender retrofitting', which is particularly relevant against a background of mounting budgets that are nowadays channelled through climate funds.

Before presenting and discussing the findings of the gender analysis in section 3, we briefly discuss different discourses and approaches towards gender and climate change in section 2.

Gender and climate change: different discourses and approaches

The rationale for the integration of a gender dimension into climate change adaptation (and mitigation) policies and activities is generally argued on the basis of welfare, equality, poverty and efficiency grounds. Browsing in more detail through the relatively recent but rapidly expanding literature on gender and climate change highlights that the different discourses resonate well with the different approaches to women/gender and development which have subsequently been designed and implemented from the 1950s onwards.

The two most frequently heard claims to promote the integration of a gender dimension in adaptation (and mitigation) policies[16] relate to women's 'vulnerability' and 'virtuousness' with respect to climate change. First, women, and particularly poor rural women in the South, are considered to be particularly vulnerable to climate change because they have less access to and control over land, money, credit and information while also having a lower personal mobility than men, which are all factors that affect the ability to adapt to climate change. They tend to be disproportionately affected by water and fuel scarcity and land degradation because they are predominantly engaged in household reproductive activities such as gathering water, fuel and other biomass resources, food preparation and caretaking.[17] Secondly, because of their higher dependency on natural resources, women are simultaneously considered to be more environmentally conscious and their contributions are considered vital for a more effective and efficient management of common property natural resources.[18]

This conceptualisation of women as 'vulnerable victims' on the one hand and 'responsible heroines' on the other hand neatly fits the pre-WID (Women in Development) welfare and WID anti-poverty and efficiency approaches. While there are important differences between the pre-WID welfare and the WID anti-poverty and efficiency approaches, at the same time they are highly similar in that they largely focus on women in isolation, while neglecting the importance of underlying gender relations to explain the observed inequalities between men and women. The importance of the sociocultural construct 'gender' has mainly been emphasised in the Gender and Development (GAD) approach, which starts from the idea that interventions in all thematic areas and at all levels (global, macro, meso and micro) are influenced by the existing structural features in societies, which differentiate among different individuals. Conversely, the assumption is that all interventions also potentially influence gender (and other) relations. Disregarding this mutually influencing relationship may lead to policy failures and a worsening of the already existing male bias in terms of allocation of resources and decision-making power.[19] This also holds for interventions in the agriculture, energy, forestry, health, water and sanitation sectors, which are those most closely associated with climate change and in which evidence exists demonstrating that the neglect of gender leads to further environmental degradation, something which in itself may intensify already existing gender-based inequalities.[20]

From the vantage point of this mutually influencing relationship between 'gender' and 'development', there is a need to integrate a gender dimension throughout the different stages (diagnosis, planning, implementation, budgeting, monitoring and evaluation) of all types of interventions at any level, i.e. gender mainstreaming. In addition to a top-down approach there is also a need for more bottom-up interventions that aim to modify the underlying gendered structures of constraint, this being particularly important in areas that are strongly regulated by gender norms. While institutional changes are never easy to achieve,[21] literature and history have shown that they are more likely to be possible when individuals act as a group through collective action. Such instances of collective action that lead to marginal institutional changes may also arise in the context of interventions in typical 'climate change sectors'. Well-known examples are cases of water and sanitation or forest conservation projects that initially started as welfare or efficiency initiatives aimed at satisfying practical gender needs, but which gradually evolve into instances of collective action where groups of women increasingly gain decision-making power with respect to water, land and forest management both inside and outside the household.[22] This also hints at the fact that interventions originally designed from a welfare or anti-poverty perspective can also gradually evolve into interventions that aim at tackling the more deep-rooted gender norms, or serve as entry points for this type of intervention.[23] However, when using instrumentalist framing to get gender issues onto the agenda, one should also be on the lookout for 'myth creation' and 'essentialism'.[24]

Discussion of findings and way forward

Despite an increasing acknowledgement of the importance of integrating a gender dimension into interventions related to climate change and reference to gender in the NAPA guidelines, the findings of our own stocktaking exercise of all 2004 to 2011 sub-Saharan African NAPAs lend credence to evidence from earlier research[25] and point at a low degree of gender sensitivity in NAPA's content with ten of the thirty-one NAPAs being entirely gender blind. When a gender dimension is included, it is mostly in sections dealing with the identification of projects and fails to be translated into budgets, indicators and targets. This dilution is indicative of the phenomenon of policy evaporation, which is particularly prevalent in the area of gender mainstreaming. When comparing gender sensitivity over different sectors, we do not come across substantial differences in gender sensitivy. While the agricultural sector outperforms the others when it comes to the selection of interventions, this pattern does not hold true for other phases.

The fact that none of the NAPAs include an in-depth analysis of gender issues in their diagnosis section already hints at the absence of a Gender and Development (GAD) approach in the NAPAs under study. As a GAD approach originates in the idea that there is a mutually influencing relationship between climate change and gender relations, some gender analysis would be expected at the outset of the NAPA which would then feed into the selection of interventions. The absence of a GAD approach does not entirely come as a surprise and is in line with Terry,[26] who highlighted that a GAD approach is not yet common in work and discussions on climate change. In the NAPAs under study, there is in particular a strong tendency to depict women as victims, a conclusion which was also arrived at by Rodenberg[27] in her review of climate change discussions and processes. Women are often lumped together with children and the elderly under a heading of 'vulnerable' and several NAPAs specifically refer to female-headed households in this respect. Interestingly, the other myth of women being 'virtuous' and more environmentally conscious is much less present in the NAPAs under study. The only prominent case is the NAPA of Mauritania, which explicitly highlights that 'women are often the chief guardians of vital local and traditional knowledge'.[28] Although at this relatively early stage of gender & climate change work, NAPAs are drawing particularly upon welfare arguments when including gender & women issues, it is highly likely that a WID efficiency approach which stresses more heavily women's virtuousness will become more prevalent in the future. What both these myths of 'vulnerability' and 'virtuousness' have in common is the fact that the importance of the underlying gendered structures which influence men's and women's constraints, opportunities and incentives with respect to adaptation remains out of the picture. This ignorance of the interplay between gender and adaptation influences the type of NAPA interventions designed, their effectiveness and their impact, both on adaptation as well as on gender equality outcomes.

Information with respect to diagnostic and decision-making processes was available only for a limited sub-sample of NAPAs, which might affect the external validity of these findings. For the specific sub-sample under study, the process was more gender sensitive than the content and no correlation was found between the gender sensitivity of the content and the process. Looking beyond the mere presence of women and gender experts shows that the urban middle-class women around the table do not necessarily have a high stake in the sectors most closely related to climate change, while gender experts might also not (yet) have enough expertise in the area of adaptation policies to steer the promotion of a gender dimension in NAPAs. The generally limited track record of gender & climate change is also evident from the absence of operational gender mainstreaming tools and approaches that are framed in 'climate change' terminology. Such framing of gender issues alongside the 'frames' of the area or ministries has proved important in triggering the implementation of gender mainstreaming by non gender experts.[29]

As Cornwall et al.[30] put it, 'when development actors seize upon feminist ideas they want them in a form that is useful for their own frameworks, analyses and overall policy objectives'.[31]

Brokering of relationships among local and central-level gender actors who have different comparative advantages when it comes to influencing climate change processes, as well as bridging gaps among gender and climate change experts, are areas in which climate change funds might invest part of their resources. It is, in particular, such exchanges and networking among actors with different knowledge and experience bases which might trigger more gender-sensitive processes with a long-term pay-off in terms of the content of future NAPAs and NAPs. Another area for further investment, research and experimentation is gender budgeting, which refers to the analysis of the differential impact of government budgets on women and men, as well as to the systematic integration of a gender perspective throughout the budget cycle. Gender budgeting is particularly relevant and timely when set against the background of the considerable amount of resources that are currently being channelled through climate change funds.

Finally, insights from the current desk study might obviously benefit from complementary field research focusing on a small number of well-selected cases, such as the relatively more gender-sensitive NAPAs of Burkina Faso and Malawi. Such in-depth field research would be interesting as a reality check for the findings of the desk study, but might also enable a better understanding of the underlying factors that have contributed towards the higher level of gender mainstreaming.

14

SHUKRI HAJI ISMAIL BANDARE and FATIMA JIBRELL

NGO leaders

Women, conflict and the environment in Somali society

Somali women have been at the forefront of environmental activism since the early 1990s. Two of these inspirational leaders are Shukri Ismail Bandare and Fatima Jibrell. They have both founded non-governmental organisations (NGOs) to help local communities protect their environment and use natural resources more sustainably. The vital role of women and gender equality in environmental protection has been at the core of their work. In the face of civil war, a fragile arid/semi-arid environment, poverty and a traditional patriarchal society, the achievements of these women and their colleagues are immense. In interviews in late 2014 and early 2015 for Friends of the Earth, they contributed their experiences and ideas on gender equality and environmental sustainability.

Shukri Haji Ismail Bandare has served as the minister for environment of Somaliland[1] since 2013. Previous to her political appointment, she was an active campaigner on environmental issues and founded a local NGO, Candlelight for Health, Education and Environment. The charity continues to deliver training, education and healthcare programmes with communities across Somaliland. Shukri served six years on the first Election Commission in Somaliland as the only woman and participated in three successful elections when Somaliland was moving from a clan-based system to a multiparty system. She explains her motivations for her work:

'The charity was born in 1995; we saw there was a real need. The Somaliland people were in the midst of war – having suffered the onslaught of the [Siad] Barre forces they were now experiencing a period of great instability involving inter-clan wars. There were no schools for children of internally displaced people (IDPs) and they were growing up with so much fear and hostilities, we didn't want another generation lost to the war.

'We set up a school. With education, we soon realised there was a dire need for a health awareness campaign and so we decided to run campaigns including the dangers involved with FGM [female genital mutilation]. The conditions of the camp made us see how important sanitation was – and the environment as a whole – and so began our work on environmental hazards. I had a lot of help from people and the charity was by no means a one-woman show. The charity is one the biggest NGOs in Somaliland and its focus continues to be on the environment.'

Fatima Jibrell is the founder of the international NGO Adeso: African Development Solutions (previously known as Horn Relief), whose mission is to work with communities to create environments in which Africans can thrive. In 2014 Fatima received the Champions of Earth award from the UN Environment Programme for her outstanding contribution to conservation. She talks about her experiences as a child in Somalia and returning as an adult:

'I was born to a pastoral nomadic family in Somalia in 1947 and until I was seven years old I lived in an area that was savannah-like, with lions, leopards, all kinds of wildlife. I first visited Somalia again about thirty years ago – the land that I had remembered as a lush green savannah was total desert, with only huge sandstorms blowing. So I became interested in seeing if it could be brought back to life. After the civil war it seemed the best time to help people. There was an influx of people from big cities like Mogadishu coming to my area. I wanted to see if I could support them in any way to understand the environment, so they don't trash it further – that was my main reason to come back.'

Trees for people and the environment

One of the main causes of Somali environmental degradation has been deforestation and desertification – in particular from people cutting down trees to make charcoal for cooking fuel.

Shukri Haji Ismail Bandare explains: 'The environment is the most essential necessity in our lives as we depend one hundred per cent on it. Without a good, healthy environment it is impossible to exist as a people. The effects of [deforestation] on a land such as ours, which can be described as arid or semi-arid land, are acute. The scarcity of forests and woodlands means any loss of trees has significant environmental deficits.

'The trees we have in mountainous areas are our equivalent of forests and they are fast being eroded. In a large part this is due to the lack of education and awareness people have about the effects of cutting trees; also some people do not have alternative livelihoods other than cutting trees to make charcoal. The people remain reluctant to use alternative means of energy due to many factors and this continues to fuel the use of coal.'

'We are content to cut down a tree but not plant one in its place. The need for trees remains the same yet that need is being unmet with our current attitudes.'

The Somali rural population is traditionally pastoral and nomadic, moving with their livestock to find grazing pastures. These communities depend upon a healthy natural environment for their survival in the hot, dry climate with irregular rainfall.

Fatima Jibrell recalls the traditional respect for trees: 'There were all kinds of laws that almost all Somalis, even those who have not been pastoralists, know about. At that time nobody dared to cut a tree more than one or two branches – they will trim and take one branch and go to another tree and take one branch, and so on, to make a fence for their temporary homestead to protect their live-stock for the night from lions and hyenas that could easily prey on their livestock. People, usually women, made ropes and other mate-rials to construct their house and this was mounted upon camels when they moved. That house was all made of trees, but they would take part of the tree bark and not actually skin the whole tree – which they do now because they don't care about the tree.

'I remember the training that my mother was given as a child, I remember her telling me: *if you want to take off the skin of the tree to make a rope, you take just a little bit off so that you can make what you want without killing the tree.* I knew from that time that we needed the trees because I was eating fruit from them, we were using them to lie down [in the shade] when the sun was out, so it was well understood! My mother expected me to be a pastoralist like her and taught me to use the environment.'

Conflict and the environment

One of Fatima's most notable accomplishments is securing a prohibition on the export of charcoal from north-east Somalia (since 1998 an autonomous region of Somalia known as Puntland), which was driving deforestation. She united people and groups, and tirelessly advocated for an end to the charcoal trade that used the region's acacia trees to make charcoal destined for the Middle East. Through her advocacy and coordination, the Puntland government prohibited the export of charcoal through Bosaso port in 2002. Fatima also recognised the need to find an alternative fuel for household cooking; so she co-founded Sun Fire Cooking to promote the use of the butterfly-design parabolic solar cooker.

Illegal charcoal exports from Somalia continue today and have been recognised by the UN Security Council as a significant source of revenue for the terrorist group Al-Shabaab. The work of Fatima and others has put this issue on the international agenda and highlighted its humanitarian, security, environmental and economic consequences.

'For example,' says Fatima, 'the urban youth are being lured into the rural areas through payments to make charcoal, yet the international community are not prioritising the environment or youth rehabilitation in their efforts.'

There are deep-rooted links between the environment and conflict in Somalia and Somaliland, as people are so reliant on their environment for their livelihoods, cultural identity and security.

Shukri Haji Ismail Bandare stresses this point: 'Environmental issues play a key role in conflict in Somaliland, I would go as far as to say such issues play a daily role in conflict situations across Somaliland. Confrontations frequently occur over disputes over grazing lands, watering holes and land that has been sealed off by individuals for private use. All these problems demonstrate the key role land features in the lives of Somalis, their existence remains tied to the land as with their nomadic forefathers.'

Challenges of environmental governance

Shukri Haji Ismail Bandare reflects on her experience as a minister: 'Our Ministry of the Environment is an emerging ministry; a lot of our efforts have been on training and building our staff capacity to facilitate an adequate working environment. Though the ministry was first created in 1997, it has not received the same level of attention or focus as the ministries for education or health, and so it has been somewhat neglected. The challenges we face within our ministry are overwhelming; we are constantly under pressure due to budgets and because we know that time is of the essence where environmental emergencies are concerned. We are facing too many environmental emergencies including prolonged droughts, flash floods across dry river beds and the increasing number of industrial factories, which require preventative measures to ensure industrial waste is properly disposed of. We face all the challenges associated with a post-conflict society but I keep telling myself: "Rome was not built in a day". Since we are all trying.'

Fatima Jibrell points out the challenges and opportunities for better environmental governance: 'Before the war and the collapse of the Somali state, there was a whole department of environment that would protect the trees. Tourists were not allowed to park everywhere. We were not allowed to consume as much as we wanted. Today it is still a challenge! Sixty per cent of jobs in Somalia come from a pastoral environment. There is no opportunity to help Somalis, particularly young people from pastoral families, to get involved in environmental or marine conservation. We have the longest coastline in Africa – that could provide a job for everyone.'

Women and the environment

'Women's livelihoods are entwined with the environment,' explains Shukri Haji Ismail Bandare. 'As a traditionally pastoral-nomadic society, it is the women who herd the livestock, they are the first to witness changes in our environment. Even in the urban setting of Hargeisa there are women (many of whom are the family's breadwinners) selling goat's milk and camel's milk from their live-stock. We are a people dependent on the environment, especially water as there is no life without water. If we do not act against environmental degradation, women will be the first casualties of any environmental disasters that result from limited actions from ourselves and the international community at large.

'Women are intimately concerned with the changes in weather pattern and rainfall, they have to personally calculate how long to walk to get water, how far to take their herd for watering and pasture. Those of us in government are also aware of the challenges facing such women. We constantly keep ourselves updated on the areas where drought is present in order to send whatever reinforcements we can.

'I think equality is not necessarily the same in everyone's eyes. As a woman I am aware of my physical limitations to that of a man and similarly I am sure a man could not match my resilience as a woman. Equality has taken on this forceful, confrontational connotation and I would like to move away from that and instead promote a complementarity between the sexes. As for the planet I don't believe we can save the planet without first creating a fair and harmonious society for humanity.'

Fatima Jibrell sees the struggle for gender equality as central to environmental protection: 'There's a very strong connection between the marginalisation of women and youth and the environmental degradation in Somalia. The degradation is making poverty even worse for so many people; politics and gender inequalities are at the heart of it.

'It's not possible to achieve environmental sustainability without gender equality, because women work in the environment, they put food on the table, bring water. Women who are doing all this and looking after children have no chance to do anything else, to get involved in politics. They are carrying the whole society on their back.'

Gender in society and politics

Women in Somali society are traditionally seen as potential peace-builders and peace emissaries, able to facilitate communication between warring groups. Women have been at the forefront of local and national peace-building across the Somali regions since the civil war. However, time and again women have been excluded from peace talks, or permitted only as observers on the sidelines rather than as equal participants with men. Unlike women, young men have no traditional role to play in conflict resolution, but like women, young men are marginalised and kept on the sidelines during peace talks.

In principle, the constitutions of the Somaliland and Puntland governments and the Federal Government of Somalia all provide for equality between men and women in relation to political participation. But in fact, all three governments are almost exclusively male forums and promises of quotas for women are variously rejected and flouted.[2] This is despite international conventions, such as the United Nations Security Council Resolution 1325 (UNSCR 1325), which calls for women's participation in peace negotiations and in post-conflict reconstruction.

From 2012 to 2014, Adeso ran a project to promote gender equality, women's empowerment and political participation in Somalia to foster the development of an inclusive, transparent and accountable society. This project, Promoting Women's Political Participation in Somalia, provided training to more than three hundred female civil society representatives and councillors in political representation, advocacy, understanding of gender equality, and the role of women in peace-building. It also offered both technical support and capacity-building to the Ministry of Women Development and Family Affairs (MOWDAFA).

The project also facilitated the construction of Community Women Centres in the four target districts of Badhan, Bocame, Carmo and Xarfo. These centres continue to be a resource for local women in Puntland, giving them a place to consult, report and share their views and experiences. The targeted women in civil society, local councillors, teachers and community leaders in the four districts learned skills to challenge and change social attitudes and cultural factors that constrain their lives, and advocate on behalf of their communities.

Fatima believes that this is the future: 'Unless men talk to women and youth, government will not improve and women will not move forward. I hope the United States and other countries that are supporting the [Federal] Government of Somalia will talk to women because each nation comes and talks to male politicians. We need every nation that comes to Somalia to talk to women separately and equally – that's how you start equality.'

Shukri Bandare shows how political and social empowerment are intricately linked: 'There was a time fifteen to sixteen years ago when the question of gender was not on the agenda; many in our society were looking at us [women in politics] as though we had committed an unspeakable taboo. But I believe we have come a long way since then. We live in a rigidly patriarchal society riddled with contradictions. On the one hand we are witnessing more girls in schools, all the way to universities, but in the end that girl is still supposed to conform to the role of stay-at-home mum. Many parents will entertain the idea of their daughters having an office job but entering politics, especially at an official decision-making level, you can be sure to face every hurdle they can throw your way.

'There have been attempts to set up a female quota in the House of Representatives but unfortunately that bill did not pass. Nonetheless, there are prominent women's associations including Nagaad Network, which is an umbrella group of many grassroots women's organisations in Somaliland. As a founding member of this network, my ministry continues to foster a close relationship with the network in the promotion of greater women's empowerment in society and politics.

'We must find a platform that encourages discussion and an open dialogue on the environmental issues we face and that is what I want to be part of, the start of that conversation.'

15

ESTHER MWANGI

Centre for International Forestry Research (CIFOR)

Gender, participation and community forestry: lessons from beneath the canopy[1]

A major concern of community/smallholder forestry is to identify and make explicit men's and women's roles in order to understand their interactions and the consequences for forest governance, people's livelihoods, sustainable use and conservation, as well as opportunities for facilitating greater gender equity. The value chains of Non-timber Forest Products (NTFPs), Reducing Emissions from Deforestation and Degradation (REDD) programmes and overall forest use and management are examples of arenas where gender relations and women's participation are increasingly seen as critical for addressing broader policy concerns such as poverty reduction, climate change mitigation and sustainable forest management. This chapter shines a light on findings from CIFOR's research on women's participation. It focuses only on one category of studies conducted by CIFOR scientists, i.e. cross-country comparative studies, in order to identify broad patterns with regard to women's participation.

Participation has long been viewed as an essential pillar of development policy and practice. Participatory processes are those in which 'stakeholders influence and share control over development initiatives and the decisions and resources [that] affect them'.[2] Participation is thought to be an important pathway through which individuals and groups, especially those marginalised, can have voice and influence over the decisions and institutions that impact their lives. The involvement of diverse stakeholders is also thought to improve the acceptability and sustainability of decisions, while contributions of local knowledge, time and resources are anticipated to lead to more effective implementation of decisions. These well-intentioned efforts at increasing participation in natural resources management and development more generally have been met with strong criticism. Participatory approaches have been demonstrated to simplify highly complicated social relations, concealing existing inequalities, and not necessarily including previously marginalised groups in decision processes.[3]

In the forestry sector, participation has equally been viewed as a pathway towards improving governance, promoting sustainable use and management while enhancing livelihoods, benefits and opportunities. It is a desired objective in natural resources management, for efficiency, equity and empowerment reasons. Women in particular are noted to be key users and managers of forest resources, often depending heavily on the same resources to meet their and their family's needs, and holding specialised knowledge of forest species, their distribution and uses. Their exclusion from decision-making arenas has been shown to result in difficulties in rule enforcement and pose challenges to conflict resolution, which are key dimensions of forest governance.[4] A large and growing literature in community forestry is now suggesting that the enthusiasm for participation is way ahead of the evidence, and there is cause for concern as exclusion, elite capture, conflict and co-optation are increasingly cited as outcomes of people's interactions in participatory forestry interventions across multiple settings.

The next section of this chapter discusses gendered constraints and opportunities in participation in NTFP value chains. The third section shares observations on gendered participation in REDD+ projects, while the fourth section highlights the factors that determine women's participation in forest use and management. It also highlights some outcomes. The final section synthesises lessons from these three cases of gendered participation in different yet equally significant arenas of community forestry.

Benefits capture in gendered NTFP value chains in Africa[5]

The marketing of forest goods and services has gained currency as an essential component of programmes intended to enhance livelihoods, reduce poverty and redirect benefits to poor, forest-adjacent communities. CIFOR's comparative work in the dry and humid forests of Africa (Burkina Faso, Cameroon, Democratic Republic of Congo, Ethiopia, Gabon, Zambia) set out to explore women's roles, benefits and how these might be expanded across value chains of about fifteen NTFPs prioritised for their socio-economic and environmental values. Using a value chains approach, the study provides details on men and women's trade in each product at different nodes, from production/harvesting, processing and packaging, to storage, transporting, wholesaling and retailing. It examined relative benefits to men and women's involvement as well as relative constraints and opportunities at different nodes of the value chain.

Findings reveal a marked gender differentiation along the value chain. For all products (except for honey harvesting in Zambia and gum olibanum harvesting in Ethiopia) the lower parts of value chains (e.g. collecting and processing) are dominated by women. Activities here are labour intensive and poorly paid. For example, collectors of gum arabic in Burkina Faso, mostly women, can earn from US$59–79 per year; in Ethiopia 87 per cent of women sorting gum olibanum earn less than US$50/month. By contrast, in the Congo Basin men dominate the harvesting of high-value products, such as charcoal in DRC, bushmeat in Gabon and pygeum (*Prunus africana*) in Cameroon. Though women harvest some high-value products, they are mainly seasonal and include mushrooms, bush mango and safou. However, women's harvesting of these products is increasingly challenged as men are now starting to harvest them owing to increasing monetary values. Where men dominate in lower parts of the value chain, such as harvesting of honey and gum olibanum in Zambia and Ethiopia respectively, physical constraints (such as climbing trees), long distances, lack of tapping skills and sub-national governments' rules that limit collection of gum olibanum to 'skilled' collectors tend to lock women out.

Marketing and sales (including transportation) of most products across both East and southern Africa and the Congo Basin are consistently dominated by men. In Burkina Faso, for example, religious and cultural barriers preclude women travelling to non-local markets and negotiating prices with primarily men buyers.

In the Congo Basin chains, benefits vary markedly for men and women involved in similar chain activities. In chains dominated by women, men generated higher profits by as much as 11 per cent. Women harvested mostly for household consumption while men were primarily motivated by income generation. Greater access to credit advantages men, allowing them to specialise in fewer products, accumulate larger volumes and operate at larger scales than women. Contrary to general findings, income generated by both men and women was used in remarkably similar ways: to meet basic household needs for food, healthcare, education, and both men and women also tended to reinvest NTFP revenues in agriculture, business and petty trade.

Though women perform a variety of functions in the value chains, their roles are not visible, either because they are operating informally, work part time or carry out their activities at home between family responsibilities. Where women's roles are more prominent, this is mainly due to gender-focused interventions by external agencies – for example, the promotion of 'modern' beehives in Zambia, which are placed closer to the ground rather than on trees. However, such external interventions are often at the production/collection stage (mostly linked to formal markets) and rarely in other nodes higher up the value chain. Other interventions have involved organising women into groups – separate from men's groups. Though these have been successful in circumventing cultural barriers that prevent women from speaking out or from involvement in decision-making, such divided groups may be inappropriate where women have minimal roles in the value chain.

Overall, in both the dry forests of East and southern Africa and in the tropical rainforests of the Congo Basin, both men and women are involved in the value chains of several important NTFPs. Activities within the value chains are gender differentiated, as are benefits, with men accruing overall greater benefits owing to better skills, literacy levels, credit and larger volumes. Both men and women appear to use their incomes to meet household needs but men have greater control over incomes than women.

Women's participation in emerging sub-national REDD+ project initiatives[6]

How does knowledge of REDD+ projects vary between women and men? Do women have a voice in decision-making in villages at REDD+ project sites? These are questions that CIFOR colleagues working on REDD+ are asking in villages that are part of a broader global comparative study on REDD+ across sixty-nine villages participating in eighteen REDD+ initiatives in five countries: Brazil, Cameroon, Indonesia, Tanzania and Vietnam. Data were collected early in the planning stages of REDD+ projects in order to provide a benchmark for assessing improvements in gender equity throughout project implementation. Clear communication of the potential benefits of REDD+ to women and men is critical to facilitate greater accountability and inclusive, gender-responsive implementation of REDD+ initiatives.[7]

Findings of this study show that even though a modest proportion of women (58 per cent) had heard about REDD+ projects in their village, women were generally less informed than men. Larger proportions of men's groups had heard about REDD+ projects (66 per cent) relative to women's groups (40 per cent). Men's groups demonstrated a basic understanding of REDD+ and were involved in consultation processes about REDD+ implementation in their villages. This disparity between basic understandings of REDD+ among men and women in villages was smallest in Brazil relative to the other countries (i.e. Cameroon, Tanzania and Indonesia). In only about nine villages (35 per cent) were women involved when REDD+ project proponents introduced and explained the project, soliciting input, or even in training events. In addition to consultation and training, men were involved in clarifying village forest tenure arrangements, in rule enforcement and in monitoring for carbon. The study shows that throughout the countries studied, women's lack of knowledge is unrelated to their level of forest use; their frequency of use is the same as men's.

At the time of data collection, none of the REDD+ project proponents had listed women as a distinct stakeholder group. Four REDD+ proponents stated fair benefits to women as a broad equity goal. Overall, the data demonstrates that even though women use forests, their knowledge of REDD+ is lower than men's, and their participation in project implementation is restricted to consultation meetings and training. Men, on the other hand, appear to participate in decisions and activities that are central to REDD+ implementation and forest governance more broadly, such as tenure clarification, rule enforcement and carbon monitoring. In the broader scheme of REDD+ these are activities and decisions that have a direct bearing on how benefits of REDD+ will be distributed in relevant villages and who will receive those benefits.

Gendered participation in forest governance: insights from the IFRI global dataset[8]

In this study, colleagues at CIFOR and IFPRI use the IFRI data set[9] to answer the following questions:

a) How do varying proportions of women (low, balanced, high) in forest user groups influence forest management?
b) Is the proportion of women in forest user groups in any way related to the governance of forests?
c) What determines women's participation in forestry institutions? What are the effects of women's participation?

Data collected from 151 user groups from sixty-seven forests in Kenya, Uganda, Bolivia and Mexico show that women-dominated user groups (i.e. with more than two-thirds female members) are less likely to adopt forest-improving technologies relative to the male-dominated ones (female proportion less than or equal to one third). Gender does not affect the regularity with which user groups undertook regeneration activities aimed at improving the forest. Gender-balanced groups (i.e. with the proportion of women between one third and two-thirds) tend to do more monitoring than men-dominated ones, and women-dominated groups are unlikely to conduct any monitoring at all. Gender does not affect the incidence of conflicts in user groups; however, descriptive analysis suggests that a higher proportion of women in user groups lowers the incidence of conflict in user groups. The authors suggest that complementarities between men and women in forest management activities – for example, men being able to monitor and sanction and women's roles in conflict resolution – may advantage gender-balanced groups. They also suggest that the weakness of women-dominated groups may stem from difficulties in sanctioning and a male bias in the delivery of extension services.

In order to answer the second question 290 forest user groups from ninety-one forests in Kenya, Uganda, Bolivia and Mexico were analysed. Results show that gender-balanced groups participate more in forestry decision-making and are more likely to exclude other groups from harvesting from the forest. Women-dominated groups participate less, sanction less and exclude less.

In order to answer the third question data from two different sources were analysed. First, more aggregated community-level data from ninety-six formal forest user group associations in ten countries in Africa, Asia and Latin America, with each association having a governing committee/council. Secondly, household surveys administered in twenty-three sites in Kenya, Uganda, Bolivia and Mexico. Results from this study show that restrictions on membership, such as membership fees and timing of meetings, lower women's attendance at forest user group (FUG) meetings. The attendance of women in more educated households is higher. Moreover, forest associations with high wealth inequality have fewer women on committees than forests with lower wealth inequality, and they are also less likely to have a women ascend to the position of committee chairperson. Women's presence in FUG committees is influenced by women's presence in previous FUG committees; however, women's presence as committee members in the past does not significantly influence the likelihood of a woman ascending to the position of chairperson of the committee. When there is competition for council seats (e.g. elections) women are likely to hold fewer seats on the council than when there is not competition. Forest associations which had women committee members in the past are less likely to have disruptive conflict, while FUGs with high wealth inequality are expected to have a higher probability of disruptive conflict. The more equal the wages between men and women the less likely there is to be disruptive conflict, while the higher the percentage of household heads that are women, the more likely there is to be disruptive conflict.

In sum, the results show that institutional requirements for competitive elections may depress women's presence in leadership positions, but that their presence on such committees serves a useful purpose in tempering the effects of conflict. The results also suggest that wealth inequality and lower education levels can depresses women's participation in forest decision-making processes. Similarly, the timing of meetings and the requirement for paid membership subscription lower women's participation. Importantly, mixed groups, especially gender-balanced groups, appear to have a positive effect on forest management.

Lessons from beneath the canopy: a synthesis of CIFOR's comparative studies

These studies explored women's participation in a broad range of settings in Africa, Asia and Latin America, and inthree domains of community forestry that are critical in light of global problem-solving, including poverty reduction, climate change mitigation and sustainable forest management. These studies considered gendered participation through different lenses, including: a) the determinants of women's participation in forestry use and management decisions; b) governance sub-outcomes of women's versus men's groups' participation in forestry decisions; c) women's versus men's participation in value chains and benefits distribution; and d) women's versus men's participation in REDD+ projects.

A broad range of indicators were used to illustrate participation. These included levels of knowledge and information (REDD+), specific nodes/activities along the value chains of NTFPs, benefits capture from value chains and their spending, meeting attendance and timing, and membership/presence on forest user group committees/councils.

What do we learn from these studies of women's participation?

First, the different types of indicators used to assess participation in the different domains of community forestry in which participation occurs speak to the multiple ways in which participation can be characterised, from the antecedents of participation such as knowledge and information to the outcomes, such as benefits capture and distribution as well as actual decision processes.

Secondly, the findings also indicate that structural considerations (such as norms and values, institutional rules, credit, education, skills, project design) can facilitate or impede women's participation. This is not a new finding, yet the fact that these cross-country enquiries point to similar findings lends further strength to prior case-based observations. The take-home message for policy-makers or practitioners implementing projects is fairly straightforward: building new initiatives on a foundation of unequal gender relationships that are rooted in the structure of society is unlikely to yield gender-equitable/equal outcomes and may instead serve to entrench such inequality. Measures to safeguard against exacerbating gender inequality will *at least* require the creation of a safe space/platform where both men and women can dialogue and work together to jointly resolve problems without threat or retribution. The Adaptive Collaborative Management, a portfolio of approaches that allow for cycles of joint problem identification, reflection, visioning, problem-solving, conflict resolution and learning, has been deployed by CIFOR colleagues to achieve gender and overall equity in forest use and management in diverse settings.[10]

Third, studies further suggest that these structural factors are animated at different levels in different ways – within communities, among individuals, and in the operation of external agents. Coordination and cooperation among actors across governance levels and spatial scales are consequently central to efforts at strengthening women's participation in community/smallholder forestry.

While these studies shine a light on factors influencing women's participation, there are additional areas of enquiry that can help deepen our analysis of gender differentials in participation in critical domains of community forestry. A thorough study of those that *fail to participate* is necessary and would provide a basis for the development of programmes targeted at encouraging their participation, as needed. Moreover, men and women are often differentiated along other lines such as wealth, class, status, education, religion, ethnicity, etc. A thorough investigation of how gender interacts with these additional lines of differentiation is necessary for a more comprehensive gender analysis of participation.

16

BARBARA STOCKING

Former CEO of Oxfam GB

Putting gender equality at the heart of Oxfam's work

Gender equality in parity organisations

If you are an organisation working on poverty internationally, you simply cannot ignore gender equality. There are more women and girls than men and boys living in poverty across the world. The disparities are extreme; women own only a tiny percentage of the world's land and assets, they are very poorly served when it comes to the resources which can support them out of poverty, from the emerging problem (though improving) of access to primary and secondary education, to the access to agricultural extension services for the 70 per cent of poor farmers in Africa who are women.

It is not surprising, then, that Oxfam has been working on gender equality for much of its history, including during the twelve years I was chief executive (2001–13) at Oxfam Great Britain. Perhaps it wasn't surprising that I was one of the first female chief executives to be appointed as CE to a major institutional NGO. The commitment to gender equality wasn't just present but, because of the position Oxfam had taken, had to be demonstrated in all it did. Throughout my time, my top team was pretty evenly balanced with men and women, and our Council, the trustee board, similarly. So that has to be the first message. You have to practise what you preach, especially in organisations which people join or support because of their values and the organisation's integrity.

Of course, leadership from the top is essential but the values of gender equality have to permeate the whole organisation. And so begins the debate of whether you should have a gender, or gender and diversity, team or unit, or should you mainstream gender? The answer for me is probably both. The essence, though, is that a gender team or, less structurally as we had it, with gender advisers in various teams, cannot be the place that 'does' gender equality; that has to be part of everyone's role. Expertise in gender issues, though, is also important. Setting a culture which expects everyone to engage with gender issues does have to come from the top and then at all levels. After all, teams in Goma, DRC, are rather a long way from head office in Oxford, so the intent has to be bought into, and expected from everyone at all levels.

So we were very serious about this in Oxfam. First the basic arguments have to be made, not just about women in poverty. In an organisation whose first belief is that 'all people are of equal value' women's rights have to be considered. Even more persuasive are the arguments about women's agency – what they can do to make the change in the world, often drawing on different skills, and their different roles in family and in community, to help lift everyone out of poverty.

However, it is no good pretending that even a basic engagement with gender equality is not countercultural in many countries where Oxfam works. The discussion has to be long and painstaking with men and women staff talking together and separately. We run for a whole period workshops called 'Let's Talk' (about gender) for several years. Even then, it is not likely that all staff (98 per cent from the countries where we work) will all believe this fully. What has to be made clear, though, is that if you work for Oxfam, certain behaviours are expected, whether that is in the working of men and women staff together or in the work with the poorest communities.

Fortunately, many men and women do see the point and it is probably then that the real work starts. Many people buy in to the idea and then they become completely confused about quite what they are supposed to do. I used to think that we needed gender confession rooms where people could go and say they really didn't understand, or didn't know what to do now – rooms where you wouldn't be put down because you didn't quite get it. And by the way, any sense of gender police in the organisation can set you back years. You have to allow discussions to be open for people to engage. It is a fine leadership judgement about when and how you draw the line.

I think the breakthrough we had a few years ago was to describe gender equality work as 'Putting poor women's rights at the heart of all we do'. This meant that everyone who was engaged in development programmes or in advocacy or campaigning was expected to look at their programme and ask the question 'what does this piece of work/action do to improve women's rights?' Our programmes and advocacy are mainly about men *and* women, though some are exclusively about women, but in each of them that question has to be asked. That is often when expertise is needed to understand what could be done differently, what other agencies have done and learnt, and of course, above all, asking women themselves what might make a difference. For example, this can range from practical matters like asking women where they would prefer latrines to be located in a new camp for refugees or displaced people, to asking small women farmers which crops would make the most sense for them to produce for supply chains, given their other commitments and ways of working.

My central message, then, is that if you want your organisation to deliver on gender equality, you have to put the long-term time and effort in, to get your organisation into the right shape. What I have described for Oxfam won't fit other organisations but there are essentials, like consistent leadership, shaping the values and sheer long-term work.

Delivering for poor women

Oxfam, of course, cannot be expert in all aspects of poverty; for long-term development it has focused above all on livelihoods, as well as pressure for basic services. Central to all of this is that poor people should have their own voices heard and should take leadership themselves. This is when 'poor women's rights' often come in, making sure that in every programme women's voice is heard and women are in leadership positions.

For example, Oxfam has worked to develop producer organisations, marketing organisations or cooperatives (depending on what is appropriate in different countries). The intent, then, is always that women should have a say, for example in meetings of those cooperatives or organisations, and that women should take leadership positions. This is long, slow work because it may take time for men to realise that women may have rather important things to say. For example, they may know better what sells in markets. Women are often illiterate too and some basic literacy and numeracy may be essential if they are to be able to take on leadership roles.

A lot, though, is about women's confidence and the level of their aspirations. I can think of so many examples where we have worked with women – for example, on a cholera outbreak in Monrovia, Liberia, or on a literacy programme with women in northern Afghanistan. As soon as you talk to them, they will say, now you have helped us this far we want you to help us with economic opportunities. In Liberia that turned out to be helping them set up a tailoring cooperative and doing very well making, for example, school uniforms for schoolchildren.

It is often women working together, in solidarity, that helps build confidence. My very first Oxfam visit was to San Juan de Laurigancho, on the edge of Lima, Peru. The area is a shanty town on the hillside, very poor and very at risk of flooding. Because the women had to travel to the city daily to carry out small-scale trading, we helped them set up community kitchens, to feed the children while their mothers were away. That was good to see in its own right but it also brought the women together for other things. In particular, they told me their story of their local mayor. He had been accused of corruption. Under Peru's laws he should therefore have stood down, but he refused to do so. The women of San Juan camped out, outside the local town hall, demanding his resignation, until he left. I don't think I have ever met such a formidable group of women anywhere in the world. Once women organise there really is no stopping them.

Another example is from a more recent visit to central Ethiopia when I met a women's agricultural cooperative. We sat in a grain store they had built. All that Oxfam had done was to link them to one of our local NGO partners for training and to provide a small bit of money for bricks and cement. They had done the work and overall their agricultural production was doing well. I asked them what had made the most difference to them. Their answer was a surprise. They said that the local NGO had given them lots more information on HIV and AIDS. HIV was becoming a real problem, not least because they were near a major trunk road with a heavy load of lorries, ideal for passing on the infection. The women became much more informed about what would help and got the whole community to agree that each person would stick to one sexual partner. The men sitting around the room when I was hearing this debate nodded that this was what they had agreed to. Of course, I have no idea whether this principle held in reality, but the power of the women to make a difference in their community was blatant, and went well beyond their agricultural output.

For women's development out of poverty they do of course need basic services. Girls must be educated, not least to contribute to the economy. Health services must be available, including contraception. Women have to have access to resources and assets from being able to have land tenure, to getting loans, etc. But for me, the learning is about enabling women to have their say, engaging them in leadership and, above all, enabling women to get together so they have so much more power and confidence, in a world where their power is almost always extremely limited. If this is true for poverty itself, it has to be similar in adaptation to climate change, in conservation and the control of national resources too. Again, the work is not easy, shifting power can have repercussions. Not all husbands are proud when their wives start bringing in money, though many of them are supportive. But the difficulties, even sometimes domestic violence, changes of power relations can bring have to be recognised and dealt with carefully. A lot of work has to go in to help men understand what is happening and why it can be so positive.

Once again, in all cases, you have to find out what is really happening. It is very easy to fool yourself. In recent years, for example, Oxfam has been developing its own outcome measures.

These are not output measures of what has been delivered (though that may be important too) but an attempt to measure deeper changes. One of them is about women having a greater say (as evidenced by themselves compared to a year ago) over community and household decisions. In one country we were working directly to increase that 'say'. By asking women, though, we found that although they said they were more involved in decisions at community level, this was not changing their say at household level. That was terribly important to know directly. You then have the ability to change and adapt your programme, simply not possible without that knowledge. A surprise to us, then, but very important to know.

Leading across the world

I have written about Oxfam's work in gender equality and about what we had to do as an organisation. There is one wider issue I would like to tackle. Surely, if we believe in women's voice locally, as we often say we do, what more can we do to achieve gender equality in the places where global decisions are made? I can think of international conferences or of my repeated attendance at the World Economic Forum in Davos (where the ratio was about 17 per cent women). You can blame the private sector partly, but even among civil society at Davos half of the leaders there were not women.

Each sector of society will have to make its own way on women's leadership but surely civil society should be leading the way. Decisions regarding the future of the planet surely must have women equally represented, yet we are a long way from that. Civil society for me then has a responsibility to get its own house in order but also to advocate for women's leadership and women's voice in all global discussions, including standing alongside women's organisations when blatant inequalities are in evidence. I look forward to women having an equal voice in 2015 at the Conference of the Parties on Climate Change in Paris!

17

NIDHI TANDON

Networked Intelligence for Development, Canada

From individual to communal rights: empowering women for sustainable use of natural resources

This contribution draws on time spent interviewing, walking with villagers and witnessing the eroding base of women's security and empowerment in rural and informal sectors in some African countries between 2009 and 2014. The countries in question share some common features: vast and valuable natural resources; high illiteracy rates among rural populations; patchy rural infrastructure; the vestiges of weakened traditional accountability systems; and investment policies that significantly favour the industrial commodity chain[1] over peasant-based food sovereignty.

Needless to say, rural women in these arenas are caught up in extremely challenging situations of feeding and providing for their families today while trying to plan for the future – a future fraught with unknowns. The narratives and experiences from women in Uganda, Tanzania, Malawi, Mozambique, Zambia, Zimbabwe, Ghana and Liberia all echo and reverberate to a common strain – their struggles are intensifying, their opportunities are limited and they are close to breaking point as their relationships with land, with natural capital[2] and with the public commons are weakened on multiple fronts.

In conversations with these women, it is apparent that they want their roles dignified, valued, recognised and supported. Where women are able to articulate their interests, or when their values and priorities are incorporated into policy-making and planning, more compelling demands are made for longer-term outcomes around health, education, food security and overall well-being for the community as a whole. In many senses, these are the bedrock factors of sustainable economies. Relative to men, women's immediate interests in these public services are especially high.

That said, rural women are *by no means* a homogeneous group. Some women are *so* disenfranchised, having no say in the decisions that affect their lives, that they will settle for labour within the globalised production system at any price. In more desperate circumstances, they will rely on humanitarian and community assistance. A growing number of women and women's networks, however, are standing up to protect their version of sustainable or natural economies; their rights to public spaces; to seed, forest and water; to health, nutrition and secure food sources, despite the increasingly tenuous situations that they may find themselves in. More often than not, they are pushed to a point where they are prepared to lay their bodies on the line to prevent further displacement and disempowerment, at great personal risk. Unregulated consumption, population growth, the commercialisation and privatisation of land and water, and deficient national policies all serve to heighten the stakes.

When government policy continues to be problematic

Liberia has one of the highest land concession rates on the continent. The government of Liberia has a range of policies and laws for the community management of natural resources and has signed up to related international agreements. It is still in the process of defining its new land policy and, notably, has not passed the 2010 Gender Equity in Politics Bill. The concentration of plantation and mining interests is extremely high; one 2012 report puts the total land allocated to rubber, oil palm and forestry concessions at approximately 25 per cent of the country.[3] A series of recent studies warn that agro-investments[4] in Liberia have not met the expectations of all communities; and that some communities have lost access to land resources and their food security in the process.[5]

Public scrutiny is pushing big companies to comply with national laws and regulations. Under pressure in Indonesia and Malaysia for their part in widespread deforestation, Asia's leading companies in the palm oil industry are turning their attention to Africa. On paper, palm oil companies have access to over 622,000 hectares and an average market capitalisation of US$8.2 billion in Liberia.[6] There are four main concession agreements at the moment with a total investment of about US$2.56 billion. If the agreement with Sime Darby to plant on 220,000 hectares goes ahead, then this is more than the total land area that the company had planted in Indonesia in 2009 (even though Indonesia is more than fifteen times the size of Liberia) and ten times more than the total area of oil palm plantations established in Ghana.[7] This gives a sense of scale to the plantation expansion in Liberia.

Traditionally, palm oil[8] is primarily a woman's crop; it ceases to be so once it enters the global supply chain. In the domestic markets across the West African region, women are the majority stakeholders in a thriving local supply chain in palm oil processing, palm fruit marketing and palm kernel processing and marketing. On the international market palm oil is increasingly traded as feedstock for biofuel although its primary use is for human consumption.

These developments could become a steep price to pay for the promised benefits of revenue and employment, as the portion of land managed by rural Liberians decreases. If community engagement around land use decisions is not integrated systemically into government policy, the resulting societal tensions could be trigger points for local grievances, conflict and violence. The long-term implications of losing land and dignity are well documented and the particular impacts for rural women are acknowledged by the international community.[9]

At the same time, with costs of living rising, the need to earn becomes more pressing. Faced with few options, and with the reality of their low employment marketability, women and men in rural communities will look to new rural investments with some expectation of employment, infrastructure development and service provision. In one palm oil plantation nursery, women are engaged in short-term seasonal work to bag, weed and administer chemicals to the palm saplings for the equivalent of US$5 a day. In one community on the borders of an oil palm plantation, one man works as a security guard; his pay is shared among his three brothers and their families, none of whom are employed. In an interview he observed: 'There are very few jobs at the plantation. We have to pay to get the job.' In Malema town, none of the women interviewed worked on the plantation. They farmed on the fringes of the plantation, supplementing their needs with charcoal burning, and had relinquished farmland to the plantation.

Rural women in Liberia already play significant roles in managing natural resources for their food, fuel, shelter and water needs. They have central and multiple relationships with natural resources that are core to their day-to-day livelihoods. They might not recognise the value of this management function themselves, and they might not be drawing the links between their farming practices, deforestation and long-term water sources. Yet on a day-to-day basis, they fulfil a wide range of activities that are directly linked to natural resource management. Asked to describe their relationships with natural resources, women invariably talk about these activities and are less likely to refer to their extractive (aggregates and mining) activities, as these activities are perhaps more mercenary or opportunistic in nature – driven by market demand and the need to supplement income. Artisanal mining continues to be a critical aspect of resource extraction in this country, requiring gender-specific policies, because of the non-formal and highly exploitative nature of the sector.

When it comes to the formal commercialisation of natural resource extraction, women's involvement becomes invisible and is put at risk, primarily because women do not have control over the decisions taken on land and natural resource access and use. Their relationship with the production and processing of these natural resources is reduced to a purely transactional one. In the process of commercialisation of these resources, women and their productive activities are invariably pushed out to marginal lands – where the environmental impacts on the physical environment can be especially taxing.

Entry points for policy intervention and regulation

Using the UN System of Integrated Environmental and Economic Accounts as a basis to categorise and analyse natural resources (Figure 17.1), four areas emerge for policy development.

Public commons

Most of the country's water, land and air are held as community property in the public commons, with distribution of natural resources traditionally governed by male elders in the non-formal economy. Women access these resources for energy, home construction and for income.

Food security

The red circles superimposed on the figure highlight those natural resources that underpin formal and non-formal rural economies. The substantive basis for food security lies in agriculture, forestry and coastal and inland fishery, whose day-to-day management is predominantly undertaken by women.

Figure 17.1 Entry points for policy intervention and regulation

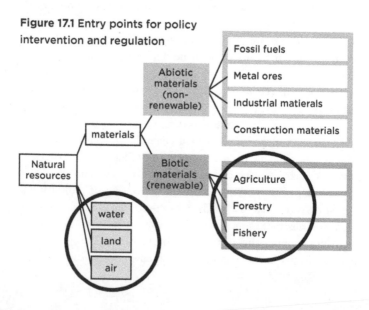

Extractive activities

The extraction of non-renewable metal ores in the non-formal sector, artisanal small-scale mining (ASM) and plantation businesses all rely heavily on the support roles of women. The benefits they derive from these activities, however, remain largely peripheral.

Non-renewable materials

As the commercial exploitation of land and non-renewable abiotic materials (represented in yellow) intensifies and grows, women's access to the public commons and to biotic materials in the non-formal (communal) sector needs protection and strengthening, while enabling women to take engaged positions in the formal (private) sector.

Roadside markets showed a 'vibrant self-employment' informal economy based on the exploitation of natural resources. Neatly tied bundles of bamboo, wood and thatch for construction, sacks of charcoal, piles of rock and slate broken into different sizes, piles of wood for burning and hills of sand of various gradients speak to an entrepreneurial drive or need to earn cash. It is not clear what implications this may have for the natural environment from which these items are extracted, whether this is regulated in any way, or whether there should even be any control over these public commons. While these existing natural resources are community assets, a question needs to be raised about the replacement value of these assets and whether there are other, more sustainable alternatives to be considered as sources of income for the poor. The entrepreneurial spirit and drive need to be complemented by awareness and action to replace and regenerate what is being mined.

Empowering women to reclaim and advance community assets and rights

With population growth, competition for natural resources and growing inequalities, the empowerment of rural women needs to take place on multiple fronts. Empowerment is the process of enabling people to be actors in their own solutions to their issues. In the case of rural women, this will mean wresting back power to take control over the decisions that affect their domestic household security, in their informal and communal (public commons) spaces as well as in the formal and political arenas.

Policies that promote women's empowerment tend to lean towards 'economic empowerment', the assumption being that with expanded economic means come more and better choices. The more financial leverage one has, the more likely one is to project power: gain voice, respect, independence and the ability to negotiate terms and a more favourable hearing. In reality, in the course of earning income in mines, plantations or in the informal natural resource economy, women are systematically exploited, have decision-making choices taken away from them and are left with denuded natural environs – a heavy price to pay for so-called empowerment.

The empowerment goal will need to be to strengthen not only women's daily management roles, but also their capacity for directly engaging in community decisions around (i) how natural resources are developed, (ii) how the benefits from extraction of natural resources are fairly shared over time, and (iii) how they might themselves engage in supply chains. Given their societal status and relative lack of assets, women are more likely to lead change as a group than as individuals. They will need to build networks of solidarity with community members across gender barriers to articulate and act on collective interests. This becomes especially difficult in rural areas, where villages are relatively isolated from each other and where transport is a significant and expensive challenge.

Women's relationships with natural resources require transformative change to current practices and policies that discriminate against or undervalue women and their productive activities. Some fundamental bases for change include:

» **Correcting gender imbalances in landholding and use** through deconstructing, reconstructing and reconceptualising existing rules of property in land under both customary and statutory law in ways that strengthen women's access to and control of land while respecting family and other social networks.[10]

» Empowerment within the holistic agro-ecological **farming framework** – integrating organic farming practices with food security and natural resource management through **changing the mode of farm practice to a holistic agro-ecological system, including tried and tested models such as organic and permaculture farming which will integrate community management of natural resources with their food production activities.**[11]

» Enhancing the proactive contribution of women in defining and implementing alternative solutions to their local fuel needs, shifting towards clean and renewable energy systems.

» **Supporting the mobilisation, political consciousness and organisation of rural and urban women** to improve their situation, influence policy and realise their rights – at decentralised, local, national and political levels.

» Raising public awareness about rights and access to natural resources as both a **public service and a civil rights issue.**

From patriarchal traditions to gender-sensitive common regimes

Now more than ever, poor women and men must claim their rights of access to natural capital within the framework and cultural context of common property, community rights and community responsibilities and solidarity.

As in many African countries, the traditional management of forest landscapes in Liberia is made up of a complex hierarchy of gender relationships, knowledge and customs. An adult male 'bush manager' is appointed by the elders to manage access to forest resources, covering a number of villages, to prevent the over-exploitation of these resources. Women are not part of this group of elders, the suggested reason being that women are 'afraid' to make decisions and because they are excluded by the male secret society. Most sacred groves of the male secret societies[12] are associated with forests, with strong oversight by members. Taboos and sanctions prohibit the exploitation of forest resources for commercial gain. When it comes to land access, both men and women have equal rights to private ownership of the flood plains for sugar cane production, although capital availability limits women's investment relative to men.[13] With the demise of these local and hierarchical structures – through changing political space and the influence of Christian and Islamic teachings – this kind of localised forest conservation service is on the decline.[14]

The questions then arise: How can the appropriate aspects of traditional value systems that policed community use of natural resources be adapted to a gender-sensitive application of rules and procedures that empowers men and women in these communities? How can the empowerment of women within the collective framework secure their rights to natural resources? How can rural communities that sustained a non-formal rural economy be supported as they enter unmediated agreements in the formal economy that expose them to the risks of global markets?

One example is provided by the Nobel laureate Elinor Ostrom, who argued that economic activity can be effectively regulated by *collective social activity*.[15] She applied the term Common Pool Regimes (CPRs) to categorise such forms of property. Her findings documented that collective community ownership of resources by rural communities may foster the evolution and adaptation of sustainable resource systems (or regimes). Along with clear rights and functioning policies for public goods and the commons, fostering collective rights to common property helps to secure the future provision of ecosystem services. Ostrom challenged the assumption that common property is poorly managed unless regulated by government or privatised, and proved that individuals can successfully form collectives that protect the resource at hand. This way of thinking sits at the heart of the way pastoralists and rural women might measure the value of natural capital – where the idea of private ownership of part or all of an ecosystem runs counter to communal access to the biosphere.

The OECD Development Assistance Committee, the World Bank and international NGOs are renewing their focus on access to natural resources as a core component of poor rural people's entitlements as citizens. Natural resources management and agriculture knowledge, technology and public services are of key importance to support natural-resource-based livelihoods, particularly in the face of environmental, climatic and market changes that require new solutions and adaptation.[16] These new solutions, behavioural changes and adaptive practices will need in the first instance to consider how women can be empowered to be community architects for the future.

18

MARIA MIES

Sociologist, activist and co-author of *Ecofeminism*

Mother Earth

For Indians and in fact for many people in the world the idea that the Earth is our Sacred Mother is still alive. As Vandana Shiva says, '*mati*' – soil – reverberates in the songs and slogans of Indian people struggling against 'development'. 'Mati Devata – Dharam Devata – Earth Goddess' were the words of the Adivasi women in the 'Save Gandhamardhan Movement' as they embraced the earth while the police tried to drag them away from the blockade of the Gandhamardhan Hills.

> We will sacrifice our lives, but not Gandhamardhan.
> We want to save this hill which gives us all we need.

'Modern development' means the 'ecological and cultural rupture of bonds with nature'.[1] It means the transformation of the living earth, of the soil, into a dead resource for industrialisation.

In India this Earth Mother can still be seen in thousands of images, representing her many manifestations. In modern Europe, however, the idea that we are not only with our body but also spiritually directly connected to nature, to the soil, is almost forgotten. And yet there was also a phase in European history when Mother Earth was venerated as our Sacred Mother, the source of food and life, of biological and cultural diversity and also of society. The Earth was female and sacred. This idea found expression in numerous old small clay statues which archaeologists found all over Europe. They called them 'Mother Goddesses'. As in India, they were conceived as the power who creates and regenerates all life forms by herself. As the All-Creator she would take her children back to herself in death and transform them again into new forms of life. Although she was one she was called by many names and appeared in different manifestations: as the 'Mother of Grain', the 'Mother of Animals' (birds, fish, cattle and other animals). But she was also the Mother of Water, because all sources, brooks, rivers and finally the sea, were goddesses.

As Marija Gimbutas, the late archaeologist, discovered, the 'Gods of Old Europe' were practically all female. Through extensive excavations in the Balkans, Greece, Crete and Anatolia, and her studies in central Europe, she was able to prove that the 'World of Old Europe was a civilisation of the Great Goddess'. Among the thousands of excavated images of gods there were hardly any male deities.

In her book *The Civilization of the Goddess – the World of Old Europe* she shows convincingly that the world of Old Europe was not a primitive world of poor peasants, hunters and fishermen who had to fight day in, day out against scarcity and the threat of hunger, having no leisure to create art, beauty and 'culture'. On the contrary, she calls the civilisation of Old Europe a 'true' civilisation because it was not based on violence, warfare, conquest and male dominance.

> Neolithic Europe was not 'before civilization' [...] It was, instead, a true civilization in the best meaning of the word. In the 5th and early 4th millennia BC just before its demise in east central Europe, Old Europeans had towns with a considerable concentration of population, temples several stories high, a sacred script, spacious houses of four or five rooms, professional ceramicists, weavers, copper and gold metallurgists and other artisans producing a range of sophisticated goods. A flourishing network of trade routes existed that circulated items such as obsidian, shells, marble, copper, and salt over hundreds of kilometers.[2]

In fact, it was a civilisation of abundance, not of scarcity.

Old European civilisation was not the creation of nomadic warriors, who, with their swift horses, their war chariots and their far-reaching weapons such as spears and bow and arrow, were able to invade the lands of the early Europeans, who were regular agriculturists. In such societies the main mystery and wonder is the regeneration of life.

> [...] with the inception of agriculture, farming man began to observe the phenomena of the miraculous Earth more closely and more intensively than the previous hunter-fisher had done. A separate deity emerged, the Goddess of vegetation, a symbol of the sacral nature of the seed and the sown field, whose ties with the Great Goddess are intimate.[3]

In her study of the *Goddesses and Gods of Old Europe*, Gimbutas shows that there were hardly any male deities among the thousands of excavated images of gods. Old European religion was a religion of the goddess. There was no Father God. The role of men in human reproduction was not yet known in the Neolithic. But there was also not the division and polarisation between female and male and the subordination of the female to the male element which we have learned to accept as 'natural' – 'Both principles were side by side.'[4] Also, the Old European civilisation does not reveal traces of a society based on warfare and conquest. In the excavations of tombs and cities no weapons to systematically kill humans – such as swords, spears, bows and arrows – were found. There were no strong fortifications of the cities or towns or villages to protect them from enemies. According to Gimbutas, Old European civilisation 'was in the main peaceful, sedentary, matrifocal, matrilinear and sexegalitarian'.[5]

Images of the Earth Mother

The earliest European image of the Earth Mother is the 'Woman of Willendorf', found in Austria. It is dated to a period around 30,000 BC. Archaeologists found such figurines at many sites in Europe. All Palaeolithic and most later Neolithic images are characterised by similar features to those of the Woman of Willendorf:

big round breasts, symbolising the giver of food, a big round belly and a pronounced vaginal triangle – the source of the generative powers of the Big Mother. She is the giver of all life. The forms of her body mean that she is not only the creator and regenerator of human life, but of plant and animal life as well. Moreover, in her body the cyclical unity of the cosmos, of the interconnectedness of all life forms, even of time and society, is expressed.

After the advent of regular agriculture (which is usually dated in the Neolithic era, c. 10,000 BC) the religion of the Old Europeans was based on the agricultural cycles: sowing, growing, harvesting, resowing. These cycles are expressed still in historical times in the names of many Greek and Roman goddesses. Thus Ceres (Rome) was the goddess of grain, Flora protected the blossoming grain, Diva Angerona was in charge of the solstices, Anna Perenna ruled over human and vegetative regeneration. Juno was the goddess of birth, Kybele, the Magna Mater, was the Mother of all life – she protected the fields.[6]

In the Rhineland (Germany) the Three Matronae were venerated till long after the beginning of the Christian era. As Young Woman, Mature Woman and Old Woman they symbolise the trinity of life, death and rebirth.

This civilisation lasted for at least 4,000 years until it was violently destroyed by invaders coming from the steppes of Russia. Gimbutas called them the 'Kurgan' people, because they built huge tombs for their leaders: 'The gentle agriculturists were easy prey to warlike Kurgan horsemen who swarmed down upon them. These invaders were armed with thrusting and cutting weapons: long dagger-knives, spears, halberds, and bows and arrows.'[7]

The thrust of the Kurgan invasions went westwards, through Ukraine, Bulgaria, Romania and eastern Hungary, following the Danube and other rivers up to the Rhine – and southwestwards into Macedonia and Greece, even reaching the Peloponnese.

The 'superiority' of the Kurgan horsemen lay not in their culture but in their control over more efficient means of destruction – arms – and better means of transport – namely the tamed horse. The armed man on the horse was a new war machine. He could not be used for any productive and peaceful purpose, only for attacking, killing, looting, invading, conquering and colonising. The civilisation which these warrior horsemen brought with them and built up in the course of their invasions all over Europe lasts till today. The latest 'inventions' of such long-distance arms are the atom bomb and the drone. These arms can destroy faraway 'targets' without fear that the enemy can retaliate. The civilisation of 'Man the Warrior' is the opposite of that of Mother Earth. It is aggressive, xenophobic, patriarchal, it creates social hierarchies based on the subordination of women, on slavery, classes and castes. Its economy is dependent on loot, tribute and on the exploitation of foreign peoples and their lands. Man the Warrior considers himself as the creator of life on Earth, of plants, animals, even of children. In all patriarchal societies, the 'father' is considered to be creator and the beginning of human life. Even today all genealogies follow the male line. Our family names are our father's, not our mother's. Thus our mothers are deleted from history. Here we see the dilemma of patriarchal men: if they want to have sons they need women, mothers. Without women they are sterile. To overcome this dilemma Man the Warrior invented ever more effective means of destruction. The new patriarchal civilisation that grew out of the killing of Mother Earth is based on the principle Creation out of Destruction. This principle was expressed most clearly by the Greek philosopher Heraclitus, who lived around 500 BC and wrote the famous phrase 'War is the father and king of all, some he has made gods, and some men; some slaves and some free'. And we can add to this patriarchal philosophy: 'Some he made men and others women'.

If we want to understand the ruling worldview on our planet today we have only to look at this sentence coined by Heraclitus. Everything is there: War is the Father and King of Everything. He has created the world and hence he is the ruler of this world. This means he who kills is the creator and king over humans and non-humans. War is the beginning of life on earth. War also creates the patriarchal and hierarchical social order of this world, which cannot be changed: once a slave, always a slave, once a god, always a god; once women are subjected to men they will always be subjected to men. This is the iron law of our patriarchal civilisation even today. Yet the secret of this civilisation is violence, not superior intelligence or creativity. Man the Warrior needs ever more destructive arms to keep his sovereignty over all things and life on Earth. Only by killing Mother Earth can he show that he is the true Father and King.

Yet we, the women, the daughters of Mother Earth counter Heraclitus by saying: 'But nature is the the mother of life'.

This truth is still accepted, or has been rediscovered, by a number of countries in today's world, particularly in South America, for instance in Bolivia and Ecuador, where Pachamama protects the Earth and all creatures on it.

Heraclitus must have known the mother goddesses of his time and region (Turkey). Therefore the main target of 'Father War' is not just human enemies but Mother Nature herself. Because the new wars are wars of conquest of new territories, populations and particularly of women. Mother Nature as the creator of life has therefore to be killed. Matricide is the most efficient 'mode of production' of patriarchy, and his latest son or avatar is capitalism. Today capitalist patriarchy is indeed considered the only source of wealth and of modern life. It can overcome the limitations of space, time and the limits of our planet Earth. The method of achieving this goal is the same today as it was thousands of years ago: kill Mother Earth, divide the parts of her body into separate bits and pieces. Thus our living Mother Earth is transformed into dead matter, material, raw material, which is necessary to produce new 'things' .The new warrior-engineers recombine these dead parts into new machines, new engines, driven by new energy. Heraclitus would be happy: destruction as creation by Man the Warrior. War unlimited[8] is the father of progress and and of life on Earth.

Yet today many people in the world realise that this victory of 'Father War' over Mother Nature also threatens the lives and the sheer existence of all creatures on Earth. Therefore the most burning question is: How can we stop this war against nature? How can we stop the ecological destruction by our modern civil-isation? How can we stop climate change, atomic pollution, air pollution, the disappearance of forests, of a number of species, of clean water and air, the poisoning of the soil by huge chemical industries like Monsanto, the destruction of biological and cultural diversity and its replacement by monoculture – in short: How can we stop those who sacrifice Mother Earth for the accumulation of money and capital?

Women, mothers, were among the first to recognise these dangers, because they ask: What future will our children have in such a world? They were also among the first who fought against the enemies of Mother Earth. But today many men and many organisations are also fighting against this ecological warfare. Many, however, believe that this is possible within the framework of capitalism. Even the German government passed laws to replace destructive energy sources with renewable ones. Like most people they want to have their cake and eat it too. Yet this will not be possible because some of the damage done to nature cannot be repaired – witness climate change and its consequences for the entire world. The only way to save life on Earth is to stop the war against nature and create a totally new civilisation, based on love and respect for Mother Earth.

19

SARAH FISHER
Population and Sustainability Network

Sexual and reproductive health and rights: a win-win for women and sustainability

Advancing sexual and reproductive health and rights (SRHR) worldwide is a win-win proposition for both women and sustainability, in more ways than you might think. To the understandable frustration of many feminists, the most common association centres around the relationships between women's fertility and family planning, global population and environmental sustainability. Yet full and universal access to SRHR is also critical for unleashing the full potential of women and girls to contribute to environmental management and decision-making. This chapter takes a closer look at how SRHR and sustainability are linked, revisits some of the common concerns and misconceptions about population issues, and proposes key strategies for drawing on the synergies between SRHR, gender equality and sustainable development.

Revisiting the population and sustainability debate

Many women in wealthier nations take their sexual and reproductive health and rights for granted. For example, they have access to information and contraceptive options to manage their own fertility; they can choose whether they marry and who; they won't put their life at great risk by giving birth to a child, and any children they do choose to have are likely to survive beyond infancy. In many areas of the world, however, particularly in the world's poorest countries, this is not the case. In developing countries, an estimated 26 per cent of women have an unmet need for contraception,[1] one in every three girls is married before the age of eighteen,[2] women are 300 times more likely to die in childbirth compared with their counterparts in an industrialised country, and their children are fourteen times more likely to die in the first twenty-eight days of life.[3]

Addressing these sexual and reproductive health issues is an urgent priority. These issues are important enough in their own right to command the necessary attention and investment for redress, irrespective of wider social, economic and environmental benefits. Some feminists and champions of SRHR are therefore understandably wary of attempts to appropriate women's rights for other means, particularly where population and the environment are concerned. This is compounded by the history of population discourse and policy, which is blighted by programmes of the 1960s and 1970s, some of which were seen as coercive, in which women were treated as objects rather than subjects: mistakes that absolutely cannot and must not be repeated. Therefore, programmes where family planning is the primary focus (perhaps with an implicit aim of reducing birth rates) can be met with mistrust.[4] Critics rightly argue that these programmes neglect the wider important sexual and reproductive health needs that should also be prioritised, including information, education and services for: the prevention and treatment of sexually transmitted infections and HIV/AIDS; safe abortion and post-abortion services; prenatal/postnatal and delivery care; infant healthcare; and prevention and treatment of infertility.

A whole range of further complexities, sensitivities and misconceptions can present barriers to constructive dialogue on the intersections between population, health, gender equality and sustainability (see Box 19.1). These factors, and others, can also make environmentalists reluctant to engage in population-related debates. Perhaps most significantly, there's the concern that a focus on population detracts from pressing consumption issues, and risks blaming women in poorer countries with large families for environmental problems that are in fact caused predominantly by the inequitable and unethical consumption patterns of the richest countries and groups.[5]

Box 19.1 Population, human rights and environmental sustainability: common questions, concerns and misconceptions[a]

Can you care about population *and* human rights?

Yes. It's commonly assumed that nothing can be done to help stabilize population growth without infringement of personal freedoms and liberties related to women's and couples' desired family size. In fact, extending and expanding access to the sexual and reproductive health services that will enable individual men and women to make their own reproductive choices is the answer. Ensuring that everyone can enjoy their right to 'decide freely and responsibly the number, spacing and timing of their children'[b] is a matter of health and human rights, and offers opportunities to advance sustainable development, by preventing unplanned pregnancies and reducing population growth and associated environmental demands and pressures.

Isn't the problem consumption, not population?

It is, and it isn't. Unsustainable, inequitable and unethical patterns of consumption and production, particularly by the world's richest nations and individuals, are a major driver of the global environmental crisis and a huge barrier to sustainable development. It's true that the vast majority of future population growth is projected to take place in the poorest countries of the world,[c] where per capita consumption rates are many times lower than in the developed world. Yet the perception that the problem and therefore the solution lies in *either* population *or* consumption is simplistic and unhelpful. Both patterns of consumption and production (including the efficiency with which resources are used) *and* numbers of people (population) influence demand for and pressures on natural resources (food, water, shelter, fuel, etc.). And it is also true that, as nations develop, per capita consumption rises. If everyone in the world today lived as the average person in the USA does, the equivalent of over 4.5 planets would be needed to support us. However, if we lived as the average person in India does, we'd be using less than half the planet's bio capacity.[d] Yet at the local level population growth does cause pressures. For example, developing countries have identified high population growth and density as undermining their capacity to adapt to climate change by exacerbating environmental problems such as soil erosion, water and land shortages.[e] What's more, to lift growing numbers of people out of poverty, the world's poorest will need to consume more,[f] making the issue of over-consumption all the more urgent if we are to avoid further major environmental threats. Given the pressing nature of the global environmental challenges we face, we should be drawing on all potentially beneficial strategies at our disposal, addressing both consumption- and population-related factors.

With global fertility on the decline, hasn't the problem been 'solved'?

It's not quite that simple; global fertility levels may be declining but fertility is not declining in all areas of the world. Forty-six per cent of the world's population now lives in countries with below-replacement fertility (where women have on average fewer than 2.1 children over their lifetimes).[e] But the population in some developing countries is still growing rapidly, and even when fertility does drop to replacement level, the population will continue to grow for several decades as the youngest generations reach reproductive age. Between now and 2050, the world population is therefore expected to increase from today's 7.3 billion to 9.7 billion.[e] More than half of this growth is projected to take place in Africa, where the population will double between now and 2050, and triple by the end of the century.[e] These levels of growth in the world's poorest countries will inevitably exacerbate the challenges already faced in alleviating poverty, ensuring food and water security, and providing access to health and education services for all. Take Niger, for example – one of the world's poorest countries. Women on average in Niger give birth to 7.6 children, only 8 per cent of sexually active women of reproductive age use a modern method of contraception and the population is growing by 4 per cent each year.[c, g]

a Some of these questions are based on materials produced by PSN with and on behalf of the Population and Sustainable Development Alliance (PSDA). See PSDA, *Population Dynamics, Reproductive Health and Sustainable Development: Critical Links and Opportunities for Post-2015*, PSN, London, 2013.

b United Nations General Assembly, *Report of the International Conference on Population and Development*, A/94/10/18, Programme of Action, UN, New York, 1994.

c United Nations, Department of Economic and Social Affairs, Population Division, 'World population prospects: the 2015 Revision, Key Findings and Advance Tables', Working Paper no. ESA/P/WP.241, UN, New York, 2015.

d WWF, *Living Planet Report 2010: Biodiversity, biocapacity and development*, WWF, Gland, 2010.

e L. Bryant, L. Carver, C. D. Butler et al., 'Climate change and family planning: least-developed countries define the agenda', *Bulletin of World Health Organization*, 87, 2009, pp. 852–7.

f Royal Society, *People and the Planet*, Royal Society, London, 2012.

g United Nations, Department of Economic and Social Affairs, Population Division, *World Contraceptive Use 2015*, POP/DB/CP/Rev2015, 2015.

These are all legitimate concerns that must be given due consideration in population and sustainability debates and related policy. Yet remaining silent about these issues and linkages is not in the interests of women, their health and rights, nor of the environment. Those who care about women's health and rights should be leading the debate rather than risk leaving it to others for whom this may not be such a concern. Increased knowledge and awareness of the wider benefits of SRHR could hasten the day when universal enjoyment of these rights becomes a reality.

Women and girls want and need their sexual and reproductive health and rights

While some people concerned with global population growth seem to think that women need educating about and convincing of the wider benefits to society and the environment of having fewer children, there are many good reasons closer to home why women want and need access to vital sexual and reproductive health information, education and services, and their sexual and reproductive rights. How can we even begin to dream of achieving gender equality unless women are able to take charge of their own bodies, sexuality and reproduction?

Considering access to contraception alone – empowering women to plan and space their children as they choose – reduces their risk of death or severe illness from giving birth, provides women with more opportunities for education, employment and personal fulfilment. Their children are more likely to be healthy, and both they and their families are more likely to be better off.[6]

The importance of SRHR starts at a young age. Early and unintended pregnancy, early and forced marriages, sexual harassment and violence, HIV/AIDs and other sexual and reproductive health issues threaten the health and rights of girls and undermine their education, exacerbating gender inequalities and female poverty. Adolescent girls are at a higher risk of death from pregnancy-related complications, as well as complications from unsafe abortions, than older women, and are at a higher risk of HIV infection than adolescent boys. They are also less likely than older women to access sexual and reproductive healthcare, including modern contraception and skilled assistance during pregnancy and childbirth. Furthermore, girls and young people often have limited information about sexual and reproductive health issues, and face stigma, discrimination and other barriers to accessing the information and services they need.[7]

There are 1.2 billion young people in the world today, the largest population of youth (persons aged fifteen to twenty-four) in history, 88 per cent of whom live in developing countries.[8] Ensuring that girls and young people have their sexual and reproductive health and

Box 19.2 How would women and sustainable development benefit from the fulfilment of unmet need for contraception?

An estimated 225 million women in developing countries have an unmet need for modern contraception. Fulfilling this need would, each year:

» Prevent 70,000 maternal deaths
» Prevent 500,000 newborn deaths
» Avert 52 million unintended pregnancies
» Avert 24 million abortions, many of which are unsafe.[a]

Increasing access to contraceptive information and choices directly benefits women, their children and families and has wider benefits for sustainable development.

The scale of the global development challenges we face is set by population trends, alongside consumption patterns and efficiencies. They shape the number and location of people, their need for access to clean water, food, health and education services, etc., and resultant environmental impacts.

Empowering women with contraceptive options and other vital reproductive health services supports progress towards a number of development priorities, reducing population growth and the overall costs of achieving development goals. For every dollar spent in family planning it is estimated that up to six dollars can be saved in interventions aimed at achieving other development goals, including those related to maternal and newborn health, gender equality, the elimination of poverty and hunger, education, HIV/AIDS and environmental sustainability.[b]

a S. Singh, J. E. Darroch and L.S. Ashford, *Adding It Up: Costs and Benefits of Investing in Sexual and Reproductive Health 2014*, Guttmacher Institute and United Nations Population Fund (UNFPA), 2014.
b S. Moreland and S. Talbird, 'Achieving the Millennium Development Goals: the contribution of fulfilling the unmet need for family planning', USAID, Washington, DC, 2006.

rights has an important yet overlooked role to play in empowering the next generation of environmental activists.

Empowering women and girls as agents of change

The critical role that women play in advancing environmental sustainability has been recognised for some time. The 1992 Rio 'Earth Summit' noted that: 'Women have a vital role in environmental management and development. Their full participation is therefore essential to achieve sustainable development.' In developing countries women play distinct roles in agriculture, in collecting water, fuel and food for domestic use and income generation and in overseeing land and water resources. Women are responsible for collecting water in almost two-thirds of households,[9] and in some countries they comprise over 60 per cent of the agricultural workforce.[10] This experience makes them an invaluable source of ecological knowledge and expertise on environmental management and appropriate conservation actions.[11] As the primary resource managers for households, women are disproportionately affected by environmental degradation, including water scarcity, deforestation, etc., and they may also have a stronger impetus to ensure that local natural resources are used sustainably.[12]

There is also evidence to suggest that women are more eco-friendly and responsive to changing their behaviour towards environmentally friendly practices. Women are more likely to recycle, buy organic food and eco-friendly products, and place a higher value on energy-efficient transport.[13] A study of 130 countries found that countries with higher female parliamentary representation are more likely to ratify international environmental treaties.[14] Local institutions of forest governance which have a higher proportion of women have been shown to be associated with significantly greater improvements in forest conditions and conservation.[15] Likewise, community water and sanitation projects run with the full participation of women are more effective and sustainable than those without.[16]

What has this got to do with sexual and reproductive health and rights?

Worldwide, women and girls bear a higher burden of unpaid domestic work and undertake most of the parenting.[17] As well as negatively impacting their health and options for pursuing educational and employment opportunities, this presents a gendered barrier to women's full participation in governing their community and society, including environmental management and decision-making. Research looking specifically at women's role in forestry management in developing countries has found that frequent pregnancies and the associated childcare and increased domestic responsibilities of women with larger families reduced the involvement of women in forest conservation efforts.[18]

In contrast, a woman who is healthy and able to choose the number and timing of her pregnancies is more resilient to natural resource constraints and climate change, and better able to manage resources effectively for her family and community. Additionally, being able to plan her family means that her domestic burden is less, she faces fewer constraints in realising her aspirations and has more capacity to engage in environmental activism and stewardship. As shown in Box 19.3, a number of 'Population Health Environment' projects in developing countries are achieving just that.

Towards a collaborative strategy for linking environmental sustainability and reproductive rights

This chapter has argued that caring about both women's rights and about population and the environment is not only compatible but essential.

But what are some of the ways forward?

Coalition building across-sectors for environmental and repro-ductive justice: Environmental, women's rights and sexual and reproductive health organisations and activists should forge new and wider partnerships, joining forces to advance shared interests and agendas, including through engagement with youth groups.

Collaboration across sectors is necessary to open dialogue, facilitate greater understanding of complementary perspectives and overcome polarised thinking about population and consumption.[19] This will help overcome the various sensitivities and complexities that

---

Box 19.3 Population Health Environment approaches: a long-awaited revolution for women and the environment?

For too long, conservation and human development agendas have been distinct from, and even in competition with, one another, failing to address the critical relationships between people, their health and well-being (including SRHR), gender equality and the environment. But this may be starting to change thanks to a small but growing movement of community-based projects in developing countries that combine reproductive health services and education with natural resource management, conservation and other sustainable development initiatives. These innovative 'Population Health Environment' (PHE) programmes take a pragmatic and holistic approach to the interconnected issues of poor health, unmet family planning needs, food insecurity, poverty, unsustainable use of natural resources and environmental degradation. Integrating these factors creates synergies and reverses this vicious cycle, improving both the health of communities and the ecosystems upon which they depend.[a] Their effectiveness over single-sector approaches is proven. A comparative study of a pioneering PHE project by Path Foundation Philippines found that integrated delivery of coastal resource management and reproductive health (including family planning) generated higher positive impacts on the ecosystem and health than delivering either in isolation.[b]

The success of these projects is by no means limited to addressing unmet need for contraception and associated fertility reductions. By responding to the priority needs of communities,

can present a barrier to environmental and development groups engaging on population, SRHR and other issues outside of their expertise. Recent work to influence the UN Open Working Group establishing a set of Sustainable Development Goals has shown

these projects are able to experience greater local trust and buy-in, helping build local ownership of conservation programmes and grassroots movements with the potential to deliver longer-lasting change.[c] This has been the finding of an integrated programme in an isolated coastal community in rural Madagascar.[d] The project by Blue Ventures started as a marine conservation programme but began working with health agencies to offer family planning services, in response to a community-articulated concern about declining fish stocks, ascribed by locals to overfishing due to rapid population growth. Offering reproductive health information and services has provided opportunities to engage women and foster their involvement in natural resource management, and in turn men have become more interested and involved in reproductive health issues.[e]

a V. Mohan, J. Castro, D. Pullanikkatil et al., *Population Health Environment Programmes: An Integrated Approach to Development Post-2015*, 2014, psda.org.uk/wp-content/uploads/2014/09/PSDA-SDSN-paper-FINAL.pdf, accessed 26 September 2014.

b L. D'Anges, H. D'Anges, J. B. Scwartz et al., 'Integrated management of coastal resources and human health yields added value: a comparative study in Palawan (Philippines)', *Environmental Conservation*, 37(4), 2010, pp. 398–409.

c R. De Souza, 'Resilience, integrated development and family planning: building long-term solutions', *Reproductive Health Matters*, 22(43), 2014, pp. 75–83.

d See blueventures.org.

e V. Mohan and T. Shellard, 'Providing family planning services to remote communities in areas of high biodiversity through a Population-Health-Environment programme in Madagascar', *Reproductive Health Matters*, 22(43), 2014, pp. 93–103.

that cross-disciplinary action is possible. To influence the post-2015 international development framework, the Population and Sustainable Development Alliance collaborated with other SRHR advocates, feminist groups and other sustainable development activists as part of the UN Women's Major Group on a wide range of compatible issues, including SRHR.[20]

Active promotion of SRHR by environmentalists: When freed from the common misperception that caring about population is intrinsically anti-women and anti-human rights, environmentalists can include population-related perspectives in their work and specifically advocate reproductive rights. This should avoid a narrow focus on family planning and emphasise the importance of universal access to SRHR and wider efforts to advance gender equality, including for girls and young people. An example is provided by the collaboration between Population and Sustainability Network and Friends of the Earth on a common position on global population, consumption and rights. The paper states: 'a rights-based approach to accelerating the positive trend of declining rates of population growth is necessary', and provides a number of shared, wide-ranging recommendations.[21]

Embracing integrated strategies: Integrated PHE approaches (see Box 19.3) offer environmental organisations a model for addressing the links between population, gender, health and environment in ways that respect and protect human rights. Responding to reproductive health needs and other local community priorities offers conservation initiatives an opportunity to increase the involvement of women while increasing effectiveness and the likelihood of long-term change.[22] PHE also offers cross-sector partnership opportunities for the necessary sharing of expertise, knowledge and programme experience. An example of how this can be achieved is provided by the PHE Ethiopia Consortium, which brings together community groups working on health, environment, gender and livelihood issues, to facilitate collaboration and build capacity to deliver integrated sustainable development interventions.[23]

Advancement of gender equality and realisation of SRHR offer rights-based ways to address population-related environmental concerns, delivering win-wins for women and the environment. By pursuing these strategies, environmental activists can help empower women and girls to make decisions that are good for them and for the planet, and to play a full role in delivering genuine and robust sustainability.

Acknowledgements

I would like to acknowledge the contributions of my colleagues Kathryn Lloyd, Karen Newman and Catherine Budgett-Meakin at Population and Sustainability Network, an international network that works to advance understanding of the relationships between population, health and sustainable development issues and to promote integrated, rights-based approaches to these interconnected challenges (www.populationandsustainability.org).

20

KATE METCALF
and colleagues

UK Women's Environmental Network

The power of grassroots action for women's empowerment and the environment

Women's Environmental Network (WEN) is the only organisation in the UK that has worked consistently to make the links between women's health, well-being, empowerment and environmental issues. WEN was established in 1988 by a group of women involved in the green movement who felt that women's perspectives were overlooked by mainstream environmental organisations. WEN's vision is of an environmentally sustainable world in which we have achieved gender equality; we attach equal importance to both and believe they can and should be achieved simultaneously. Achieving one without the other is not possible or desirable.

Those groups that are most disadvantaged in global society, such as women, children and indigenous peoples, are affected in ways that are linked to their inequality. The logical belief that arises from this observation is that if we can increase equality, we can lessen their suffering. And that is the task to which WEN, along with a number of other charities and organisations, has dedicated itself. That is why environmentalism is a feminist issue. And equally, feminism is an environmental issue. There are multitudes of ways in which women are affected by environmental issues such as climate change owing to unequal social roles and responsibilities. Even without extensive research into the gendered aspect of climate change, it seems common sense that solving something as massive as climate change should require the efforts of 100 per cent of the population. When half the world is inhibited in its ability to speak out, to take action, even just to educate itself, then we have only half the 'manpower' we might. Achieving gender equality is a way to maximise our efficacy in fighting climate change and other environmental challenges. Even if women were not the first affected, we should still all be equally consulted. Unfortunately, this simply is not the case.

WEN aims to inspire women to make environmentally informed choices about their health, and to empower women to become agents of change in their families, networks and society, and to participate equally in an environmentally sustainable future. Below we outline some examples of how we have done this in practice.

Past projects and successes

Since forming in 1988, the Women's Environmental Network has campaigned, published high-quality information and run practical sessions on issues which lie at the nexus between women and the environment. We have brought a gendered analysis to environmental debates such as climate change, where a gender-blind focus has been the norm, but also have broadened the scope of what is considered an 'environmental issue'. This focus has seen us tackling a range of subjects such as sanitary products, menstruation, harmful chemicals in cosmetics, breast cancer as an environmental disease, stress incontinence, cloth nappies, food growing and seed saving.

Enviromenstrual issues

Many of WEN's campaigns have centred on products which cause both health risks and waste. In 1989, WEN campaigned for dioxin-free and unbleached products and achieved the widespread agreement of manufacturers to use chlorine-free pulp in papers. In the same year we published a briefing about the hazards caused by the production, use and disposal of sanitary products to the environment and women's health. Since then, WEN has provided regularly updated information on alternatives to sanitary towels and tampons which are both environmentally friendly and avoid the numerous associated health problems. This work has helped to break down the taboos surrounding menstruation.

In 1992, WEN persuaded tampon manufacturers to provide clear health warnings about toxic shock syndrome on the outside of all tampon packs, also pushing for new research on this condition. WEN's briefing 'No laughing matter' provided free information on preventing and managing stress incontinence, another taboo issue which affects nearly 17 per cent of women over eighteen and has extensive environmental and social impacts.[1] An awareness-raising campaign examining the environmental causes of breast cancer in 1995 continued to explore the links between women's health and the environment and pushed for precautionary chemical regulation.

Waste and real nappies

Moreover, at the beginning of the 1990s WEN launched its first packaging waste campaign, Wrapping is a Rip Off, which involved the promotion of reusable products such as cloth handkerchiefs. We initiated the Waste Prevention Bill, which was first presented to Parliament in 1995 and evolved into the 1998 Waste Minimization Act, which gave local authorities power to introduce waste reduction measures.

WEN has consistently campaigned to raise awareness of the environmental impacts of disposable nappies, and in 2003 pressure from WEN resulted in the government prioritising nappy waste in its Waste Implementation Programme. WEN launched Real Nappy Week, which takes place at the end of April and has become a mainstream event supported by over 90 per cent of UK local authorities, and developed Real Nappies for London and the Real Nappy Exchange to provide parents with information and access to local real nappy sellers.

Harmful chemicals

WEN's work around chemical hazards has included a 1993 campaign around the pesticides, lindane in particular, used on cocoa which then end up in chocolate. A year of campaigning led to the regular testing of chocolate by the Ministry of Agriculture, Fisheries and Food. Lindane also had an adverse effect on the women cocoa harvesters as it was alleged to cause miscarriage. Towards the end of the 1990s, WEN also published a set of briefings on genetic engineering and was one of the founding members of the Five Year Freeze. In 2005 this became the GM Freeze campaign, which continues to push for a precautionary approach with regard to the propagation of genetically modified food and the patenting of genetic resources.

WEN's work on harmful chemicals in cosmetics began with our 2002 report, *Pretty Nasty*, which exposed the use of phthalates in European cosmetic products.[2] This was followed by *Getting Lippy: Cosmetics, toiletries and the environment*, a briefing addressing both the social pressure on women to use cosmetic products and the specific health risks accompanying them.[3] Alongside this, WEN began providing resources and workshops on making your own natural beauty products, known as Fruity Beauty, and also Toxic Tour workshops inviting women to undertake a toxic tour of their bathroom cabinets to find out about the potential harmful effects of the chemicals in their toiletries.[4]

Gender and climate change

WEN has pushed for the promotion of gender awareness in climate change action and policy. In 2007, we launched a Women's Manifesto on Climate Change in partnership with the National Federation of Women's Institutes, calling on the UK government to involve women in decision-making on climate change and provide economic incentives and carbon labelling to enable them to reduce their environmental impact.[5] During the 2009 Copenhagen Summit, this was developed into a comprehensive report (*Gender and the Climate Change Agenda*), which found that climate change is exacerbating existing gender inequality and demanded efforts to address this inequality, as well as gender-sensitive climate change mitigation and adaptation strategies.[6] We condensed this report into a four-page briefing, 'Why women and climate change', in order to make it more accessible to a wider audience.[7] The briefing outlined how women are more affected by climate change owing to gender inequality, have contributed less to it and are not equally involved in decisions about solutions to address it, despite often being best placed to report on and tackle the problems. For example: women are more likely to suffer from an increased workload as a result of climate-change-related disasters such as an increased burden of water and fuel collection, and they are more likely to suffer violence, including sexual violence, in resource conflicts exacerbated by climate change.

Current grassroots work: the Local Food project

For the past fifteen years, WEN has been working on food-growing projects with low-income and unemployed women from black, Asian and minority ethnic (BAME) backgrounds in the London Boroughs of Tower Hamlets and Hackney, both of which have some of the highest levels of deprivation in England.[8] It is estimated that 40 per cent of Asian and black women live in poverty in the UK, and Pakistani and Bangladeshi women are the most disadvantaged, earning the lowest salaries of any ethnic group and experiencing poverty at greater rates.[9] Thirty per cent of Tower Hamlets' residents are Bangladeshi.[10] Therefore, WEN's food-growing project aims to address the problems of poor health, social exclusion and barriers to education associated with this deprivation, as well as female marginalisation and climate change.[11]

The WEN Local Food project encompasses a number of smaller projects, which complement and enchance one another. As the local lead for Capital Growth in the borough, WEN coordinates the Tower Hamlets Food Growing Network: a network of food growers supported by four seasonal gatherings a year, a community seed library, email updates and a resource directory. The Network is comprised of individuals, community groups, community gardens, mental health groups, housing associations, council representatives and Tower Hamlets Public Health. The Network is an easily replicable model which serves to enhance and promote the community food-growing activity already taking place in the borough, as well as to raise the profile of food growing and access to healthy, fresh food for people on low-incomes. WEN also offers Spice it Up! organic food growing training, which empowers disadvantaged women to grow their own organic food and to share their knowledge and expertise with others. The project addresses the social isolation of marginalised groups such as Somali and Bangladeshi women, while also promoting biodiversity and green spaces in a densely populated urban area. It aims to help the many women in East London who lack access to formal horticultural and other training owing to gender, language, cultural and financial barriers. Spice it Up! provides a space for women to develop new skills and confidence and places value on their cultural food-growing knowledge.[12]

WEN has a unique role in the area, providing women-only activities for disadvantaged BAME women, who are often reluctant to attend mixed-sex groups and who face particular cultural, practical, psychological and institutional barriers to learning.[13] The social and health benefits of community food growing are becoming widely known and locally valued. In an evaluation of the Tower Hamlets Healthy Borough Programme, coordinated by NHS East London and the City, community food growing was found to be particularly positive, generating a wide range of health and social benefits, strong community enthusiasm and buy-in from social housing landlords. Given the wide recognition of the importance of community food growing, the London Borough of Tower Hamlets recently commissioned a community gardening service which WEN successfully bid for in partnership with a number of local Registered Social Landlords (RSLs), including Eastend Homes, Poplar HARCA and Tower Hamlets Community Housing, and Capital Growth/Sustain. WEN coordinated this project, 'Gardens for Life: Tower Hamlets Community Gardens', creating fifteen new community gardens with residents on housing estates, at community centres and in sheltered accommodation centres. Beneficiaries of this project received training and ongoing support and were linked into the Tower Hamlets Food Growing Network to ensure sustainability. The Network has been a great way to integrate people of different cultural, social and economic backgrounds, but above all a safe space for women and men to share.

Food growing for domestic use can provide its own economic benefits, such as improved access to healthy affordable food. Organic food is often regarded as a luxury, but growing food without the use of chemical pesticides and fertilisers is a straight-forward cost-saving measure for the majority of small-scale and low-income growers. From our experience, Bangladeshi women in particular are expert organic gardeners, using agricultural skills and a culture of gardening that have been passed down through the generations in Bangladesh. Valuing traditional knowledge of this kind is important in empowering women, fostering community and making the most of community diversity.

Developing skills

Volunteering at community food-growing and urban agriculture projects has also been found to increase employability of individuals and aid the transition to work through the development of transfer-able skills, increased confidence and social support, the development of technical skills and formal qualifications, and linking participants to networks that increase their chances of finding employment opportunities.[14] This has particular significance for BAME women, who are more likely to face cultural and psychological barriers to formal employment, but for whom food growing can offer an enjoyable and culturally appropriate form of engagement, with the potential to lead on to further opportunities.

Women's role in the alternative food economy: successes and constraints

One goal of WEN is to facilitate the self-empowerment of women as social, economic and environmental actors in accordance with femi-nist principles. WEN also seeks to build communities both among women as well as among larger communities of interest where women and the environment are prioritised. These efforts have been and continue to be successful in many respects, but challenges and constraints are ever present. Constraints include working with women who don't speak English, making empowerment efforts challenging. Time constraints mean that many women have very little spare time and often have to be back at noon to cook lunch. Successes include training hundreds of local women in organic food growing as well as building relationships through Spice it Up! and helping to set up numerous community gardens. Working with partner organisations, WEN is building a borough-wide network of community gardens, as well as a network of women who support each other in their food-growing efforts. WEN is also very proud of their community seed library, which is continuously developing. There are, however, ongoing challenges to our goals, primarily in relation to sustainability. Women's organisations and services across the board are facing huge funding crises. It is not an easy sell when people and funders think that gender equality issues have been solved and mainstreamed, so therefore do not see the need for a separate women's organisation or a specific gender focus on environmental issues.

Gardening allows ethnic minorities to express their cultural identities in the crops (e.g. okra, chilli, coriander, sweet potato, callaloo) they choose to grow and how they organise their gardens.[15] Programmes such as Spice it Up! celebrate cultural diversity and women's knowledge and allow Asian women, in particular, the opportunity to share their gardening and culinary culture with their neighbours. Gardening in a community of women can also give women the confidence to become involved in larger community greening efforts.

Through these same avenues of renegotiation, acts of growing and other forms of self- sufficiency by women can also be seen as a feminist act.[16] By taking the power of production back from some of the large-scale exploitative economic processes, women can gain a greater say in their own economies. This is not without its tensions, as women have historically and still largely remain responsible for food provision,[17], making tough choices concerning nutritional value when providing food on a tight budget.[18] Valuing these women's existing food-growing skills is vital as these skills are routinely devalued in the mainstream economy.

It is easy to see how food growing positively impacts women in terms of their familial food budget. It can, however, be a challenge to translate those skills into direct economic power for women outside of the home. Possible economic benefits might involve selling produce locally, or perhaps finding paid employment using agricultural skills. One possible means of making community gardens financially sustainable is to sell produce to local restaurants or markets, as mentioned above, and we are beginning to see relationships develop between community gardens and local business, yet more work needs to be done in this area to help ensure success. WEN would also like to see food provision and other domestic tasks shared equally with men to reduce women's burden.

Spice it Up! revalues food-growing skills that are going to become increasingly important in the face of peak oil and climate change – challenges which our current economic system cannot resolve. Small-scale food growing projects are one way of reinvigorating local communities to take more control of their food security and put sustainability at the forefront. Crucially these projects develop vital skills such as cooperation, working with nature and fostering community resilience in the face of the above challenges. Local small-scale action is often devalued in the global economy, along with women's skills and knowledge. We believe that projects such as Spice it Up! are valuable not just economically, but above all socially, culturally and environmentally, and play a small part in creating an alternative food economy with women at the forefront.

Conclusion

At the grass roots is where Women's Environmental Network currently works, educating and enabling women and men (through the Tower Hamlets Food Growing Network) in disadvantaged areas of London to take back control over their food, positively impacting their health and the environment by growing their own food in community gardens.

We would advocate that similar approaches be used more extensively in environmental and gender equality struggles. WEN is creating and facilitating spaces where women can share and value their knowledge and skills, which are routinely devalued by the mainstream economy and patriarchal society. Food growing and gardening are non-threatening, non-controversial ways to engage with many women who are isolated and not participating in wider societal structures. It is a useful strategy to address their practical gender needs, although we also aim ultimately to address their strategic gender needs. It provides not only a platform to talk about wider environmental issues in an accessible way with very concrete examples rooted in people's lives, but also works as a tool for language learning, healthy eating and social inclusion.

We have also found that while many women we work with would be uncomfortable attending any social activism events such as an anti-GM protest, they do feel strongly about the topics and are keen to engage in a practical way. We take them on a journey, because for many women just getting out of the house is a big hurdle to overcome. We have seen that the Tower Hamlets Community Seed Library empowers women by providing a way for them to take action by saving and sharing seeds with one another; engaging with the environmental issues in a way that they are comfortable with. WEN would like to see similar inclusive approaches bringing people together to build networks for sustainability and gender equality. In this context, using a covert feminist approach is more effective than an overt one, although we do endeavour to engage the women we work with in wider political and environmental issues such as biofuels, seed sovereignty, climate change and gender equality. Our vision is an environmentally sustainable world in which we have achieved gender equality. Not an easy task, but one where we are going to need multifaceted approaches to foster an awareness of the importance and benefits of working towards this vision. This entails working with both women and men to promote this agenda.

WEN is calling for recognition of the fact that the future of the planet, and everyone on it, relies on policy-makers and governments including women in decision-making, and empowering them, through achieving greater gender equality, to make the changes that need to be made for all our sakes. This means we need more women at the top level in policy-making, and, crucially, we need grassroots movements to educate and empower women at ground level. It is for these reasons that, for WEN, feminism and environmentalism go hand in hand.

21

MARYLYN HAINES EVANS

National Federation of Women's Institutes

One hundred years of collective action for environmental change

> We are yet bound together in one great, unbreakable sisterhood.
>
> Grace Hadow

In writing these words, NFWI's first vice-chair, Grace Hadow, recognised the strength of women coming together – and captured the imagination of a generation of women united in the WI's vision of a movement that could unlock the potential of all women and so create a strong, informed and active civil society. Since the 1920s, this has included taking responsibility for our impact on the planet and empowering women as agents of environmental change.

The ethos of the WI has always been to inspire, to educate, and to improve the lives of women and those around them. One hundred years on, the organisation has changed in many ways yet this ethos, and the ideals of community and friendship underpinning it, still holds true.

Grace's recognition of the value of collective action for bringing about change still permeates every level of the WI. A look back through the WI's history books offers a case study on how the empowerment of women can be harnessed to bring about environmental change.

The WI set out to empower women to get to grips with issues of concern to members and their communities. The founding members recognised: 'if one person alone cannot make her wants heard it becomes much easier when there are numbers wanting the same kind of things. That is why large numbers of women organised in bodies such as the National Federation of Women's Institutes can become a real power.' At a time when few women participated in public life and the vote for women had not yet been won, the organisation took a democratic and coordinated approach to mobilising women in the belief that if women learnt how to conduct meetings and run committees, and gained confidence in speaking in public, these skills would equip them for a changing world and stand them in good stead for participating in other areas of public life. This approach offered British women training in democracy and the exercise of the vote, enabling members, who perhaps had little prior experience of exerting power, to exercise influence and through the WI come together with other women in the numbers needed to become a force to be reckoned with; gradually forging the organisation a reputation as an effective force for change.

> This meeting, realising the significant changes which are rapidly taking place in agriculture and rural life, calls on the NFWI Executive Committee and the County Federations to encourage WI members to study these changes and to help to adapt new conditions to old.
>
> 1938 AGM

The WI's initial focus centred on the war effort. In 1917, with word out that only three weeks' food supply remained in the country, the newly formed National Federation of Women's Institutes began urging WIs to get behind food production efforts. WIs began growing more for villages and communities and, at a time when fruit conservation was something of a novel concept, members began bottling and preserving excess fruit in tremendous volumes; during the Second World War efforts were again stepped up with members preserving nearly twelve million pounds of fruit for the nation between 1940 and 1945. The jam-making label stuck. While it is now something of a stereotype, it's one which the WI is rightly proud of – demonstrating the organisation's commitment to encouraging members to give help where needed, tackling some of society's major challenges along the way.

Since then, the WI has campaigned on a wide range of issues that matter to women and their communities. With its roots in the countryside, the WI has been at the forefront of protecting and promoting the countryside, and understanding the symbiotic relationship between humans and nature. As early as 1927, the WI was speaking out on the threats our seas and coastal shores faced (at the time being polluted by waste oil from ships) and the impact on sea-life. Concerned by the need for greater planning regulation to protect the countryside from urban expansions and the effect this had on the health of people and wildlife, in 1938 WI members called for the preservation of 'wide areas of special beauty'. A decade later, Areas of Outstanding Beauty were established as part of the National Parks and Access to the Countryside Act 1949.

Often these campaigns have not only triggered important national conversations, but have responded to local need and, in many cases, left a rich legacy. One of the most memorable and long-standing WI initiatives stems from a resolution calling for a campaign to 'preserve the countryside against desecration by litter'. This resolution, passed in 1954 under the then chair, Elizabeth Brunner, led to the formation of the Keep Britain Tidy campaign, now an independent charity that celebrated its Diamond Jubilee in 2014.

In more recent years, WI campaigns have ranged from tackling the plight of the honey bee to reducing waste and conserving the countryside. A 2005 resolution on protecting natural resources inspired a nationwide action day that saw WIs up and down the country return excess packaging to supermarkets, as part of efforts to encourage retailers to reduce waste. The WI Carbon Challenge, launched in 2008, saw 10,000 members signed up, pledging to reduce their carbon footprint by 20 per cent. The savings achieved were equivalent to filling the Royal Albert Hall 108 times with CO_2. Each campaign, and the resolutions that inspire them, is underpinned by the founding members' vision of the potential of an empowered group of women; agents of change with the ambition to build a well-informed and active society that takes responsibility for our impact on the planet.

> Members must learn to realise their responsibility toward the community in which they live and, from an interest in their own village and their own county, come to see the connection between their affairs and those of the nation at large.
>
> Grace Hadow

Worldwide, women are both an influential and positive force for change and some of the most vulnerable individuals in the face of our changing climate. Globally, women remain influential consumers of domestic products and utilities, responsible for the tremendous spending power that accompanies their holding the purse strings on the vast majority of consumer spending. Management professor Gloria Moss suggests women buy 93 per cent of all groceries and 92 per cent of holidays, along with, perhaps more surprisingly, 60 per cent of new cars and 55 per cent of home computers. With UK women so critical to household spending, and so influential on others' purchases, women's economic and social capital means they hold the potential for powering tremendous environmental change through individual lifestyle and consumer choices.

The social roles women play as primary caregivers for children and older people in most societies throughout the world also offer women a unique perspective on sustainability, and the power to positively influence the way in which today's children consider their coexistence with our planet. NFWI research, undertaken ahead of the People's Climate Marches and the UN Climate Summit in New York City in September 2014, revealed that 74 per cent of British women believe that responsibility for tackling climate change cannot be left to future generations. And when asked what worried women the most when thinking about the effects of climate change, 35 per cent were concerned about the challenges that will face the future generations set to inherit a warmer planet, with all the difficulties around both resource and human security that will accompany this.

This awareness of the legacy that we leave with the choices we make has been a constant theme within the WI movement over the past 100 years. While we may feel that individually we are unable to have an impact or change the course of events, by working together it's easier to see how every person making seemingly small changes can contribute towards a huge collective effect.

Looking again at the NFWI's women and climate polling, it starts to become apparent why the formula to which the WI works is effective. The study found that women were more likely than men to believe that they as individuals could make a difference in tackling climate change (16 per cent of men felt that individuals cannot do much about climate change, compared to 9 per cent of women). It also found that women believed that the government had an important role to play in supporting the public to make more sustainable choices in their day-to-day lives, such as through improved recycling schemes or making it easier for people to use public transport.

> Women's Institutes have awakened the members' responsibility towards the community. It has led them to realise their power and to exert it for the improvement of conditions of rural life.
>
> WI Handbook, 1953/54

The WI campaigns model frequently sees members take a twofold approach: pressing for change from decision-makers; while examining the role of individuals as change agents, leading the way in their own communities by driving environmental changes by taking their own lives as a start point for practical action.

Take the WI's SOS for Honey Bees campaign, for example. Members across England and Wales, concerned at the accelerating decline in the UK honey bee population, backed an AGM resolution that launched a campaign calling on the government to increase funding for research into bee health in 2008. By 2013, with the research funding in place but the situation for bees and other pollinators remaining bleak, members got behind national campaigning for more comprehensive action for bees, through the development of a government-led national pollinator strategy. This important national campaigning was underpinned by awareness-raising among the public to build understanding about the declining honey bee population and the vital role that pollinators play in the country's ecosystem and food production.

Thousands of WI members have embraced the campaign by taking action in their own homes and communities. Henllan WI in Denbighshire offers one such example, taking SOS for Honey Bees to the centre of the community with their vision to create Wales' first bee-friendly village. After securing funding from the Welsh Assembly's Rural Development Plan, the newly formed village conservation group began planting lavender and wildflowers in beds across the village, holding flower planting and gardening sessions, involving the whole community, from young to old.

Many more WIs took up the challenge, turning unused land into community bee paradises, securing hives or donated plants, and mobilising the whole community to transform once neglected space into areas to be proud of. Others encouraged local authorities to plant bee-friendly flowers, giving out seed packs and planting guides at village fetes and county fairs. Campaigns such as these are rooted in the recognition that we all have a role to play in protecting our environment, and that collective action brings about wider change in society and government policy.

> Although for 55 years we've worked to improve the conditions of the countryside, now we must hurry. We can't afford to be slow [...] Let's make thousands know what we're doing, positively, to conserve the countryside.
>
> Mrs Jacob, 1972 (at the launch of the
> 'This Green and Pleasant Land' competition)

The concept of women as agents of change is one that resonates strongly with members. Right from the start, the WI was about giving women a voice and ensuring that women used that voice. And that this voice be an informed voice. But just as importantly, the NFWI worked hard to make sure that this informed voice was heard. This was not always easy, however, even with the strong leadership of resourceful and connected women such as Lady Denman, Dame Frances Farrer and Lady Brunner – and a look through the NFWI archives highlights moments when the NFWI rebuked ministers for their lack of female representation on influential committees or international delegations. In one such letter, addressed to The Rt Hon. Anthony Wedgwood Benn, MP (then Secretary of State for Energy), NFWI chairman Mrs Patricia Batty Shaw urged action to address the poor representation of women on the Energy Commission, noting 'that the representation of the non-industrial consumer might well be strengthened, possibly by the inclusion of another woman, as we have noted that there is only one on the Commission at present'.

In 2015, the Women's Institute celebrates 100 years of action. Despite its many successes, further action is needed, in particular to give women a proper place and a voice at decision-making tables, whether in government, in business or elsewhere. Only then can women's potential to create a fairer, more sustainable world be fully realised.

22

JULIET DAVENPORT
CEO of Good Energy

The impact of gender balance in the renewable energy sector

Broadly, what's your vision for energy, for our energy system?
My vision broadly has always been renewable. I do believe we could have a 100 per cent renewable Britain and I think that's good on many levels. Firstly, from the climate point of view, secondly from an energy security and global security point of view, and thirdly it's about ownership. It's about the fact that renewable energy doesn't have to be owned by one person; it can be developed by people in their own homes, it can be developed by communities. It gives access at all different levels of society. My vision is one of lots of people generating their own power, becoming much more responsible for the power they use and using renewables to achieve this.

Among the problems that we face in getting to that vision, how important is the issue of gender inequality, do you think?
It's a really interesting question. I can't say directly that these issues are just driven by men, because this is about a wider part of society taking responsibility – both men and women. So it's not just about women being in positions of power. It's also about women understanding that they hold as much responsibility as the people who have traditionally worked in this area. By bringing women into the workforce, particularly in energy, you bring first of all a different view, but also you bring a wider sense of responsibility about issues like energy use, where it's produced and how it impacts on other people's lives.

How important is gender equality within the context of Good Energy itself? Do you actively promote gender equality? What do you do about it?

As part of the energy industry, I got very used to being the lone female voice in a fairly male-dominated area, but there are now more women employed across the sector. From Good Energy's perspective, we're now doing pretty well on gender balance. I remember back in our early days sitting down at a meeting, and realising that I was pretty much the only female face there. We did some analysis of gender equality in the company, and started to measure it, which is the first stage for any organisation. Where are we losing women? When are they coming in? What we found is that we had gender equality at the start stage, among students and graduates and, as time went on, we slowly lost our women, so a lot of our staff in senior positions were male. So I wanted to look at how we could support women through coming back to work, making sure that they got career progression and ensuring they were interested in what they were doing. We now have a Board with three women out of seven, so nearly a 50 per cent split and we're getting more women into other senior positions.

We've not deliberately set out to promote women but I put it on the agendas of our headhunters and our HR team and told them I wanted to see a balance. You always want to choose the best person, but also to make sure that you're seeing enough people. Then within the company, we've also tried to give people a lot of support in coming back to work: mentoring about how to manage childcare, because that is the key issue for women coming back to work. How do you make sure that, firstly, their job is interesting enough for them to want to come back to work, because otherwise they will want to stay at home. Secondly, how do they actually do that? There's a lot of administration involved and you have to make sure that people understand how to manage that.

Can you see an impact from an improved gender balance in a company? Has that had an impact on the business?

We've definitely seen more senior women come in who've had a very can-do attitude, which has been great, and it's broken down some of the barriers in terms of getting things moving. It also means people have got to think slightly more holistically, seeing it all from slightly different angles, so you get a much better debate on areas of risk. If you get too much of a male environment, it can sometimes be the case that people are worried about asking the 'stupid questions which can quite often be the most important ones'. They're worried about looking silly and that becomes a major issue, because then you don't discover what's really going on. I don't know if it's the same if you get too much of a female environment, that's probably got its negatives as well.

And you'd attribute that to a difference in gender, that in a way we're wired differently?
I think so, I do see that. When you put one gender in place, you get all the assets reinforced and all the negatives reinforced. Where you get a balance between men and women working together, they balance each other out really well and bring different aspects to the table. If you only have one gender, you tend to start to see biases. To say it's a gender bias isn't quite correct, because there are different types of biases, but you do run the risk of everybody beginning to say the same thing, rather than challenge anyone.

Is it true that the energy business is very male-dominated?
Although more women work in the sector than ever before, it's still very much dominated by men.

If so, what made you personally want to get involved in it? Was that a challenge that you welcomed, or was there a barrier in it, deterrent to you?
My working life and my career started when I studied science at university and there was probably a worse gender balance then than there is currently in the energy industry. I studied physics, and 10 per cent of us were women – maybe even less. But I really enjoyed physics. I then studied climate change and, if you want to do something about climate change, you end up in the energy sector. It wasn't because I was wanted to be a female in a

male-dominated area but because it was the area that I was interested in. In terms of gender equality, it is quite dull being in the minority all the time and it's quite hard work. When there are more women around, you feel slightly more confident that you may be heard. If you sit in a room with twelve people and you're the only woman, you stick your hand up to say something, you stand out. You do. You can't help it. So having more women in the room, you feel more normalised.

You started off as a scientist. What kind of action would you say is needed to get more women into science, technology, business, politics?
It's a wider societal issue. I see girls being indoctrinated into the fact that science is boring at the age of ten. I think we need to look at primary schools and how we teach science. I think science is absolutely fundamental. Our lives are so based around science. Everything we do in our lives – whether it's an iPad, an iPhone, the electricity we supply our houses with – everything needs sciences to exist. Yet the majority of the people who use it don't understand it and I think that makes us very vulnerable to people who do understand it and people who can blind us with science.

In my view, if society's going to shift its perception, we need to celebrate scientists as much as we celebrate the arts – writers, actors, personalities. We need to see science as a really positive thing. Brian Cox is a good example, where you see a focus on somebody who is a scientist – we need to see more of that coming through. We need to make programmes about science that are really interesting and help people see that it is part of their lives, not just something that someone else does. It's vital that this starts at a really early age, because by the time children are eleven, most of them have made their decision about whether they're going to be a writer or not. Well, not quite, but they've already got that scientific or non-scientific bent.

I've worked with South East Physics Network, SEPnet, which is about getting more people into science – and about getting more women into science. If you look at a lot of companies and businesses worldwide, a lot of people who run them, or are involved in them, have got some type of scientific background, because you need to be hugely numerate, you need to be able to understand how things work. The more we can see women coming through to science, the more we'll see women at high levels in business.

The political world, which obviously shapes energy policy, is also obviously male-dominated. Has this made your job and your vision more difficult to achieve, do you think?
I look at politics and think, 'I don't want to be a politician. It's bad enough being a business leader!' You get your life put in the spotlight and that can be hard. I guess that's true no matter what sex you are.

I think politics has got to look at itself very hard if it wants to encourage more women into it. Whether it's made my job more difficult? I don't know. You have to try harder to relate to a man than a woman, and a lot of talking to politicians is about related-ness, an understanding of where they're coming from. So it does make it a little harder, yes.

Switching tack slightly, are you aware of any gender bias in your customer base, particularly among those involved ... you spoke about community ownership earlier. Is there a gender bias in the customer base, do you know of, among those involved in micro-generation?
There used to be. When we first set up, we definitely had a gender bias with more men as customers. That has shifted over the years, as we've seen more women get involved in energy. I'm not seeing a bias at the moment. From our recent analysis of our customer base, we're seeing fewer families, more singles, more couples without families and young couples. If you look at that mix, the family side may be where we're missing out, because if you've got someone at home running the family, we're not obviously appealing to them. It would be interesting to see whether we can get women more engaged. Working with organisations such as the WI to get more people engaged in running your home – and electricity is part of running your home – might be part of the solution.

And that's with regard to micro-generation specifically?
Yes, but also energy customers, as well. There's real opportunity to engage women running homes - it's how you use energy, what appliances you have in your home, how much energy you use – and so on.

So can you say, broadly speaking, for example, the decision for a family to install solar panels or to sign up to a green tariff would be led by the male partner or the female partner?
It's really difficult, actually. I used to be able to, but I can't any more. It's a very interesting question. It's quite tricky to figure out, because quite often, you'll have two people on the bill, male and female. So it's much more difficult to see who the decision-makers are. We're seeing it as much more of a joint decision now.

More broadly than energy, do you think women have a particular role to play in creating a green economy?
Yes. There have been a lot of women leaders in fashion, in the arts, in companies like People Tree, Body Shop, in terms of beauty products – we've seen quite a lot of female leaders break through in those areas, maybe partly because those are traditionally more female areas. You could say that, in some senses, we've seen green ideas coming through earlier, where there's a greater balance of women in those sectors. It would be good to unpick how that comes about. Is it the case that if you've got more of a balance of women involved in an industry, they actually start looking at the environment as something that should be looked after as much as the economy? What drives this different approach and how can we encourage more organisations to expand their gender balance so that they can benefit from the green economy?

If you could do one thing to improve the number of women in positions of power, or gender equality more generally, what would that be?
To be honest, I would take a fiscal measure. I would make childcare – particularly for those on middle and low incomes – tax deductible. I know that we've already got various childcare support mechanisms,

but this is one of the biggest issues women face when returning to work. When you're working your way through to becoming more senior – so late twenties, early thirties – if you decided to have a child, coming back to work becomes a huge decision on a personal basis, on a financial basis, and on the basis that you like your job, as well, because I think that's really important. If we can make at least one of those an easier decision and start to encourage people, to make it easier for them to go back to work if they want to then I think that would be brilliant. I read somewhere that if you have a chauffeur, that's tax deductible! If you have childcare, that should be tax deductible, as well. That would deliver a much more balanced society.

And conversely, would you like to see it incentivised for men to be at home, or do more of the childcare?
How do you incentivise that? I think you have to make it acceptable. I think that has to become a more societal norm, so how do you teach that? That's about education. Trying to make it tax-appealing? Maybe there could be a tax break for people staying at home. But I think a lot of it is getting over the stigma men feel if they decide to stay at home. If we can get over that, as a society, then why not? To a certain extent, it's a bit like having a sabbatical, but with children on the side. We can take time out. We can see it as enriching our lives to spend it with our children, and then make sure that going back to work is straightforward and not seen as a negative thing.

So to come back to the overarching question we're looking at in this book, is it possible for you to say, we think we'll get better environmental outcomes if there were greater gender balance? If there were more women in positions of power, in energy particularly, in business, politics, more generally?
I think the answer is yes, because we bring in a wider balance of society. We bring in different views, we bring in different challenges and the idea of 'group speak' begins to diminish. That's the danger in organisations where you have a gender bias. You begin to move to 'group speak', where you just reinforce what you think already,

and you don't question it. For me, gender balance is all about questioning and challenging things, asking if this is the best way to do something and checking what impact an action or idea might have somewhere else. Having more women across the board – whether that's in energy companies, in all companies, in government – is a really good thing. Having a proper gender balance throughout your organisation, from top to bottom, makes a real difference. We need women on the board, as managers and as senior leaders if we really want to get the right business and environmental outcomes.

23

EMMA HOWARD BOYD

30% Club for women in business leadership

More women in business for a sustainable economy

'We cannot return to the old macho ways'

In February 2009, the then business editor of the *Observer*, Ruth Sunderland, invited me to join a round-table discussion with seven women from the world of business and finance to discuss 'City culture, machismo's role in the financial crisis and how women can help bring about a resolution'.[1]

For a while, Ruth had been observing that women's voices had been conspicuously absent from the debate on what went wrong with the banking system. If men were the architects of a risky and fragile financial system whose flaws have now been laid bare, should we be looking to women to help create a more balanced and sustainable economy?

Our discussion was wide-ranging, covering several pages of the newspaper, but with a core theme: that the financial crisis highlighted the dangers of homogeneous boards and the need for diversity of thinking. The *zeitgeist* was right for change.

One of the comments I made during the discussion focused on the contribution gender diversity can make to diversity of perspective, bringing a greater understanding of a broad range of issues, including those relating to environmental sustainability:

> I would hope that we get a mind-set that comes into this debate that allows a different type of thinking about other

areas, about the environment, about green issues. We are going through a financial crunch but there are a whole range of other crunches coming up around carbon, around water and a lot of those will impact first on developing countries. We need to think about some of the risks that have built up in the financial system and also to understand the other risks that are building up.[2]

While I plan to explore whether greater representation of women at senior levels of business can help in the transition to a sustainable economy, later in this chapter, before I do, I want to describe the important work of the 30% Club.

Since the spring of 2011, I have been a member of the steering committee of the 30% Club, founded by Helena Morrissey, CBE, CEO of Newton Investment Management. The 30% Club launched in the UK in 2010 with an initial goal of FTSE-100 boards having female representation of 30 per cent or more by the end of 2015.

Over this period, the under-representation of women at senior levels in almost every area of society – business, politics, the public sector, professional services, sports bodies, academia and the arts – has attracted a huge amount of attention, not just here in the UK, but globally.

But after decades of snail-like progress, accelerated results over this relatively short time indicate that finally we are taking the right actions to address the issue – in a sustainable and meaningful way.

So first, let's look at what has been achieved in the FTSE-100 and FTSE-250, the UK's largest and next tier of public companies:[3]

» 46 FTSE-100 companies have at least 25 per cent women on their board
» 25 have reached 30 per cent
» By May 2015 we had reached 24.7 per cent of the FTSE-100 total (up from 12.5 per cent at the 30% Club's launch in 2010
» And, since May 2014, no all-male FTSE-100 boards, as the last bastion fell

» And in the FTSE-250 strong momentum, with only 20 all-male boards left, down from 131 (yes, over half)
» Rather encouragingly, since 1 March 2013, 33 per cent of all board appointments to the FTSE-100 have been women
» And of great importance, all delivered without resorting to quotas – a real achievement.

There is no doubt that a key breakthrough has been the acceptance that better gender balance at senior levels is a business issue, not just a women's issue – taking the issue beyond a specialist diversity effort and into mainstream talent management.

There is increasing agreement that diversity at board and top executive level in terms of skills, gender and nationality is a key factor in the quality and performance of boards. Improved board-room dynamics, greater diversity of perspective, varying attitudes to risk and a better ability to connect with consumers are all acknowl-edged as powerful benefits of a mixed-gender board.

As a result, we have seen a radical shift in the way business leaders are approaching the issue of what makes a more effective corporate board – including by institutional shareholders, who simply want the opportunity to invest in more successful companies.

So what has been the catalyst behind this breakthrough? How have we improved outcomes and moved away from a period where efforts exceeded results?

While there has been no 'silver bullet', there has been a combina-tion of factors coming together to powerful effect – a formula for change that might prove useful elsewhere.

» The most important driver was undoubtedly senior business leaders' involvement – those who could make a real differ-ence in terms of female appointments. There are now over one hundred members of the 30% Club – chairs of listed companies, professional services firms and public sector bodies. The impact of their visible commitment – most of them are, of course, men – cannot be overstated. Their public support has made a big impact, for example on the board recruitment process, especially that of the executive search firms.

» The focus of a specific and measurable goal – an aspirational target, not a mandatory quota – has provided real impetus for change. The original emphasis on boards has widened to include developing the executive pipeline of female talent; the aim is now 30 per cent women at all senior levels.

There were a number of other key ingredients:

» One has been timing. The financial crisis highlighted the dangers of homogeneous boards – 'groupthink' – and the status quo. In 'The moral DNA of performance',[4] a report published by the Chartered Management Institute in October 2014, one of the top ten steps to an ethical organisation was to 'harness diversity to challenge "groupthink"'.

» Similarly, the European Commission threatening to introduce quotas, which the 30% Club does not support, has brought a sense of urgency to the debate, and helped highlight voluntary action as the preferred way.

» This increased political attention was a key driver behind Lord Davies publishing his excellent report into the (then) scarcity of 'women on boards'. The Davies Report[5] set out ten clear recommendations in 2011 – a useful and replicable blueprint for change.

» Where no initiative existed around a Davies recommendation, we set out to address this. For example, establishing an investor group, which I chair, representing over £5 trillion in assets, to engage with companies.

» Importantly, the UK's Financial Reporting Council (FRC) made changes to the UK Corporate Governance Code which reflect the view that gender diversity strengthens board effectiveness by reducing the risk of 'groupthink', making fuller use of the talent pool and keeping companies in touch with their customers.

» The 30% Club investor group's approach is one of constructive engagement with listed companies as part of a broader analysis of a company's governance and development of future top talent. We have been encouraging improved disclosure beneath the board and executive committee levels. Where insufficient action is taken, individual members of the investor group are prepared to use their voting rights to encourage greater response. This approach is set out in our paper 'Diversity and stewardship – the next steps'.[6]

Growing the female talent pipeline needs to be high on the agenda for every board and executive committee

While progress has been made in increasing female representation on boards over the last three years, this has, on the whole, been achieved through an increase in the appointment of female non-executive directors.

The FTSE-100 has moved from 12.5 per cent female directors in 2010 to 24.7 per cent as of May 2015, while only 8.6 per cent of executive directors in the FTSE-100 are women. Attention now needs to be focused on achieving real, measurable progress – not by 'fixing the women' or 'beating up the men', but through men and women working together to improve business culture and achieve more diversity of thought at all company levels.

For a real step change to occur, more women must progress from senior management to executive board roles. Having the focus of a specific and measurable goal – an aspirational target, not a mandatory quota – can provide real impetus for change.

As the CBI noted in its position paper 'Building on progress: boosting diversity in our workplace',[7] published in June 2014: 'More firms should take on the example set by some leading firms of extending diversity targets, on a comply-or-explain basis, down through their middle and senior management cohorts.'

Notable examples include Sky, which in 2015 set a target of 50:50 gender split in its top 500 senior management roles, increasing from the current level of a third.

The CBI is leading by example and has committed to becoming a more diverse organisation. Currently eight of its thirteen senior managers are women, it has recently appointed its first female director general and the CBI board has approved a target of 30 per cent female representation at its events and in its policy-making processes.

This chimes with our own ambition. Our original emphasis on boards (with an initial goal of FTSE-100 boards having female representation of 30 per cent or more by the end of 2015) has widened to include developing the executive pipeline of female talent.

Investors are in a unique position to encourage companies to improve their gender diversity – but not just at board level

In July 2014, the 30% Club held its fourth annual London seminar in which we set out the next steps for accelerating change towards better gender balance from 'schoolroom to boardroom', demonstrating that the momentum behind our campaign has spread to a number of initiatives based on a collaborative approach.

In his introductory remarks to our seminar one of our founding chairmen, Sir Roger Carr, reminded the audience of the moment when the critical role of investors was underlined:

'Now, whilst chairmen can influence board behaviour, the Club recognised that it is ultimately the owners who really call the shots – and reinforcement of the message was powerfully nailed when Martin Gilbert of Aberdeen Asset Management stood up at an earlier meeting of this type [our first annual seminar] and encouraged investors to challenge boards and demand action.'

Investors are in a unique position to encourage companies to improve their gender diversity – but not just at board level. The 30% Club's investor group has the clout to make a big impact – now with more than twenty members, including PIMCO and Blackrock, and combined assets under management of around £5 trillion.

So what is it that investors, in particular, can focus on?

» Investors are increasingly aware that talent management is a mainstream issue and are in a unique position to encourage companies to improve their gender diversity – but not just at board level. Whilst many companies say that their people are their most valuable asset, in which they invest significantly, there is no established framework for reporting on human capital. This makes it difficult in turn for investors to assess this vital aspect of a company's future prospects. The Investment Association has been leading a project to consider ways of addressing this shortcoming, working with a small group of investors and representatives from other groups. Growing the female talent pipeline needs to be high on the agenda for every board and executive committee, and seen as a crucial part of business strategy and a key determinant of future performance.

» With the focus moving from boardroom to senior management teams it was agreed that this issue needs to be considered by mainstream fund managers, not just by specialist governance teams, and raised in meetings with CEOs, as well as chairmen, as part of the assessment of companies' longer-term prospects.

» There is a need for greater transparency surrounding talent management in companies. This will be helped by the new requirements for companies to report on the number of male and female directors, senior managers and employees that they have, as set out in the guidance on the strategic report, published by the UK Financial Reporting Council in June 2014.[8]

» A focus on board refreshment could accelerate the pace of change. Data published by BoardEx in January 2015 shows that out of 839 non-executive FTSE-100 directorships, 83 non-executive directors (NEDs) – 10 per cent – have served on the board for more than nine years, the maximum recommended term under the UK Corporate Governance Code. Of these, seventy-four are men.

More women in business makes for better business overall

A whole raft of research has been published linking women leaders with business success.[9]

Most recently, a study of companies in the UK, US and India found that companies perform better when they have at least one female executive on the board. Only one in ten of the companies surveyed had female board executives, and the report concluded that those publicly traded companies with male-only executive directors missed out on £430 billion of investment returns last year.[10]

McKinsey also published a report making the economic case for advancing women's equality. In a 'full potential' scenario in which women participate in the economy identically to men, as much as 26 per cent would be added to global gross domestic product by 2025 compared with a business-as-usual scenario.

This is equivalent to adding the combined value of the US and Chinese economies. Taking a more realistic 'best in region' scenario in which all countries simply match the rate of improvement in gender equality of the best-performing countries in their region, McKinsey finds that $12 trillion of additional GDP growth would be achieved by 2025.[11]

Other studies have looked at whether women leaders create positive return beyond financial performance, i.e. whether women are making companies 'better' or 'better companies' have stronger female representation on the board.

One 2012 study, 'Women create a sustainable future',[12] investigated the correlation between having at least one woman on a board and improved environmental, social and governance (ESG) performance among 1,200 Fortune companies.

Environmental performance proved most statistically significant – the research concluded that businesses with more women on their board of directors are more likely to: manage and improve their energy efficiency; measure and reduce their carbon emissions; reduce their packaging impacts; invest in renewable power.

Social performance came in second: businesses with more women on their board of directors are more likely to improve access to healthcare in developing countries; have strong partnerships with local communities; offer products with nutritional or health benefits; proactively manage human capital development.

Finally, on governance issues, women on boards correlate to: less fraud, corruption and misreporting of numbers. In short, fewer CEOs charged with misconduct.

The 'MSCI 2014 survey of women on boards'[13] explored this area further and found some interesting correlations between women on boards and broader ESG metrics.

» Boards with gender diversity above and beyond regulatory mandates or market norms had fewer instances of governance-related scandals such as bribery, corruption, fraud, and shareholder battles.
» There was preliminary evidence that companies with more women on their boards tend to display overall stronger management of ESG-related risks.
» Companies with a higher percentage of women on their boards tend to have higher ESG ratings than their peers.
» Interestingly, subsequent to appointing a female CEO, companies exhibit a greater rate of female director appointments compared to male-led companies.

Catalyst's latest research published in January 2015 ('Companies behaving responsibly: gender diversity on boards'[14]) also suggests that gender-diverse boards are good for business *and* society. The research highlights that what is good for women is good for men, business, communities and, indeed, good for the world. Companies with both women and men in the boardroom are better equipped to oversee corporate actions and ensure corporate citizenship standards are not only met, but exceeded – building stronger, more sustainable companies.

A company that holds its supply chain accountable, values customer loyalty, and improves both the community and the environment creates a positive cycle of influence. This approach not only makes the world a better place, but also increases the likelihood of sustainable big wins for the company and its stakeholders. Research published in Australia in July 2015, based on a sample of 128 Australian publicly listed companies, confirmed that having larger representations of women on corporate boards is associated with lower occurrences of fraud.[15]

Gender-diverse boards can help companies and stakeholders alike

Are companies that empower women more likely to be companies that act sustainably? As explored earlier, empirical evidence suggests that companies with at least one woman on their boards achieve superior financial results than those with all-male boards. While causality cannot be proved at this stage – that this is due to the women – it is noticeable that those companies which 'get' this particular issue also tend to be more forward-looking on other aspects of good governance, including sustainability. And that, in itself, is a big prize, well worth having.

24

FIONA REYNOLDS
Former director general of the National Trust

Sustainability is about people

As a woman who's spent all my working life within or close to the environmental movement in the UK, I have never experienced discrimination or difficulty in getting my voice heard. I think that's because our movement is a place where women can thrive and make a difference. Indeed, women *have* thrived and made a difference from the beginning; perhaps because fundamentally sustainability is about people. Women are, and always have been, critical in understanding the necessity of a high-quality environment for good health and well-being. And women are critical to bringing about change to achieve this, whether as national activists or in families and communities everywhere. Leading more sustainable lives is about leading healthier, more rewarding lives, identifying what really matters in life and valuing the things that money can't buy – such as a beautiful view or time spent with friends and family.

I've learned this lesson personally, through more than thirty years in the voluntary sector. I joined the movement in 1980, when I was appointed Secretary to the Council for National Parks (CNP), a tiny charity campaigning to protect National Parks. I was fresh from university and thrilled by the chance to work on newly emerging environmental policy: the Wildlife and Countryside Bill was about to be introduced into the House of Lords, and there was growing public and political interest in all aspects of the countryside and environment.

And there was much to do. Farmers were ploughing up Exmoor's heather moorland, grubbing out hedgerows and farm ponds, draining precious wetlands and overstocking the hills. They weren't doing these things out of malice, but because agricultural subsidies paid them more the more they produced. Mineral companies were trying to extend quarries in the Peak District and Yorkshire Dales National Parks because limestone was needed to meet the huge demand for road building. Foresters wanted to plant conifers high in the Brecon Beacons National Park and in the Flow Country in Scotland. And there were continual pressures to build housing estates on the Green Belt and in beautiful countryside. These were tangible threats, and what was needed was policy change – change that reflected the public mood for a beautiful countryside and better conservation.

For the next eighteen years, during which I moved from CNP to become director of CPRE (now the Campaign to Protect Rural England), there was always plenty to do. We did well: we got agricultural policy switched from encouraging intensification to paying farmers to look after particularly beautiful or precious parts of the countryside. We secured safeguards in National Parks whereby some minerals could be extracted only for specialist end uses, not for road building. We achieved the abolition of the tax regime which had enticed investors to afforest the hills and uplands of the UK with conifers. And we successively fought off threats to reduce the potency of Green Belt protection and secured commitments for more development on brownfield land rather than in the countryside.

In the process, we became experts in every aspect of public policy that affected the countryside. I can remember arguing with ministers over obscure sections of the Treaty of Rome, which unpins our membership of the European Union; urging MPs and peers to support amendments to Bills that would place new duties on public bodies to think about the environment, or to improve the planning regime; and endless meetings in Brussels over the finer details of the Environmental Impact Assessment Regulations.

All this was entrancing, and exciting. And important: this work needed to be done. But we were becoming so technically proficient and professional, arguing about ever more abstruse questions, that I sometimes wondered whether we were seeing the wood for the trees and how much difference we were actually making.

I even went into Whitehall for a brief spell, keen to find out what it was *really* like. But then I got the chance of a lifetime: the chance to lead one of the country's largest and most effective charities, the National Trust. I'd been involved in the Trust as a volunteer since my early twenties, when working for CNP. I was first a member of a regional committee, then a Council member, and I loved the immediacy and practicality of the Trust's work. If we agreed to take on a house or landscape we would look after it well and safeguard it for ever. If we planted trees they would shape the landscape for decades to come. If we repaired stone walls and managed hay meadows they would be a lasting feature of our landscape, bringing joy to people and providing a safe haven for wildlife. There was something reassuringly solid and permanent about what the National Trust could do.

Becoming director general, in 2001, therefore, was both a thrill and a responsibility. But there were challenges too. What the Trust needed to do, I believed, was match its extraordinary expertise in conservation with a passion for people. It risked losing support by being too stiff and formal – all those 'don't touch' signs. And what I also wanted to do, in helping the Trust become warmer and friendlier, was to remember the sense of passion that had shaped the early National Trust.

Because the Trust stands for the things in life that really matter but money can't buy: a beautiful view; time spent in idyllic surroundings with family and friends; priceless works of art and architecture easily accessible; the peace and beauty of protected countryside. These were things the Trust's founders had felt passionately about. And although the reasons are completely different today, it was National Trust research that highlighted that too many of today's children are also deprived of fresh air, green grass and open spaces to play in. Today children spend less than 5 per cent of their time playing in wild places (it was 50 per cent a generation ago) and the area over which we let our children roam unsupervised has shrunk by 90 per cent in a generation.

I soon realised that if we wanted to follow the lead of our founders and think about the big challenges the world is facing we wouldn't

Octavia Hill, co-founder of the National Trust, had said: 'The need of quiet, the need of air, the need of exercise, the sight of sky and of things growing seem human needs, common to all.' As a young woman, she'd led children from the ragged school where she taught out of London on Sunday afternoons simply to experience grass beneath their feet, flowers growing wild and the beauty of open spaces – such a contrast to the desperate, crowded, filthy conditions in which many of them lived. Later, her remarkable work in establishing social housing and co-founding the National Trust sprang directly from her desire to right the wrongs of extreme deprivation. At a time before women had the right to stand for election or even had the vote, Octavia Hill found other ways to help the poor, protect green spaces and bring about social reform.

achieve that simply by changing public policy; or by lecturing people on the merits of a greener life. We need to inspire people to engage with nature, and to seek out the simple pleasures of life. As David Attenborough has said, 'people will only protect what they care about, and they will only care about what they have experienced'.

And so the National Trust began to promote local food, grow-your-own, walking and cycling, and launched the wonderful children's campaign '50 things to do before you're 11¾'. All these are things that the women in a family often lead on: they are about family priorities and relationships, about inspiring people to think about the way they live their lives.

The debate about what really matters in life is not, of course, new. The question is whether we can learn from history or will repeat the mistakes of the past.

The first crunch came at the end of the nineteenth century, when Britain witnessed the unprecedented exploitation of natural and imperial resources, intensive industrialisation and urbanisation. Huge wealth was generated for some, but the human costs were enormous.

Brave Victorian radicals challenged the status quo: on slavery, desperate living conditions, appalling housing, the spread of diseases such as cholera, and high mortality rates. Some, like John Ruskin and William Morris, argued for mechanisation to be rejected, arguing for a utopian vision where people led simpler lives, dependent on the skills of craftsmen and practical efforts. They didn't succeed, but there was a huge burst of charitable activity, leading to the establishment of many social, health and welfare charities, e.g. Barnado's, the NSPCC, the National Trust, the RSPB and the RSPCA.

Gradually planning legislation, sanitation, housing, children's welfare, public health and education systems began to be established, but conventional economic progress remained the overwhelming measure of success.

The second attempt to define a different future came out of the tragedy of two world wars. By the early 1940s two generations had laid down their lives for their country, and members of the cross-party War Coalition were determined that at least as much effort should be put into planning the peace as had been put into winning the war: in other words that post-war reconstruction should be for the benefit of everyone.

And so when Labour won the 1945 election it brought in a raft of legislation to achieve this. This included the universal right to education, the establishment of the free National Health Service, industrial policy which dispersed investment and jobs throughout the UK, investment in farming to feed a nation used to rationing, a major housing improvement and construction programme, the protection of the country's natural and historic sites, and the designation of National Parks for spiritual and physical refreshment and to safeguard Britain's most beautiful landscapes. Taken as a whole, the programme reflected a rounded view of what society needed, reflecting material and non-material needs.

But how successful was this harmonising, integrated programme? In practice, as before, some elements proved more powerful than others.

It was not long before Britain's population had its first taste of growth not only trickling down but reaching the working population.

In 1957 Prime Minister Harold Macmillan was telling the nation that they had 'never had it so good'. In the 1980s Margaret Thatcher brought new wealth to families able to buy their council houses at discounted prices. And because of the post-war reforms there was steadily improving public health and education: each generation was healthier, longer lived and better educated than its parents.

Against these tangible signs of progress the environmental elements of the post-war settlement struggled to gain purchase. Conservation *was* part of the 1940s vision, but it was modest in scope, and there was a naive assumption that farming and forestry would be compatible with the protection of nature and landscapes.

So the safeguards put in place in the 1940s proved inadequate to meet the pressures on land and natural resources that flowed from the pace of growth that took place from the 1950s onwards. As I'd discovered when I joined CNP's staff, farming had become industrialised, and countryside was being built over to provide homes, jobs, roads and factories. But there was more: seas were overfished; rare and vulnerable species were pushed to the brink of extinction; natural resources such as coal and building materials were extracted at an ever faster rate; and energy consumption galloped forward.

The alarm was sounded, with increasing urgency. In 1972 the Club of Rome published *Limits to Growth*, coinciding with the first oil crisis; and in the early 1970s the environmental movement was born in the UK: FOE in 1971, with its returnable bottles campaign, and Greenpeace's *Rainbow Warrior* taking on the commercial whalers.

And so the second half of the twentieth century was a time of fights: about waste and power stations, overfishing, against road expansion and quarries, against commercial agriculture and forestry, and for public access and the better protection of important buildings, wildlife and landscapes. My experience fitted neatly into this paradigm: the environment was a victim and the fight was by David against the Goliath of the overwhelming pressure for development and growth.

And, as I've described, we made some progress. For a while, even, being 'green' was not only fashionable but politically attractive: there was a record high Green vote of 15 per cent in the 1989

European elections; and all the political parties established green think tanks and had green policies in their manifestos.

But it didn't last. Once again the environment has slipped from public attention and the economy has assumed overwhelming importance. How and why did this happen?

At its heart was the 2008 recession, which represented a much more serious challenge to the system than previous economic stumbles. This time it was not just that economic conditions became more difficult, but that the very foundations of the post-war economy were challenged. It required a profound overhaul of many of the things we had taken for granted; and the imperative to get the economy back on its feet forced a short-term view.

This left environmental arguments and the non-quantifiable dimensions of policy exposed and vulnerable. Much of the progress we achieved had, it was clear, been on the back of a growing and prosperous economy. When the economy collapsed, the case for being green – especially if it required money – risked collapse too.

Yet we are now exposing deeper human challenges. After decades of improving quality of life some of the progress made in the twentieth century is unravelling. We are now predicting poorer health and shortening lifespans, and that young people today will be less well off than their parents. There is a particular pressure on our children, with conditions like rickets, obesity and mental health problems becoming more prevalent.

So, as I learned at the National Trust, we need a different approach: a third great 'moment' which, like those of the nineteenth and mid-twentieth centuries, can create the space for a new paradigm, this time built on the foundations of sustainability. And this time the revolution in thinking and action has to come from us.

For it seems to me that the twenty-first-century challenge is not the technical question of sustainability but the human one. We learned a lot in the twentieth century about conservation and its technical needs and challenges; and we were adroit at managing the status quo. But if climate change has failed to become a strong enough rallying point it may be because we have couched it too much in technical, not human, language.

So the challenge for the twenty-first century is about people, about the need to harmonise our multiple, complex aspirations to help us all achieve more sustainable lifestyles. People are, in fact, realistic: more so than they are often given credit for. We know we are unlikely to get materially richer over the next few years, and that our children are likely to be less well off than we are. So already we are adapting – taking up activities and seeking experiences that don't cost a fortune but are beyond price in their value. It is no surprise that organisations like the National Trust (with 4 million members), the RSPB and the Wildlife Trusts have attracted more support since the recession hit.

We need also to value the things we *can* measure but which we have not previously recognised as important. In 2011 Defra published the National Ecosystem Assessment, which identified the value and vulnerability of the natural capital – soils, peat, forests, water, habitat – on which we all depend. The Natural Capital Committee and the Ecosystem Markets Taskforce need to help us insert these values into mainstream decision-making.

So we are not bereft of ideas. But we cannot force them on people: we will not succeed if we fail to inspire people to seek out more sustainable lifestyles. We need to show that there is a bigger prize for humanity than short-term growth built on unsustainable foundations. And so I believe we can make changes; all drawing on skills women have in abundance. Here are three ideas:

First, we need a new definition of progress. GDP is widely recognised as inadequate, yet remains in use. There are definitions of success other than economic progress: measures of happiness and well-being are both now credible alternatives. And we are beginning to understand how we can influence people's behaviour towards more sustainable lifestyles, such as healthy eating and taking more exercise.

Secondly, we need to turn the telescope round and put place-making at the heart of policy. Places are where we live and make our lives, yet at the moment we apply sectoral, silo'd policies *to* places. We should involve people in creating places we want to live in – urban, rural and suburban – designing systems that will feed us, supply us with water and infrastructure, and provide the services and facilities (housing, jobs, education, healthcare, shops, as well as access to nature and green space) we need to live rewarding and more sustainable lives.

Finally we need to engage as citizens, not consumers, in the future of our world. We have become hooked on consumption, assailed by marketing and media messages, forgetting that we are citizens of a shared and vulnerable planet. We've turned people off with scientific, technocratic arguments about climate change, and we have turned ourselves into consumers with a depressingly short attention span and an unrealisable desire for instant gratification. As citizens, we can help shape our future.

But I have one final plea, drawn from the inspiration of Octavia Hill. If we do nothing else, we owe it to the next generation to look at the way we educate and bring up our children. In recent times educational ambitions have narrowed and in our effort to protect our children we have deprived them of the joy of playing outside, experiencing nature at first hand and the delight of self-discovery.

We will only achieve change if we engage people in designing a future defined by sustainability and a recognition of the planet's finite resources. And the challenge starts at home, with the way we live our lives and the values and experiences we instil in the next generation. Octavia Hill once said: 'new occasions teach new duties'. It's time, and the moment, to find those new duties and lead the change we know is necessary.

25

CATHY NEWMAN
Journalist and TV presenter for
Channel 4 News, UK

Sexism and gender equality in British politics

You've worked tirelessly to expose sexual harassment in Parliament. Other journalists showed a passing interest in that, but you've really stuck at it. What kept you going?
I pay tribute to the women who came forward to complain after sexual harassment by Liberal Democrat Lord Rennard, because they hadn't got a hearing, and I felt it would be doing them an injustice not to take their complaints seriously. The Liberal Democrats hadn't taken their complaints seriously, as they now admit, so they felt they had no alternative but to come to me. I really wanted to do my utmost to get them the revolution in parliamentary attitudes that they wanted, to hear their story, and to make sure it was raised and acted upon at the right levels. I suppose I was only partially successful in that, but at least they now feel they've had a proper hearing.

How bad do you think the problem is in Parliament?
Sexism and harassment are prevalent in Westminster, as they are in all sections of society, really. I think one thing at Westminster that makes it worse is that it's a particularly unusual workplace. There's sexism and harassment in any workplace, and that's something we've put up with for decades, but in Westminster, it's worse, because it's a bit like a public school. There are way more men than women. I think less than a quarter of parliamentarians are

women, so it's a lot of men who get together. They're far from home. There are lots of late-night votes. It's very antisocial hours. There's lots of drinking, and I think that does contribute to an unhealthy culture when it comes to women and harassment. So I think there is a problem that it's worse at Westminster, but it's not one that's unique to Westminster.

What kind of reception did you get from politicians to the work you were doing?

I think privately a lot of politicians said, 'Good on you. That needed to be exposed. Well done.' Publicly, I felt they were a lot more reticent. The Liberal Democrats' leadership publicly did talk about self-appointed detectives, which was a bit of a gibe at me and the team, but they also, reluctantly, praised Channel 4 for doing what we did. They recognised that they'd got it wrong. But other parties were a little bit more reluctant, in a way, to go public on the problems of sexism in Westminster, I think because they were nervous about their own records being exposed. They knew that allegations of harassment were not unique to the Liberal Democrats. I think they were slightly nervous about where the story was going to lead next. Privately people were much more supportive than they were publicly.

Did you get any outright hostility?

I got quite a lot of hostility from senior Liberal Democrats. I can't remember exactly the words they used, but there was a reference to a mild version of sexual harassment, a sense that we'd gone on a crusade and had an agenda. Lord Carlisle, who acted for Lord Rennard, was rather patronising, and accused me of not listening in an interview when he tried to defend his friend. So there was quite a lot of open hostility from senior Liberal Democrats – particularly peers. A lot of the MPs were a lot more supportive, people like Tim Farron, the [former] party president, who was quite open about how wrong the party had got it, and apologised repeatedly to the women.

Do you think that a Parliament that was more gender equal would have a very different kind of feel about it, and atmosphere, and also focus on different things?
Yes, I do think that ... I think it's wrong, for a start, that Parliament is supposed to represent the people who vote MPs in, and more than 50 per cent of people in the population are women, so it seems wrong that that's not represented in Westminster. Also, with more women coming through the ranks, there has been a greater focus on issues that shouldn't really be 'women's issues' like childcare. But those are issues that have been neglected by a male-dominated Westminster, and I think that now that is beginning to change, but it's not changing fast enough.

Some of the academic literature suggests that parliaments with a greater proportion of women in them also take environmental issues more seriously. Do you think this is true?
I'm not sure that I have a sense of that, to be honest. I'm sure if you asked a pollster, you might get a better answer. Whenever I've talked to pollsters like Peter Kellner about what issues women care about most, he does say that ranking is different from men. But I'd always feel a little bit uneasy about saying, 'Women care more about environmental issues.' I can think of as many men who talk about problems of climate change in Parliament as women. Apart from Caroline Lucas, I couldn't actually name many female MPs who have made the environment a big campaigning agenda. I'm thinking of Zac Goldsmith, for example. He's a very prominent environmental campaigner. I can't think of too many women who have embraced a similar stance. I'm not sure that I would see it as a gender issue.

What do you think needs to change to get greater gender equality?
Instinctively I'm opposed to the idea of all-women shortlists, because I think all women want to be there on merit, so then it's about just changing the culture. The leader's got to promote good women up the ranks, so that they've got a chance to shine,

and for people out there who might be thinking of becoming MPs, they've got to be able to see that women are well treated, that they're given jobs, that they're not less valued. Prime Minister David Cameron recently decided to pay the new leader of the House of Lords less than her predecessor, who was a man. Things like that have got to stop. There's got to be a real sense that women can rise up the ranks in Parliament. It's a shop window. It's a chance for people who might be thinking about a career in politics to see that this could be for them, if they're a woman, just as if they're a man.

As for working hours, it is difficult. If you've got a family, you've got to keep two homes. You've got to split your kids between two homes. They're late hours, although they're not to be as late as they used to be. But then, I don't see why that should be more of an issue than it is for male MPs who are fathers as it is for women who are mothers.

I think Miriam Clegg, the wife of [former] Liberal Democrat leader Nick Clegg, got it right when she was saying that men have to pull their weight when it comes to their partners having a career. Because if you're a female MP, you're going to do best if you have a very supportive partner or a husband, who's going to help out, and pull their weight with the childcare. So I'm not sure that the onus is on Westminster there. I think the onus is on the culture changing. It's still the case that, as a woman, you're always asked how you balance family life with working, and that isn't a question that's asked for men – although it's slightly changing in politics. Nick Clegg was insistent on getting home for bedtime, and reading stories, and doing the bath several nights a week. It was good that he talked about that. Miriam Clegg is a great role model for women, in terms of having a great career of her own, and she's not going to take any nonsense from Nick Clegg when it comes to work–life balance.

Also, in terms of making Westminster a more amenable place for women, the parties have got to take a grip when there are allegations of harassment, or examples of harassment. Having women in senior positions where they can root out these problems would help. Unfortunately there are too few women who are promoted within the parties. I mean, will there be another female party leader soon? Perhaps Theresa May. Margaret Thatcher still looks like a bit of a one-off.

26

SARAH RICHARDSON

Historian, University of Warwick

Mistresses of their own destiny: a history of women's empowerment in nineteenth-century British politics

Women's role and contribution to society have been marginalised, both historically and in the present. Their increased education, civil and political rights, economic muscle and social status are universally accepted as fundamental to transforming society and achieving environmental sustainability. However, they often struggle to have their voices heard. The emphasis has thus traditionally been focused on the barriers which stand in the way of gender equality and on female marginalisation. It is easy to discover the obstacles to women's full participation. The attainment of global female suffrage has been painfully slow. In Europe, Lichtenstein and Switzerland permitted women to vote only in the 1980s and 1990s respectively and women's political rights are still severely restricted in Saudi Arabia, Brunei, the United Arab Emirates and Lebanon among other nations. Access to secondary and tertiary levels of education is restricted largely to boys in many developing regions. The gender pay gap and inequality in the working environment are universal, with women of all ages receiving lower pay, fewer social benefits and higher levels of job insecurity. However, while identifying impediments to female social, economic and political progression is helpful, it is important not to overlook the many ways in which women *are* able to contribute and the strategies they employ to survive and sometimes prosper in a male-dominated world.

Thus, rather than focusing on the impediments to women's political participation (which are well documented and understood), this chapter considers the approaches that women in the past used to circumvent their lack of political and civil rights and to contribute to the public life of the nation (using the case study of Britain). Women in nineteenth-century Britain were largely disenfranchised but by focusing on issues and campaigns that interested and affected them, they were able to change and contribute to policy agendas. However, their contribution has been overlooked and ignored. This has resonances today. Given that women are central to achieving environmental sustainability, more attention needs to be given to the impact they are already making in their own communities. By measuring and assessing where women are active (as opposed to concentrating on their lack of progress in some formal political institutions) it is possible to redefine the perception of what is 'political'. Issues that matter to women, such as the closure of local schools or playgroups or cuts in spending on welfare, are often marginalised by the establishment and viewed as 'apolitical'. This overlooks the contribution that women make (and made) to political life, as well as the importance of such activities in providing them with experience in public affairs. Women, partly because of their under-representation in formal political arenas and owing partly to their own interests and commitments, are most active in their homes, neighbourhoods and communities. These are formative sites of female political action. There are (and were) often direct connections between the home and pressure groups, such as those considering the environment, ethical consumption or for action against poverty.

The established position on women's contribution to political life in the nineteenth century is to emphasise the restrictions. There were no women prime ministers or MPs, women did not vote in parliamentary elections and thus they were highly restricted in the public sphere – although, of course, women could hold the central and most powerful position of monarch, and Queen Victoria reigned for much of the period. However, many commentators view her contribution negatively, emphasising her domestic rather than her public persona. The author of *The Laws Respecting Women*, published by Joseph Johnson in 1777, summed up women's legal status effectively: 'by marriage the very being or legal existence of a woman is suspended'. Every wife, except a reigning queen, was under the legal authority of her husband: 'she can't let, set, sell, give away, or alienate anything without her husband's consent. Her very necessary apparel, by the law is not hers in property.' Marriage stripped women of legal identity and thus, by definition, married women could never be a citizen or possess political rights. Only in the bleakest way possible was a woman's freedom of political action in Great Britain formally acknowledged. If she committed high treason she could be put on trial and burnt. She could be punished for plotting against the state but could never play an active part within it.

However, this rather dismal picture does not represent the social realities. Women could and did play a public role in politics, despite the legal position and the increasing public debate about manners and polite society which sought to exclude women from taking a public role. Politics is here defined broadly and inclusively: definitions of what construes the political are inherently problematic, often being themselves derived from a particular ideological viewpoint. Political history is frequently dominated by the concerns of 'high politics' – an arena which is written largely by men about men. Women in this period regularly engaged with parliamentary agendas and electoral politics but their political activities were far broader, encompassing such issues as vegetarianism, animal rights, alternative medicine and consumerism. This is not to say that women's potential for political involvement was unrestricted. It goes without saying that they did not have the same opportunities as their male contemporaries, but we should also recognise that the barriers against their activities were not as inflexible as has been commonly assumed. The boundaries between public and private worlds merged and overlapped.

To illustrate some of the ways in which women were politically active and major contributors to policy areas in nineteenth-century Britain, this chapter will consider three areas:

» Women's contributions to the campaigns against slavery
» Female politicised philanthropy
» 'Lifestyle' politics, including women's championing of issues such as vegetarianism and homeopathy.

Women campaign against the slave trade

The slave trade in Britain was abolished in 1807. In the 1820s campaigners started to mobilise against British colonial slavery with the foundation in 1823 of the Society for the Mitigation and Gradual Abolition of Slavery Throughout the British Dominions (known as the Anti-Slavery Society). Its efforts were eventually rewarded in 1833 with the passing of the Emancipation Act, which granted a modified freedom with full freedom being granted in 1838. Women, though not members of national committees, nevertheless played an extensive and active role throughout these years in anti-slavery ladies' associations, through involvement in widespread national petitioning, and in their writing and campaigning. The growth of a network of ladies' associations alongside all-male local associations was an entirely new development. Between 1825 and 1833 at least seventy-three such associations were active. The first group was the Birmingham Ladies Society for the Relief of Negro Slaves, which was founded by the evangelical Anglican Lucy Townsend and the Quaker Mary Lloyd, building on their joint interests in interdenominational and evangelical philanthropy. The Birmingham society saw its role very clearly as the promotion of further such ladies' associations throughout the country. Though at first they were greeted with some hostility by some male leaders such as Wilberforce, there was increasing support for the ladies' organisations in the anti-slavery society throughout the 1820s because of their effective extra-parliamentary campaigning. Such associations had as their models middle-class pressure groups, and philanthropic and charitable societies. They had an organisational structure similar to male associations with officers, including a treasurer and a committee. The Birmingham society appointed its own paid agents, all men, as travelling anti-slavery lecturers. Raising money was an important part of their work. However, although they contributed significantly to the funds of the national anti-slavery society, they also had their own objectives, reflecting the concerns of their members. Chief among these was relief and educational work – for example, the establishment of Sunday schools and female refuges, the purchase of books, and the foundation of benevolent societies to support the black populations of the British West Indies. Ladies' associations also gave funds to help individual slaves and free black men and women. Their work was often linked to missionary activity, although they were anxious also to maintain their primary aim, the abolition of slavery.

One of the outstanding activists in this period was Elizabeth Heyrick, a Leicester Quaker and district treasurer for the Female Society of Birmingham. Heyrick was born in Leicester to wealthy Unitarian parents. At the age of eighteen, she married John Heyrick, but he died of a heart attack, leaving her a widow at the age of twenty-six. She returned to her parents a widow and converted to Quakerism. She began to participate in a number of political activities: campaigning against cruelty to animals, agitating for a 'living wage' and visiting prisons, often supporting the causes financially with the allowance given to her by her parents. In the 1820s she began to write pamphlets on a variety of subjects including her *Appeal to the Electors*, which urged men to vote for anti-Corn Law candidates. She was deeply involved in the campaign to abstain from slave-grown sugar, and urged ladies' associations to use the sugar boycott to force planters to move their production from slave to free labour. She also intervened to shift the policy of the leadership of the Anti-Slavery Society, which had from its inception argued for the gradual abolition of slavery. In her pamphlet *Immediate, not Gradual Abolition; or an Inquiry into the shortest, safest, and most effectual means of getting rid of West-Indian Slavery*, written in 1824, she called for immediate action through mass abstention, attacking the leadership for placing political expediency ahead of Christian principles and the natural rights of all. She followed up her pamphlet by personally carrying out a door-to-door survey of households in her home town of Leicester, finding support for the idea of a consumer boycott. Many of the ladies' associations followed her call and finally, from 1830, the national policy shifted.

In the early 1830s, the female strategy in the anti-slavery movement progressed to a mass petitioning campaign. Before 1830 petitioning had largely been seen as an entirely masculine activity. Yet on this issue, and in a renewal of activity, women organised their own petitions as well as signing many mixed-sex ones. This crusade culminated in a national female petition, organised by the London Female Anti-slavery Society in 1833, which had 187,157 signatures. In 1838 there was a women's petition to the new female monarch, Queen Victoria, against the apprenticeship system (a modified form of slavery), which had been introduced in 1833. Although the number of female-only petitions was not high, women represented almost a third of the signatories to the anti-slavery petitions in 1833 and two-thirds of signatories to the anti-apprenticeship petitions of 1838.

The political anti-slavery movement continued to be supported by a corresponding cultural movement against slavery, consisting of poetry, short stories and powerful campaigning tracts, many written by women. When the Female Society of Birmingham made its annual report in 1828 it was headed by a poem written by Susannah Watts, entitled 'The Slave's Address to British Ladies'. Mary Anne Rawson, who led the Sheffield Female Anti-Slavery Society, edited a collection of anti-slavery poetry entitled *The Bow in the Cloud* in 1834. Many women from different dissenting and evangelical backgrounds contributed to this collection. Poems, hymns and tracts were all actively distributed by ladies' associations, sometimes in workbags sewn in East Indian (and therefore not slave-grown) cotton or silk. Such writing drew heavily upon the religious and moral impetus of the movement. If anti-slavery was represented as a philanthropic cause, it could be seen as entirely compatible with active intervention and organisation by women.

Female philanthropy and politics

Women's benevolence in the nineteenth century was a complex phenomenon, but analyses of the motives underlying the charitable impulse have tended to neglect the role of politics and ideology. There has been widespread appreciation of the contribution middle-class women made to social welfare through their philanthropic actions. Examples of Bible societies, house-to-house visiting and clothing clubs have been well documented, along with numerous case studies of individual women and their charitable enterprises. However, it has been assumed that the philanthropic activities of middle-class women acted merely as a distraction from, or extension of, their domestic lives and experiences. Thus it is argued that leisured women of the middle class used their feminine skills to care for the young, the sick and the elderly. Their mission to reform the morals of wider industrial society is seen merely as an extension of their domestic role. It has been frequently asserted that women were in an informal, casual and non-theoretical relationship with philanthropy in the nineteenth century. Commentators have discerned a cleavage between 'male' and 'female' approaches to charitable relief, with the former considered institution-focused, principled and policy-based and the latter as personal, intuitive and auxiliary. These stereotypical models do little to appreciate the varied intentions underpinning the charitable actions of women in the nineteenth century.

Women should not be seen merely as practitioners of philanthropy, but also as contributors to the intellectual and ideological arguments that prompted and sustained such work. Contemporary considerations of the role of the state, centralisation, local government and economic theories were significantly enriched by female contributions. For many women, then, philanthropy was an expression of their wider concern with social and civic affairs. Philanthropy was inextricably bound up with the public sphere. One area where women made a significant contribution to contemporary policy debates was concerning responsibility to the poor. In the early nineteenth century these deliberations were largely constructed within the discourse of political economy. The term 'political economy' originated in the French and Scottish Enlightenments, the key figures being François Quesnay and the French Physiocrats, and Adam Smith. This new field of enquiry made connections between the economy and the state and sought to explain questions of wealth and poverty. The discipline quickly became a fashionable topic of discussion in the salons, drawing rooms and dinner parties of the early nineteenth century. For example, Maria Edgeworth wrote in 1822: 'It has now become high fashion with blue ladies to talk political economy. Meantime fine ladies now require that their daughters' governesses should teach political economy.' Interpretations of the various strands of political economy dominated women's efforts to theorise approaches towards philanthropy and the poor in early-nineteenth-century Britain. More often than not, women (and men) turned to female writers to instruct and inform them in these debates. Women writers played a central role in popularising the ideas of Adam Smith, Ricardo, Malthus and the other economic giants of the Industrial Revolution.

One of the most popular works was Margracia Loudon's *Philanthropic Economy*, published one year after the passage of the Poor Law Amendment Act. Her treatise was an innovative attempt to redefine the very nature of government activity and to recast the bases of political economy. Little is known about Loudon: she was probably a Unitarian, and lived in Leamington Spa, Paris and London before her death in Cheltenham in 1861. She was married to Charles Loudon, a doctor and commissioner on the inquiry into the employment of factory children in 1830. She appealed especially to women readers, linking directly their local charitable activities with reform of the social, economic and political infrastructure. She called not only for universal rights, municipal reform and the abolition of the House of Lords, but also argued that government itself should lead the way in inaugurating a new era of benevolence. Outlining a theory of the redistribution of wealth, Loudon called for direct taxes to be replaced with a property tax and for allotments of land to be made available to the poor. Loudon invited a new definition of political economy – one that would recognise the needs and wants of all. Her notion of 'active benevolence' depended upon a nation of caring, equal citizens who would follow in the footsteps of government in ensuring that all were treated with justice and equality. Although *Philanthropic Economy* is largely forgotten today – as are many female contributions to politics and policy – it was an important addition to the debates on the Poor Law and was widely reviewed and highly praised in the contemporary radical and liberal press. Loudon's work became more widely known when the Anti-Corn Law League extracted the section on the Corn Laws and printed 9 million copies for distribution to electors via the new technology of the Penny Post.

Lifestyle politics

A distinctive characteristic of many female contributions to political discourse in the period was that the evidence they presented was drawn from areas concerned with the reform of everyday life. There was a burgeoning interest in alternative approaches to topics such as health, diet, consumption and child-rearing, and women placed these concerns in a wider political context. This concept of what would today be termed 'lifestyle politics' involved the politicisation of leisure and consumption practices and the promotion of the social responsibilities associated with all aspects of domestic life. By focusing on these 'domestic' concerns women reformers were able to entwine the private domain of the home and family with public policy concerns. Many female activists made connections between the lack of control they had over their own healthcare, diet and welfare and their limited political and civic rights. Thus they argued that the health of their own bodies was dependent upon them wresting control from the authorities and taking over the management of their own well-being. One of the key elements that emerged in this struggle between the establishment and women's activists centred on that vital element for survival: food. The Food Reform Movement emerged in Germany in the 1820s, and was quickly adopted by British radicals keen to accompany political change with a democratisation of the 'care and feeding of the body'. Food and health reform formed essential components of female public identities around the time of the 1832 Reform Act, leading to the politicisation of the household as a site for activism. Dietetic reformers encompassed a diverse group of campaigners: vegetarians, vegans, fruitarians, schools meals activists and, by extension, those against cruelty to animals, including anti-vivisectionists. There were strong links between the personnel of these movements and wider female political reform organisations. Food reform enabled women to highlight fundamental issues about their participation in the public sphere, their subjugation and lack of a voice on civic matters by evoking similarities between their own treatment and that of animals. Moreover, in making these connections, they were drawing upon a rich discourse which had long linked corruption and decay in the political establishment with unhealthy and unbalanced diets. Purity in the body politic depended upon democracy and simplicity; similar virtues could be applied to the health of the physical body.

The individual whose life and work perhaps most comprehensively summarises the connections between food, feminism and politics was Annie Cobden-Sanderson. She was one of five surviving daughters of the noted free trade politician Richard Cobden. She had been a vegetarian since the age of twenty, and an interest in food reform underpinned much of her activism. In 1906, she was arrested along with nine other suffragettes after a disturbance in the lobby of the House of Commons. The forcible detention of Cobden's daughter triggered a wave of public sympathy for the disproportionate reaction to the demonstration. Although Cobden-Sanderson was imprisoned before the suffragettes' adoption of the tactic of using hunger strikes to publicise their cause further, she nevertheless suffered immense privation in prison, the more so because of her vegetarian diet. In an open letter to the press, her husband detailed her treatment, including twenty-three hours of solitary confinement per day and meals of dry bread, tea or cocoa and potatoes. Millicent Garrett Fawcett visited her in prison, and was appalled that her dinner consisted of three potatoes, the prison authorities being ill equipped to deal with a vegetarian prisoner. Annie resisted her harsh treatment while in prison, and continued to raise awareness about the poor conditions once free. Her cell was infested by cockroaches, so she complained to the prison governor, but refused the offer of a move, recognising that whoever later occupied her cell would face the same conditions. On her release, she wrote a series of letters to the newspapers exposing the poor environment in prison, including the freezing temperatures on the hospital wards. Her motivation was to improve the treatment of women prisoners but also to draw attention to the fact that they were incarcerated as a result of legislation enacted by an entirely male government and judiciary.

In her juvenile diaries and letters Annie had expressed concern for animals, nature and the environment, causes which forged her early political identity. In her brief memoir explaining how she became vegetarian, it was clear that animal rights activism formed part of her belief system, infusing all aspects of her ideological outlook. Food reform continued to be an important strand to her political pursuits throughout her career. In 1908 she was instrumental in establishing the New Food Reform Movement with Sarah Grand, and fellow vegetarians Charlotte Despard, Beatrice Webb and Seebohm Rowntree. The professed aim of the movement was 'to enlighten public opinion on matters of diet' and 'to point out the dangers of our present system of food supply'. Eugenics and social Darwinism formed a key theme of the movement. One supporter argued that vegetarianism was a natural consequence of the evolution of the human race, which was moving away from barbarous practices such as the slaughter and consumption of animals. A vegetarian diet had social benefits, with followers more open to progress and exercising higher moral values.

Food reformers like Annie believed diet could solve many of the problems of the age, and also that women were best placed to tackle these. She was particularly interested in the question of children's food. In a paper she wrote for the *British Health Review* entitled 'Housekeeping for the nation's children' she echoed some of the eugenicist sentiments of the food reformers, arguing that 'we must look to the change in diet as the chief cause for the present degeneracy'. Her ideas were in line with many on the left, particularly the Fabians Sidney and Beatrice Webb, who were the leading socialist promoters of 'national efficiency'. In her paper, Annie suggested five dinner menus which would solve the problem, most containing a small amount of fish or meat but also reliant on a large amount of root vegetables, fruit, wholemeal bread and porridge.

She suggested using the 'less refined' kind of bread, which should be made crusty by rebaking in the oven, serving to 'cleanse the teeth, and at the same time oblige the children to eat slowly, and properly masticate their food'.

Annie crusaded against the traditionally heavy, rich meat diet of the period, arguing that it was wasteful, harmful to health and bad for the digestion. In 1908 she spoke at a conference calling for the scientific feeding of school children organised in response to the introduction of school meals by the National Food Reform Association. She reiterated her view of the danger of the food provided for children by local authorities: 'Children in elementary schools had long been underfed. But there was now a danger of their being overfed in the schools by being given food which was too heavy for them.' She later elaborated her views on the need for a scientific approach to the feeding of schoolchildren in a pamphlet she wrote with Margaret McMillan for the Independent Labour Party entitled *London's Children. How to Feed Them and How Not to Feed Them.* Here, she contended, 'The feeding of children [...] is a NATIONAL question, which has for its object the building up of a strong and healthy race; and the child, and not the education of the parent, must see the object of our solicitude.' Cobden-Sanderson's emphasis on the practicalities of feeding the poor schoolchildren of London was underpinned by her strong belief that a healthy diet was at the heart of political regeneration. Thus the focus on school meals had a far wider objective, that of transforming national politics. This was also a feminist agenda. The establishment were charged with failing to nurture the nation's most precious resource: its people. The practical activities of campaigners such as McMillan and Cobden-Sanderson aimed to demonstrate that women were aware of the key social and economic challenges of the age, and knew how to resolve them.

This brief survey of three distinct areas of female engagement in a period when the political landscape appeared to exclude them fully from participation has lessons for today's activists.

» First, the emphasis should be on measuring and assessing where women are active, as well as counting their lack of progress in some formal political institutions. Many female campaigners enter 'mainstream' politics after becoming active in local and neighbourhood organizations. The marginalisation of these overlooks the contribution that women make to political life. Such community enterprises are also important in giving women experience in public affairs and the confidence to articulate their views.

» Secondly, even where women play a full part in political life, such as in voting or holding office, they tend to be written out of the official record. They are assumed to be absent from politics, when in fact their voice is unheard and their actions unrecognised. Thus there needs to be greater recognition and reward for female activism.

» Thirdly, a broader definition of politics and political culture needs to be established. The areas discussed in this chapter are often excluded from analyses of nineteenth-century politics and government. This compounds the marginalisation of women and overlooks their important contributions. The home, the neighbourhood and the community are formative sites of female political action and should be acknowledged as such.

» Lastly, it should be recognised that while most female political activity is unacknowledged and ignored, now and in the nineteenth century, there are real barriers to women's full participation in public life. The invisibility of politically active women means that political parties and institutions need to be much more proactive – for example, by recognising women's contributions and reforming processes and practices which exclude them from political life.

NOTES

INTRODUCTION

1 See also A. Sundstrom and A. M. McCright, 'Gender differences in environmental concern among Swedish citizens and politicians', *Environmental Politics*, 23(6), 2014.

2 Suzanne Goldenberg, 'Why are so many white men trying to save the planet without the rest of us?', *Guardian*, 8 May 2014, www.theguardian. com/commentisfree/2014/may/08/white-men-environmental-movement-leadership

3 H. Tallis and J. Lubchenko, 'Working together: a call for inclusive conservation', *Nature*, November 2014.

1 DIANE ELSON

1 UNCED (United Nations Conference on Environment and Development), *Rio Declaration on Environment and Development*, A/CONF.151/26, 1992, www.un-documents.net/rio-dec.htm

2 IUCN (International Union for Conservation of Nature), *The Environment and Gender Index (EGI) 2013 Pilot*, IUCN, Washington, DC, 2013.

3 United Nations Conference on Sustainable Development, *Outcome Document: The Future We Want*, Resolution adopted by the General Assembly, A/RES/66/288, 2012, sustainabledevelopment.un.org/futurewewant. html, paras 31, 45.

4 UNDP (United Nations Development Programme), *Powerful Synergies: Gender Equality, Economic Development and Environmental Sustainability*, ed. B. Cela, I. Dankelman and J. Stern, New York, 2012, p. 40.

5 L. Schalatek, *The Post-2015 Framework: Merging care and green economy approaches to finance gender-equitable sustainable development*, Heinrich Böll Stiftung, Washington, DC, 2013; World Bank, *Gender and climate change: 3 things you should know*, World Bank, Washington, DC, 2011.

6 IUCN, *The Environment and Gender Index (EGI) 2013 Pilot*.

7 B. Agarwal, *Gender and Green Governance: The political economy of women's presence within and beyond community forestry*, Oxford University Press, New Delhi, 2010.

8 UN Women, *World Survey on the Role of Women in Development*, UN Women, New York, 2014, p. 40.

9 Committee on the Elimination of Discrimination Against Women (2004) *General Recommendation 25* on Article 4, paragraph 1, of the Convention on the Elimination of All Forms of Discrimination against Women, on temporary special measures, para. 8, www.un.org/womenwatch/daw/cedaw/recommendations/General%20recommendation%2025%20%28English%29.pdf, para. 8.

10 Ibid., para. 10.

11 M. Sepulveda Carmona, *Report of UN Special Rapporteur on Extreme Poverty and Human Rights to UN General Assembly*, A/68/293, 2013.

12 J. W. Rockström et al., 'Planetary boundaries: exploring the safe operating space for humanity', *Ecology and Society*, 14(2), 2009, p. 32.

13 K. Raworth, 'A safe and just space for humanity: can we live within the doughnut?', Oxfam Discussion Paper, Oxfam, Oxford, 2012.

14 WCED (World Commission on Environment and Development), *Our Common Future: Report of the WCED* (Brundtland Report), Oxford University Press, Oxford, 1987, ch. 2, para. 1.

15 S. Fukuda-Parr, J. Heintz and S. Seguino, 'Critical perspectives on financial and economic crises: heterodox macroeconomics meets feminist economics', *Feminist Economics*, 19(3), 2013, pp. 4–31.

16 UN Women, 'Gender equality and the global economic crisis', Research paper, UN Women, New York, 2014.

17 See, for example, ILO, *Working towards Sustainable Development: Opportunities for decent work and social inclusion in a green economy*, International Labour Organization, Geneva, 2012.

18 World Bank, *World Development Report 2012: Gender equality and development*, World Bank, Washington, DC, 2012.

19 UNEP (United Nations Environment Programme), 'Global green new deal', Policy brief, Nairobi, 2009.

20 Ibid.

21 Ibid., p. 6.

22 O. Strietska-Ilina et al., 'Skills for green jobs: a global view', Synthesis report based on twenty-one country studies, ILO, Geneva, 2011, p. 126.

23 ILO, *Working towards Sustainable Development*.

24 Ibid.

25 UN Women, *World Survey on the Role of Women in Development*, pp. 74–5.

26 D. Elson, 'Economics for a post-crisis world: putting social justice first', in D. Jain and D. Elson (eds), *Harvesting Feminist Knowledge for Public Policy*, Sage, New Delhi, 2011.

2 WANJIRA MAATHAI

1 UN, *Forests: Action Statements and Action Plans*, Climate Summit 2014, UN Headquarters, New York, 2014 http://www.un.org/climatechange/summit/wp-content/uploads/sites/2/2014/07/New-York-Declaration-on-Forests_8-Oct-2015.pdf

2 D. Sperling and D. Gordon, *Two Billion Cars: Driving Towards Sustainability*, Oxford University Press, 2009

3 K. Reytar, *7 Unexpected Places for Forest Landscape Restoration*, World Resources Institute, 2014 http://www.wri.org/blog/2014/05/7-unexpected-places-forest-landscape-restoration

4 T. T. Deressa, *Climate Change And Growth In Africa: Challenges And The Way Forward*, Africa Growth Initiative, The Brookings Institution Washington DC, 2014 www.brookings.edu/~/media/Research/Files/Reports/2014/foresight%20africa%202014/09%20foresight%20climate%20change%20growth%20africa%20deressa.pdf

5 World Bank, *Turn down the heat : climate extremes, regional impacts, and the case for resilience*, Working Paper No. 78422, World Bank 2013.

6 R. Winterbottom, *Restoration: It's About More Than Just The Trees*, World Resources Institute, 2014, http://www.wri.org/blog/2014/05/restoration-it%E2%80%99s-about-more-just-trees

7 P. Smith et al.,*Agriculture, Forestry and Other Land Use (AFOLU)*, in O. Edenhofer et al. (eds), *Climate Change 2014: Mitigation of Climate Change. Contribution of Working Group III to the Fifth Assessment Report of the Intergovernmental Panel on Climate Change*, Cambridge University Press, Cambridge, UK, 2014.

8 Green Belt Movement, *Promoting Sustainable Development through Environment-relevant policies: Annual Report 2012*, www.greenbeltmovement.org/sites/greenbeltmovement.org/files/2012%20Annual%20Report.pdf

9 World Bank, *Making Development Climate-Resilient in Sub-Saharan Africa: A World Bank Strategy for Sub-Saharan Africa*, Report No. 46967-AFR, World Bank, 2009, http://web.worldbank.org/WBSITE/EXTERNAL/COUNTRIES/AFRICAEXT/0,,contentMDK:22410211~pagePK:146736~piPK:146830~theSitePK:258644,00.html.

10 K. Buckingham, *Bamboo: The Secret Weapon in Forest and Landscape Restoration?*, World Resources Institute, 2009 http://www.wri.org/blog/2014/02/bamboo-secret-weapon-forest-and-landscape-restoration

3 LYLA MEHTA AND MELISSA LEACH

1 This chapter draws on M. Leach et al., 'Gender equality and sustainable development: a pathways approach', Background working paper for UN Women World Survey on the Role of Women in Development, 2014.

2 B. Unmüßig, W. Sachs and T. Fatheuer, *Critique of the Green Ecology – Toward Social and Environmental Equity*, Ecology Series no. 22, Heinrich Böll Stiftung, Berlin, 2012.

3 Ibid.

4 See ibid.; W. Harcourt (ed.), *Feminist Perspectives on Sustainable Development*, Zed Books, London.

5 See C. Wichterich, *The Future We Want. A feminist perspective*, Ecology Series no. 21, Heinrich Böll Stiftung, Berlin, 2012.

6 See ibid.; UN Women, *World Survey on the Role of Women in Development 2014: Gender Equality and Sustainable Development*, New York, 2014.

7 J. Rockström et al., 'A safe operating space for humanity', *Nature*, 461, 209.

8 C. Folke et al., 'Reconnecting to the biosphere', *Ambio*, 40, 2011.

9 K. Raworth, 'A safe and just space for humanity: can we live within the doughnut?', Oxfam Discussion Paper, Oxfam, Oxford, 2012.

10 Unmüßig et al., *Critique of the Green Ecology*.

11 UNEP, *What is the Green Economy Initiative?*, www.unep.org/greeneconomy/AboutGEI/WhatisGEI/tabid/29784/Default.aspx, 2013.

12 J. Clancy, *Economy or Environment? It's a false choice*, National Union of Public and General Employees, Canada, 2009 nupge.ca/content/815/economy-or-environment-its-false-choice .

13 T. Jackson, *Prosperity without Growth: Economics for a Finite Planet*, Earthscan/Routledge, London, 2009.

14 Wichterich, *The Future We Want*; Unmüßig et al., *Critique of the Green Ecology*.

15 For example Natural Capital Committee, *The State of Natural Capital: Towards a framework for measurement and valuation*, Defra, London, 2013, www.defra.gov.uk/naturalcapitalcommittee

16 See J. Fairhead and M. Leach, *Misreading the African Landscape: Society and ecology in a forest-savanna mosaic*, Cambridge University Press, Cambridge, 1996; L. Mehta, G. J. Veldwisch and J. Franco, 'Introduction to the Special Issue: Water grabbing? Focus on the (re)appropriation of finite water resources', *Water Alternatives*, 5(2), 2012; S. M. Borras, Jr, R. Hall, I. Scoones, B. White and W. Wolford, 'Towards a better understanding of global land grabbing: an editorial introduction', *Journal of Peasant Studies*, 38(2), 2011.

17 See M. Naret Guerrero and A. Stock, 'Green economy from a gender perspective', www.academia.edu/1604568/Green_economy_from_a_Gender_perspective, 2012, accessed February 2015.

18 See L. Schalatek, *The Post-2015 Framework: Merging Care and Green Economy Approaches to Finance Gender-Equitable Sustainable Development*, Heinrich Böll Foundation, 2013.

19 See Unmüßig et al., *Critique of the Green Ecology*.

20 For example G. Vaughan (ed.), *Women and the Gift Economy: A Radically Difference Worldview Is Possible*, Inanna Publications & Education Incorporated, 2007; M. Mellor, 'Ecofeminist political economy and the politics of money', in A. Salleh (ed.), *Eco-Sufficiency and Global Justice: Women write political ecology*, Pluto Press, London, 2009.

21 See L. Mehta, *The Limits to Scarcity. Contesting the Politics of Allocation*, Earthscan, London, 2010; A. Salleh (ed.), Eco-Sufficiency and Global Justice: Women write political ecology, Pluto Press, London, 2009.

22 See Wichterich, *The Future We Want*.

23 See B. Agarwal, 'Gender inequality, cooperation and environmental sustainability', Workshop on 'Inequality, collective action and environmental sustainability', Working Paper 02-10-058, Santa Fe Institute, New Mexico, November 2002; S. Buckingham-Hatfield, 'Gender equality: a prerequisite for sustainable development', *Geography*, 2002, pp. 227–33; UNDP, 'Powerful synergies: gender equality, economic development and environmental sustainability', New York, 2012, www.undp.org/content/dam/undp/library/gender/Gender%20and%20Environment/Powerful-Synergies.pdf; G. Johnsson-Latham, 'A study on gender equality as a prerequisite for sustainable development: Report to the Environment Advisory Council, Sweden 2007:2', Ministry of the Environment, Sweden.

24 M. Leach, I. Scoones and A. Stirling, *Dynamic Sustainabilities: Technology, environment, social justice*, Earthscan, London, 2010.

25 M. Leach, L. Mehta and P. Prabhakaran, 'Gender equality and sustainable development: a pathways approach', Background working paper for UN Women World Survey on the Role of Women in Development, 2014; UN Women, *World Survey on the Role of Women in Development 2014*.

5 SUSAN BUCKINGHAM

1 JCC (Joint Curriculum Council), 2013, www.jcq.org.uk/Download/examination-results/a-levels/a-as-and-aea-results-summer-2013&rct=j&q=&esrc=s&sa=U&ei=zNs_VPSOCMeN7Aaun4HgBA&ved=0CEEQFjAI&usg=AFQjCNHiME-Z373jhu98XuG5vqiGM7sBwg, accessed 17 October 2014.

2 European Commission, *Horizon2020*, 2013.

3 However, women comprise only 19 per cent in the business sector, where across the EU-27 research spending is highest, though this is not the case for a handful of countries, including the UK. Ibid.

4 Derived from data presented in Eurostat, *Statistics on research and development*, in ibid.

5 F. Denton, 'Climate change, vulnerability, impacts, and adaptation: why does gender matter?', in R. Masika (ed.), *Gender, Development and Climate Change*, Oxfam, Oxford, 2002.

6 A. Fouillet, G. Rey, F. Laurent, G. Pavillon, S. Bellec, C. Guihenneuc-Jouvaux, J. Clavel, E. Jougla and D. Hemon, 'Excess mortality related to the August 2003 heat wave in France', *International Archives of Occupational and Environmental Health*, 80(1), 2006, pp. 16–24.

7 See Elaine Enarson's work, including 'Women and girls last?: averting the second post-Katrina disaster', Social Science Research Council, 2006, forums.ssrc.org/understandingkatrina/contributors/essays June 11, 2006.

8 M. Fordham, 'Making women visible in disasters: problematising the private domain', *Disasters*, 22(2), 1998, pp. 126–43.

9 I. Sánchez de Madariaga, in I. Sánchez de Madariaga and M. Roberts (eds), *Fair Shared Cities*, Ashgate, Aldershot, 2013.

10 European Commission, *Horizon2020*.

11 Gendered Innovations in Science, Health and Medicine, Engineering and Environment, *Sex and Gender Analysis Policies in Peer Reviewed Journals*, 2014, genderedinnovations.stanford.edu/sex-and-gender-analysis-policies-peer-reviewed-journals.html, accessed 28 October 2014.

12 See European Commission, 'Europeans' attitudes towards climate change', *EUROBAROMETER 300* special, European Commission, Brussels, 2008.

13 A number of initiatives across Europe have been developed on the basis that more gender-balanced company boards will contribute to more financially stable businesses, more innovative and responsive to a wider community. E. M. Davies, 'Women on boards', Equality and Human Rights Commission, 2011; European Union, 6 COM(2012) 614, 2012, ec.europa.eu/justice/gender-equality/gender-decision-making/index_en.htm

14 In the UK, 30 per cent of employees in the transport industry are women; 27 per cent of employees in the water and energy industries are women. In the nuclear power industry, 22.5 per cent of employees are women. By 2010, the proportion of practising architects who were women had dropped to c. 20 per cent from over 25 per cent the previous year. (The Fees Bureau/RIBA, http://www.feesbureau.co.uk/Earns2012-1.asp, 2010.)

15 Buckingham, S., D. Reeves and A. Batchelor, 'Wasting women: the environmental justice of including women in municipal waste management', *Local Environment*, 10(4), 2005, pp. 427–44.

16 R. Kulcur, 'Environmental injustice? An analysis of gender in environmental non-governmental organisations (ENGOS) in the United Kingdom and Turkey', PhD thesis, Brunel University, London, 2013, bura.brunel.ac.uk/handle/2438/7680

17 D. Massey, 'Masculinity, dualisms and high technology', *Transactions of the Institute of British Geographers*, 20(4), 1995, pp. 487–99.

18 G. L. Magnusdottir and A. Kronsell, 'The (in)visibility of gender in Scandinavian climate policy-making', *International Feminist Journal of Politics*, 17(2), 2015, pp. 308–26.

19 E. Saragossi, 'Mothers on boards. Comparing the level of support for working mothers to the proportion of women in senior management in eight OECD countries', 30% Club, 2013.

20 See also H. Kurtz, 'Gender and environment justice in Louisiana: blurring the boundaries of public and private spheres', *Gender, Place and Culture*, 14(4), 2007, pp. 409–26; J. Sze, 'Gender, asthma politics, and urban environmental justice activism', in R. Stein (ed.), *New Perspectives on Environmental Justice. Gender, Sexuality, and Activism*, Rutgers University Press, New Brunswick, NJ, 2004, pp. 177–90; and, on 'citizen science', A. Irwin, *Citizen Science: A study of people, expertise and sustainable development*, Routledge, London, 1995.

6 YVONNE ORENGO

1 www.andrylalanatohana.org
2 The traditionally nomadic ethnic group inhabiting Androy, southern Madagascar.
3 Systeme Alerte Precoce (SAP) Southern Madagascar monitors annual harvests, food shortages, etc.: www.gripweb.org/gripweb/sites/default/files/databases_info_systems/Madagascar%20SAP.pdf
4 See Feteline's testimony in a video at andrewleestrust.org/voices.htm
5 Project Village Voices for Development at andrewleestrust.org/voices.htm
6 Project Radio at andrewleestrust.org/radio.htm
7 Project HEPA at andrewleestrust.org/hepa.htm
8 UNDP Communications for Empowerment National Study 2008, Oslo Governance Centre.
9 www.instat.mg/index.php
10 SNU Vision Stratégique Madagascar 2010–2011.
11 Øyvind Dahl, *Malagasy Meanings*, Centre for Intercultural Communication School of Mission & Theology, 1993.
12 Y. Orengo and N. Harford, 'A study in the use of radio to promote human rights and enable citizens to act on their rights to information and freedom of speech in S. Madagascar', 2013.
13 L. Metcalf, N. Harford and M. Myers, 'The contribution of radio to the achievement of Millennium Development Goals in S. Madagascar', 2007.
14 Collectif Tany/SIF, 'Land grabbing in Madagascar, echoes and testimonies from the field', 2013.
15 INSTAT Madagascar, www.instat.mg/index.php?option=com_content&view=article&id=17&Itemid=94
16 FAO, 'Women in agriculture – closing the gap for development', in *The State of Food and Agriculture*, 2013.
17 ALT Drought Mitigation Programme and Project Apemba Soa.
18 ALT Project Energy, andrewleestrust.org/energy.htm
19 Metcalf et al., 'The contribution of Radio'.
20 Ibid.
21 N. Harford, 'ALT Project Radio Monitoring and Evaluation Consultancy – report of briefing visit', London and Madagascar, ALT, 2005.

7 JULIE A. NELSON

1 Earlier research underlying this chapter was funded by a grant from the Institute for New Thinking in Economics (INET).
2 G. Lakoff, *Women, Fire, and Dangerous Things: What Categories Reveal About the Mind*, University of Chicago Press, Chicago, IL, 1987; K. M. Knutson, L. Mah et al., 'Neural correlates of automatic beliefs about gender and race', *Human Brain Mapping*, 28, 2007, pp. 915–30; J. E. B. Wilkie and G. V. Bodenhausen, 'Are numbers gendered?', *Journal of Experimental Psychology: General*, 2011, advance online publication.

3 Heterodox approaches – including Marxist, feminist and ecological approaches to economics – exist, but are much marginalized within the profession.

4 W. D. Nordhaus, *A Question of Balance: Weighing the Options on Global Warming Policies*, Yale University Press, New Haven, CT, 2008; US Department of Energy, 'Final Rule Technical Support Document (TSD): Energy Efficiency Program for Commercial and Industrial Equipment: Small Electric Motors', Appendix 15A (by the Interagency Working Group on Social Cost of Carbon): 'Social Cost of Carbon for Regulatory Impact Analysis Under Executive Order 12866', 2010.

5 IPCC, 'Final Draft Report of the Working Group III contribution to the IPCC 5th Assessment Report, "Climate Change 2014: Mitigation of Climate Change"', Intergovernmental Panel on Climate Change, 12 April 2014.

6 E. Stanton, 'Negishi welfare weights in integrated assessment models: the mathematics of global inequality', *Climatic Change*, 2010, online.

7 Some economists with strong mainstream credentials have recently publicly split from some or all of these views. But they are not yet carrying the day, nor do they tend to re-evaluate the mainstream assumptions as a whole. See, for example, Nicolas Stern, 'The structure of economic modeling of the potential impacts of climate change: grafting gross underestimation of risk onto already narrow science models', Journal of Economic Literature, 51(3), 2013, pp. 838–59.

8 J. A. Nelson, 'Economists, value judgments, and climate change: a view from feminist economics', *Ecological Economics*, 65(3), 2008, pp. 441–7.

9 E. F. Keller, *Reflections on Gender and Science*, Yale University Press, New Haven, CT, 1985.

10 S. Harding, *The Science Question in Feminism*, Cornell University Press, Ithaca, NY, 1986.

11 J. A. Nelson, 'Gender, metaphor, and the definition of economics', *Economics and Philosophy*, 8, 1982, pp. 103–25; A. L. Jennings, 'Public or private? Institutional economics and feminism', in M. A. Ferber and J. A. Nelson (eds), *Beyond Economic Man*, University of Chicago Press, Chicago, IL, 1993, pp. 111–29.

12 J. A. Nelson, 'Does profit-seeking rule out love? Evidence (or not) from economics and law', *Washington University Journal of Law and Policy*, 35(69), 2011, pp. 69–107.

13 J. A. Nelson, *Economics for Humans*, University of Chicago Press, Chicago, IL, 2006; H.-J. Chang, *23 Things They Don't Tell You about Capitalism*, Bloomsbury Press, New York, 2010; V. A. R. Zelizer, *Economic Lives: How Culture Shapes the Economy*, Princeton University Press, Princeton, NJ, 2011.

14 R. E. Freeman, *Strategic Management: A Stakeholder Approach*, Pitman, Boston, MA, 1984; L. Stout, *The Shareholder Value Myth: How Putting Shareholders First Harms Investors, Corporations, and the Public*, Berrett-Koehler, San Francisco, 2012.

15 Y. Smith, *Econned: How Unenlightened Self Interest Undermined Democracy and Corrupted Capitalism*, Palgrave Macmillan, New York, 2010.

16 E.g. J. Gillespie and D. Zweig, *Money for Nothing: How CEOs and Boards Are Bankrupting America*, Free Press, New York, 2011.

17 S. Sivaraksa, 'Alternatives to consumerism', in A. H. Badiner (ed.), *Mindfulness in the Marketplace: Compassionate Responses to Consumerism*, Parallax Press, Berkeley, CA, 2002, pp. 135–41; M. Bookchin, 'What is social ecology?', in M. E. Zimmerman, J. B. Callicot, K. J. Warren, I. J. Klaver and J. Clark (eds), *Environmental Philosophy: From Animal Rights to Radical Ecology*, Pearson Prentice Hall, Upper Saddle River, NJ, 2005, pp. 462–78; 463, 474.

18 J. A. Nelson, 'Ethics and the economist: what climate change demands of us', *Ecological Economics*, 85, January 2013, pp. 145–54.

8 ANNA FITZPATRICK

1 www.londonfashionweek.co.uk/news/623/Facts--Figures-AW14

2 S. Bruzzi and P. Church-Gibson, *Fashion Cultures Revisited: Theories, Explorations and Analysis*, Routledge, London, 2013.

3 G. Lipovetsky, *The Empire of Fashion: Dressing Modern Democracy*, Princeton, NJ, Princeton University Press, 1994.

4 Personal communication.

5 www.oecd.org/social/40881538.pdf

6 Y. Kawamura, *Fashion-ology: An Introduction to Fashion Studies*, Berg, 2005.

7 Personal communication, April 2015.

8 K. Fletcher, *Sustainable Fashion and Textiles: Design Journeys*, Routledge, London, 2013.

9 As stated in S. Bell and S. Morse, *Sustainability Indicators: Measuring the Immeasurable?*, Routledge, London, 2012, p. 79.

10 A. Fuad-Luke, *Design Activism. Beautiful strangeness for a sustainable world*, Earthscan, London, 2009.

11 www.ecoliteracy.org/article/designers-challenge-four-problems-you-must-solve

12 Fletcher, *Sustainable Fashion and Textiles*.

13 As quoted in D. Mukherjee-Biswas, *Unleash the Power of Diversity*, Author House, 2013, p. 189.

9 CELIA ALLDRIDGE

1 WMW International Actions take place every five years, starting in 2000, and International Meetings take place every two to three years.

2 The WMW Rules and By-laws were revised at the 8th IM in the Philippines in 2011, where delegates acknowledged the continuing relevance of Objective #7 and opted to maintain it in the version of the Rules and By-laws (where it became Goals 'h' and 'i').

3 The WMW Action Area documents were published in 2009 and are available on the WMW international website.

4 WMW, 'Women in the fight against the commodification of nature and life!', WMW Report from Rio+20, 2012.

5 Activist drumming group using recycled materials as drums and percussion.

6 A. Salleh, *Rio+20 and the Green Economy: Technocrats, Meta-industrials, WSF and Occupy*, 2012, zcomm.org/znetarticle/rio-20-and-the-green-economy-technocrats-meta-industrials-wsf-and-occupy-by-ariel-salleh/

7 A. Bosch, C. Carrasco and E. Grau, 'Verde te quiero violeta: encuentros y desencuentros entre feminismo y ecologismo', in E. Tello, *La Historia Cuenta: Del crecimiento económico al desarrollo humano sostenible*, El Viejo Topo, Barcelona, 2005.

8 7th National Congress Declaration, CONAMURI (a member organization of the Paraguayan WMW National Coordinating Body).

9 D. Harvey, *The New Imperialism*, Oxford University Press, Oxford, 2003.

10 WMW, *Preparatory document for the 4th International Action*, 2013, www.marchemondiale.org/structure/9rencontre/context/en

11 MAB (Movimento dos Atingidos por Barragens – Movement of People Affected by Dams), in SOF (Sempreviva Organização Feminista), *Nosso Corpo Nos Pertence*, Video, 2014, www.youtube.com/watch?v=UvS4hwSa8So

12 www.abc.com.py/edicion-impresa/politica/paraguay-es-facil-es-una-mujer-bonita-dice-cartes-632556.html

13 www.ultimahora.com/cartes-empresarios-brasilenos-usen-y-abusen-paraguay-n767800.html

14 S. Federici, *Caliban and the Witch: Women, the Body and Primitive Accumulation*, Autonomedia, New York, 2004; S. Federici, 'Feminism and the politics of the commons', www.commoner.org, 2010.

15 Federici, *Caliban and the Witch*, p. 97, emphasis in original.

16 Ibid.

17 Federici, 'Feminism and the politics of the commons'.

18 Ibid., p. 5.

19 CONAMURI (Coordinadora Nacional de Organizaciones de Mujeres Trabajadoras Rurales e Indígenas), *7th National Congress Political Declaration*, 2014.

11 QUINN BERNIER, CHIARA KOVARIK, RUTH MEINZEN-DICK, AGNES QUISUMBING

1 R. Meinzen-Dick, C. Kovarik and A. R. Quisumbing, 'Gender and sustainability', *Annual Review of Environment and Resources*, 39, 2014, pp. 29–55.

2 Ibid., p. 31.

3 D. Budlender, 'The debate about household headship', *Social Dynamics*, 29(2), 2003, pp. 48–72; M. Buvinić and G. R. Gupta, 'Female-headed households and female-maintained families: are they worth targeting to reduce poverty in developing countries?', in *Economic Development*

and Cultural Change, 45(2), 1997, pp. 259–80; C. Diana Deere, G. E. Alvarado and J. Twyman, 'Gender inequality in asset ownership in Latin America: female owners vs household heads', *Development and Change*, 43(2), 2012, pp. 505–30.

4   Meinzen-Dick et al., 'Gender and sustainability'.

5   WCED (World Commission on Environment and Development, *Our Common Future*, Oxford University Press, New York, 1987.

6   G. B. Villamor, F. Desrianti, R. Akiefnawati, S. Amaruzaman and M. van Noordwijk, 'Gender influences decision to change land use practices in the tropical forest margins of Jambi, Indonesia', *Mitig. Adapt. Strateg. Glob. Change*, 2013, doi: 10.1007/s11027-013-9478-7

7   L. German and H. Taye, 'A framework for evaluating effectiveness and inclusiveness of collective action in watershed management', *J. Int. Dev.*, 20(1), 2008, pp. 99–116.

8   V. T. D. Huong, 'Gendered knowledge in the management of medicinal plants: a case study of a Dzao community in the buffer zone of Bavi National Park, Northern Vietnam', Presented at the regional seminar 'Regionalization of development: redefining local culture, space and identity in the Mekong region', 22–24 April 2006, Luang Prabang, Laos; B. Agarwal, 'The gender and environment debate: lessons from India', *Fem. Stud.*, 18(1), 1992, pp. 119–58; R. Brara, *Shifting Sands: A study of right in common pastures*, Inst. Dev. Stud., Jaipur, India, 1987; as cited in B. Agarwal, 'Conceptualising environmental collective action: why gender matters', *Cambridge J. Econ.*, 24, 2000, pp. 283–310.

9   G. Feder and A. Nishio, *The Benefits of Land Registration and Titling: Economic and Social Perspectives*, World Bank, Washington, DC, 1997; G. Feder, T. Onchan, Y. Chamlamwong and C. Hongladarom, *Land Policies and Farm Productivity in Thailand*, Johns Hopkins University Press, Baltimore, MD, 1988.

10 A. R. Quisumbing, E. Payongayong, J. B. Aidoo and K. Otsuka, 'Women's land rights in the transition to individualized ownership: implications for tree-resource management in western Ghana', *Econ. Dev. Cult. Change*, 50(1), 2001, pp. 157–82.

11 M. Goldstein and C. Udry, 'The profits of power: land rights and agricultural investment in Ghana', *J. Polit. Econ.*, 116(6), 2008, pp. 981–1022.

12 Meinzen-Dick et al., 'Gender and sustainability'.

13 L. Fortmann, C. Antinori and N. Nabane, 'Fruits of their labors: gender, property rights, and tree planting in two Zimbabwe villages', *Rural Sociol.*, 62(3), 1997, pp. 295–314.

14 A. Deininger, D. A. Ali and T. Yamano, 'Legal knowledge and economic development: the case of land rights in Uganda', *Land Econ.*, 84(4), 2008, pp. 593–619.

15 D. A. Ali, K. Deininger and M. Goldstein, 'Environmental and gender impacts of land tenure regularization in Africa: pilot evidence from

Rwanda', Policy Res. Working Paper 5765, World Bank,Washington, DC, 2011.

16 K. Deininger, D. A. Ali, S. Holden and J. Zevenbergen, 'Rural land certification in Ethiopia: process, initial impact, and implications for other African countries', *World Dev.*, 36(10), 2008, pp. 1786–1812.

17 A. R. Quisumbing and N. Kumar, 'Did the Ethiopian land registration improve women's land rights and increase adoption of soil conservation?', Presented at 'Agricultural development within the rural–urban continuum', Stuttgart-Hohenheim, 17–19 September 2013.

18 Agarwal, 'Conceptualising environmental collective action'.

19 J. Dey, 'Women in African rice farming systems', in *Women in rice farming: Proceedings of a conference on women in rice farming systems*, International Rice Research Institute, Gower Publishers, Brookfield, 1985; J. von Braun and P. J. R. Webb, 'The impact of new crop technology on the agricultural division of labor in a West African setting', *Economic Development and Cultural Change*, 37, 1989, pp. 513–34; C. Jones, 'The mobilization of women's labor for cash crop production: a game theoretic approach', *American Journal of Agricultural Economics*, 65(5), 1983, pp. 1049–54.

20 M. Di Gregorio, K. Hagedorn, M. Kiri, B. Korf, N. McCarthy, R. Meinzen-Dick, B. Swallow, E. Mwangi and H. Markelova, 'Property rights and collective action for poverty reduction: a framework for analysis', in E. Mwangi, H. Markelova and R. Meinzen-Dick (eds), *Collective Action and Property Rights for Poverty Reduction: Insights from Africa and Asia*, Penn Press for International Food Policy Research Institute, Philadelphia, PA, 2012, pp. 25–48.

21 R. Meinzen-Dick, J. A. Behrman, L. Pandolfelli, A. Peterman and A. Quisumbing, 'Gender and social capital for agricultural development', in A. Quisumbing, R. Meinzen-Dick, T. Raney, A. Croppenstedt, J. Behrman and A. Peterman (eds), *Gender in Agriculture and Food Security: Closing the knowledge gap*, Springer and FAO, Dordrecht, 2014.

22 B. Agarwal, *Gender and Green Governance*, Oxford University Press, Oxford, 2010.

23 H. J. Malapit, K. Sproule, C. Kovarik, R. Meinzen-Dick, A. Quisumbing et al., 'Measuring progress toward empowerment', WEAI Baseline Report, International Food Policy Research Institute, Washington, DC, 2014, feedthefuture.gov/sites/default/files/resource/files/ftf_progress_weai_baselinereport_may2014.pdf

24 Agarwal, 'The gender and environment debate'.

25 S. K. Kumar and D. Hotchkiss, 'Consequences of deforestation for women's time allocation, agricultural production, and nutrition in hill areas of Nepal', IFPRI Research Report no. 69, International Food Policy Research Institute, Washington, DC, 1988.

26 F. S. Arku and C. Arku, 'I cannot drink water on an empty stomach: a gender perspective on living with drought', *Gender and Development*, 18(1), 2010, pp. 115–24.

27 S. Joekes, N. Heyzer, R. Oniang'o and V. Salles, 'Gender, environment and population', *Dev. Change*, 25(1), 1994, pp. 137–65.

28 Quisumbing and Kumar, 'Did the Ethiopian land registration improve women's land rights …'

29 M. G. Fisher, R. L. Warner and W. A. Masters, 'Gender and agricultural change: crop–livestock integration in Senegal', *Soc. Nat. Resour.*, 13(3), 2000, pp. 203–22.

30 Meinzen-Dick et al., 'Gender and sustainability'.

12 ISABEL BOTTOMS AND AMENA SHARAF

1 ECESR & CESR, 'Factsheet no. 13, Egypt', 2013, p. 2, www.cesr.org/downloads/Egypt.Factsheet.web.pdf

2 L. Ersado, 'Income inequality and inequality of opportunity: cues from Egypt's Arab Spring', World Bank blog, 2012, blogs.worldbank.org/developmenttalk/income-inequality-and-inequality-of-opportunity-cues-from-egypt-s-arab-spring

3 S. Amin and N. H. Al-Bassusi, 'Education, wage work, and marriage: perspectives of Egyptian working women', *Journal of Marriage and Family*, 66(5), December 2004, pp. 1287–99.

4 R. Hendy, 'Rethinking the time allocation of Egyptian females: a matching analysis', Gender and Work in the MENA Region working paper series no. 17, Population Council, June 2011, p. 14.

5 Ibid., p. 13.

6 Amin and Al-Bassusi, p. 1296.

7 F. El-Zanaty and A. Way, 'Egypt Demographic and Health Survey 2008', Ministry of Health, El-Zanaty and Associates, and Macro International, Cairo, 2008, p. 100.

8 M. Assaad and J. Bruce, 'Empowering the next generation: girls of the Maqattam garbage settlement', Population Council, p. 16, www.popcouncil.org/uploads/pdfs/seeds/SEEDS19.pdf

9 www.giz.de/en/worldwide/16278.html.

10 E. Ellabany and M. Abdel-Nasser, 'Community based survey study on non-communicable diseases and their Risk Factors', World Health Organization, 2005/06, Table 24, p. 43.

11 El-Zanaty and Way, 'Egypt Demographic and Health Survey 2008', p. 235.

12 I. Mohsen, 'Epidemiology of hypertension in Egypt', Cairo University, p. 4, www.ehs-egypt.net/pdf/rv2.pdf

13 R. Barsoum, 'Burden of chronic kidney disease: North Africa', *Kidney International Supplements*, 3, 2013, pp. 164–6, www.nature.com/kisup/journal/v3/n2/full/kisup20135a.html

13 NATHALIE HOLVOET AND LIESBETH INBERG

1 This contribution is based on our paper in *Climate and Development*, 6(3), 2014, pp. 266–76.

2 UNDP, *Human Development Report*, New York, UNDP, 2011; World Bank, 'Local institutions and climate change adaptation', *Social Dimensions of Climate Change*, 113, World Bank, Washington, DC, 2008.

3 The UNFCC was agreed upon during the 1992 United Nations Conference on Environment and Development (UNCED), yet it neglected the UNCED Rio principle that 'women have a vital role in environmental management and development', and that 'their full participation is therefore essential to achieve sustainable development'. UNCED, *Rio Declaration on Environment and Development*, UNCED, Rio de Janeiro, 1992, p. 4.

4 IUCN, *Draft Guidelines to Mainstreaming Gender in the Development of National Adaptation Plans (NAPs)*, UNFCCC, Bonn, 2011.

5 UNFCCC, *Report of the Conference of the Parties on its sixteenth session, held in Cancún from 29 November to 10 December 2010. Addendum. Part Two: Action taken by the Conference of the Parties at its sixteenth session*, UNFCCC, Cancún, 2010, pp. 3–4.

6 UNFCCC, *Draft decision –CP.18. Promoting gender balance and improving the participation of women in UNFCCC negotiations and in the representation of Parties in bodies established pursuant to the Convention or the Kyoto Protocol*, UNFCCC, Qatar, 2012.

7 UNFPA and WEDO, *Climate Change Connections*, UNFPA and WEDO, New York, 2009.

8 The guidelines prescribe the following structure: 1) Introduction and setting; 2) Framework for adaptation programme; 3) Identification of key adaptation needs; 4) Criteria for selecting priority activities; 5) List of priority activities; and 6) NAPA preparation process. Least Developed Countries Expert Group, *Annotated guideless for the preparation of national adaptation programmes of action*, UNFCCC, Bonn, 2002.

9 Ibid.

10 Skinner, E., *Gender and Climate Change Overview Report*, Institute of Development Studies, Brighton, 2011.

11 IUCN, *Draft Guidelines to Mainstreaming Gender in the Development of National Adaptation Plans (NAPs)*.

12 UNFPA and WEDO, *Climate Change Connections*, p. 28.

13 The sub-Saharan African countries that have elaborated a NAPA in the period 2004–11 are (in alphabetical order): Angola, Benin, Burkina Faso, Burundi, Cape Verde, Central African Republic, Chad, Comoros, Democratic Republic of Congo, Djibouti, Eritrea, Ethiopia, Gambia, Guinea, Guinea-Bissau, Lesotho, Liberia, Madagascar, Malawi, Mali, Mauritania, Mozambique, Niger, Rwanda, Senegal, Sierre Leone, Sudan, Tanzania, Togo, Uganda, Zambia.

14 The IUCN is the partner of the three Rio conventions and the Global Environment Facility (GEF) in mainstreaming gender into the implementation of the three conventions. IUCN Gender Office, *Harmonizing Gender in the Three Rio Conventions and the GEF*, IUCN, n.d.

15 National Adaptation Plans were agreed upon in the context of the 2010 Cancún Adaptation Framework and, in contrast to NAPAs, they are focused on the middle and long term (S. Kreft, A. O. Kaloga and S. Harmeling, 'National Adaptation Plans towards effective guidelines and modalities', Discussion paper, Germanwatch and WWF International, 2011). In 2011, the Gender Office of the International Union for Conservation of Nature (IUCN) elaborated draft gender guidelines for these National Adaptation Plans (IUCN, *Draft Guidelines to Mainstreaming Gender in the Development of National Adaptation Plans (NAPs)*).

16 As discussed in detail in S. Arora-Jonsson, 'Virtue and vulnerability: discourse on women, gender and climate change', *Global Environmental Change*, 21, 2011, pp. 744–51.

17 See J. Demetriades and E. Esplen, 'The gender dimension of poverty and climate change adaptation', *IDS Bulletin*, 39(4), 2008, pp. 24–31.

18 See H. Djoudi and M. Brockhaus, 'Is adaptation to climate change gender neutral? Lessons from communities dependent on livestock and forests in northern Mali', *International Forestry Review*, 13(2), 2011, pp. 123–35.

19 See, e.g., D. Elson, 'Male bias in macroeconomics: the case of structural adjustment', in D. Elson (ed.), *Male Bias in the Development Process*, Manchester University Press, Manchester, 1991.

20 See M. Hemmati and U. Röhr, 'Engendering the climate-change negotiations: experiences, challenges, and steps forward', *Gender and Development*, 17(1), 2009, pp. 19–32; G. Terry, *Climate Change and Gender Justice*, Practical Action Publishing in association with Oxfam GB, Warwickshire, 2009; UNFPA and WEDO, *Climate Change Connections*; UNDP, *Powerful Synergies. Gender Equality, Economic Development and Environmental Sustainability*, UNDP, New York, 2012.

21 See C. D. North, *Institutions, Institutional Change and Economic Performance*, Cambridge University Press, Cambridge, 1990.

22 See, e.g., B. Agarwal, *A Field of One's Own: Gender and Land Rights in South Asia*, Cambridge University Press, Cambridge, 1994.

23 L. Lessa and C. Rocha, 'Food security and gender mainstreaming: possibilities for social transformation in Brazil', *International Social Work*, 55(3), 2012, pp. 337–52.

24 See also A. Cornwall, E. Harrison and A. Whitehead, 'Gender myths and feminist fables. The struggle for interpretive power in gender and development', *Development and Change*, 38(1), 2007, pp. 1–20.

25 UNFPA and WEDO, *Climate Change Connections*.

26 Terry, *Climate Change and Gender Justice*.

27 B. Rodenberg, *Climate Change Adaptation from a Gender Perspective. A cross-cutting analysis of development-policy instruments*, German Development Institute, Bonn, 2009.

28 *NAPA-RIM*, Islamic Republic of Mauritania, Ministry of Rural Development and of Environment, Department of the Environment Project Coordination Unit, Nouackchott, 2004, p. 7.

29 See S. Theobald, R. Tolhurst, H. Elsey and H. Standing, 'Engendering the bureaucracy? Challenges and opportunities for mainstreaming gender in Ministries of Health under sector-wide approaches', *Health Policy and Planning*, 20(3), May 2005, pp. 141–9.

30 Cornwall et al., 'Gender myths and feminist fables'.

31 Ibid., p. 16.

14 SHUKRI HAJI ISMAIL BANDARE AND FATIMA JIBRELL

1 As a consequence of the civil war, in 1991 north-western Somalia broke off its union with the rest of Somalia and declared independence. Its secession remains internationally unrecognized. Instead it is defined as an autonomous region of Somalia.

2 See F. Musse and J, Gardner, *A Gender Profile for Somalia*, EC Somalia Unit, 2014.

15 ESTHER MWANGI

1 This chapter presents some of the emerging lessons from the Centre for International Forestry Research (CIFOR) research effort aimed at understanding gender relations in community/smallholder forestry; www. cifor.org/gender/home.html. I acknowledge the support of the CGIAR Consortium Research Programme on Forest, Trees and Agroforestry and the Austrian Development Agency.

2 World Bank, *The World Bank Participation Sourcebook*, World Bank, Washington, DC, 1996.

3 L. Mayoux, 'Beyond naivety: women, gender inequality and participatory development', *Development and Change*, 26(2), 1995, pp. 235–58; U. 'Power, knowledge and social control in participatory development', in B. Cooke and U. Kothari (eds), *Participation: The new tyranny?*, Zed Books, London, 2001, pp. 139–52; B. Agarwal, 'Participatory exclusions, community forestry, and gender: an analysis for south Asia and conceptual framework', *World Development*, 29(10), 2001, pp. 1623–48.

4 B. Agarwal, 'Gender and forest conservation: the impact of women's participation in community forest governance', *Ecological Economics*, 68(11), 2009, pp. 2785–99.

5 This section draws heavily on the following publications: S. Shackleton, F. Paumgarten, H. Kassa, M. Husselman and M. Zida, 'Opportunities for enhancing poor women's socioeconomic empowerment in the value chains of three African non-timber forest products (NTFPs)', *International*

Forestry Review, 13(2), 2011, pp. 136–51; V. Ingram, J. Schure, J. Tieguhong, O. Ndoye, A. Awono and D. M. Iponga, 'Gender implications of forest product value chains in the Congo Basin', *Forest, Trees and Livelihoods*, under review.

6   This section draws heavily on A. M. Larson, T. Dokken, S. Atmadja, I. A. Resosudarmo, P. Cronkleton, W. Sunderlin, M. Brockhaus, G. Selaya, A. Awono and A. Duchelle, 'Gender and REDD+: analyzing women's roles in sub-national initiatives', under review.

7   UNREDD, *The Business Case for Mainstreaming Gender in REDD+*, 2011, www.unredd.net/index.php?option=com_docman&task=doc_download&gid=6436&Itemid=53

8   This section draws heavily on E. Mwangi, R. Meinzen-Dick and Y. Sun, 'Gender and sustainable forest management in East Africa and Latin America', *Ecology and Society*, 16(1), 2011, pp. 17–25, www.ecologyandsociety.org/vol16/iss1/art17/; Y. Sun, E. Mwangi, R. Meinzen-Dick, P. Bose, P. Shanley, F. C. da Silva, and T. MacDonald, 'Forests, gender, property rights, and access', Info Brief no. 47. CIFOR, Bogor, Indonesia, February 2012, www.cifor.org/publications/pdf_files/Infobrief/3750-infobrief.pdf; E. Coleman and E. Mwangi, 'Women's participation in forest management: a cross-country analysis', *Global Environmental Change*, 23(1), 2013, p. 193, www.sciencedirect.com/science/article/pii/S0959378012001185

9   See www.sitemaker.umich.edu/ifri/home.

10   C. Colfer (ed.), 'The equitable forests: diversity, community and resource management', Resources for the Future, Washington, DC, 2005; K. Evans, A. Larson, E. Mwangi, P. Cronkleton, T. Maravanyika, X. Hernandez, P. Müller, A. Pikitle, R. Marchena, C. Mukasa, A. Tibazalika and A. Banana, 'Field guide to Adaptive Collaborative Management and improving women's participation', CIFOR Report, CIFOR, Bogor, Indonesia, 2014.

17 NIDHI TANDON

1   The industrial nature and mode of agricultural investment often go beyond the visible immediacy of land grab to the destruction of land itself. The use of inorganic fertilizers, synthetic pesticides and herbicides, increased landscape homogeneity, reduced fallow periods, the wholesale drainage of water systems and decimation of ecological diversity, all contribute to damaging soils and ecosystems, the effects lasting long after the industrial investors have left. The intensification of agriculture and subsequent degradation of ecosystem services further erode local food systems.

2   UNEP's *Towards a Green Economy* (2011) defines natural capital as natural assets such as forests, lakes, wetlands and river basins, essential components of natural capital at an ecosystem level. These underlying ecosystems provide services and values in the diversity and abundance of species and variability in genes that can be used for different services and products.

3   R. Knight et al., *Protecting Community Lands and Resources*, Namati and International Development Law Organization, 2013.

4   Studies such as S. Kpanan'Ayoung Siakor, *Uncertain Futures: The impacts of Sime Darby on communities in Liberia*, World Rainforest Movement and Sustainable Development Institute, 2012, and L. Balachandran, E. Herb, S. Timirzi and E. O'Reilly, *Everyone must eat? Liberia, Food Security and Palm Oil*, Columbia/Sipa, 2012.

5   The long-term implications of losing land and dignity and the particular impacts for rural women are being acknowledged by the international community. See Oxfam, *Promises, Power, and Poverty: Corporate land deals and rural women in Africa*, 2013, and Action Aid, *From under their feet: A think piece on the gender dimensions of land grabs in Africa*, 2012.

6   Rights and Resources Initiative, *Investments into the Agribusiness, Extractive and Infrastructure Sectors of Liberia: An Overview*, February 2013, www.rightsandresources.org/publication/investments-into-the-agribusiness-extractive-and-infrastructure-sectors-of-liberia/

7   Ministry of Agriculture stats, Ghana (2010), puts total nucleus (hectares) of land under oil palm plantations at 21,574 hectares.

8   The global palm oil industry has recently witnessed unprecedented growth, with a cumulative annual growth rate (CAGR) of 8 per cent, although West Africa's CAGR is 1.5 per cent. The competitive landscape is dominated by South-East Asian producers who have better production efficiency (higher productivity at comparable costs of production, hence able to capture larger shares of the world market) and ideal climatic conditions. K. Ofosu-Budu and D. Sarpong, 'Oil palm industry growth in Africa: a value chain and smallholders study for Ghana', in A. Elbehri (ed.), *Rebuilding West Africa's Food Potential*, FAO/IFAD, 2013.

9   See www.youtube.com/watch?v=ocDWFcbGts8 and, e.g., Oxfam, *Promises, Power, and Poverty*, and Action Aid, *From under their feet*.

10 www.uneca.org/sites/default/files/uploaded-documents/fg_on_land_policy_eng.pdf. This would be consistent with commitments made by African states in the AU's 2003 Maputo protocol to the ACHPR on the Rights of Women in Africa and the 2004 Solemn Declaration on Gender Equality in Africa, which call for action to address gender inequalities, including women's unequal access to land.

11 The UN's International Assessment of Agricultural Knowledge, Science and Technology for Development (IAASTD) concludes that 'small-scale farmers and organic, agro-ecological methods are the way forward to solve the current food crisis and meet the needs of local communities'. Greening agriculture in developing countries and concentrating on smallholders can reduce poverty while investing in the natural capital on which the poor depend. Greening the small farm sector through promotion and dissemination of sustainable practices could be the most effective way to make more food available to the poor and hungry, reduce poverty, increase carbon

sequestration and access growing international markets for green products. See www.unep.org/greeneconomy/Portals/88/documents/ger/GER_synthesis_en.pdf

12 The '*poro*' association for men has declined in significance in large part because the political situation in the past made such associations illegal. However, there may be a role for other sacred institutions, including the '*sande*' for women, and in Garpu Town, a sacred institution called '*nigi*' is organized around a river in the forest – it is forbidden to fish or hunt in the vicinity of the grove. (See IUCN, 'Understanding diversity: a study of livelihoods and forest landscapes in Liberia', 2009, p. 39, cmsdata.iucn.org/downloads/liberia_lls_report_sept_2009.pdf.) The '*sande*' societies, for instance, retain knowledge of plant species for medicinal purposes and valuable traditional folklore.

13 IUCN, 'Understanding diversity', p. 20.

14 Ibid., p. 30.

15 E. Ostrom, *Governing the Commons: The Evolution of Institutions for Collective Action*, Cambridge University Press, Cambridge, 1990.

16 OECD, 'Empowerment of poor rural people through initiatives in agriculture and natural resource management', 2012, p. 2.

18 MARIA MIES

1 Shiva, in M. Mies and V. Shiva, *Ecofeminism*, Zed Books, London, 1993, 2nd edn 2014, p. 99.

2 M. Gimbutas, *The Civilization of the Goddess – The World of Old Europe*, Harper, San Francisco, CA, 1991.

3 M. Gimbutas, *The Goddesses and Gods of Old Europe 6500–3500 B.C. Myths and Cult Images*, Thames & Hudson, London, 1984, p. 237.

4 Ibid., p. 237.

5 Gimbutas, *The Civilization of the Goddess*, p. 352.

6 Frauenmuseum Wiesbaden (eds), *Von Erdgöttinnen und Kornmüttern. Aus dem Reich der Fülle* [Of earth goddesses and grain-mothers. From the realm of abundance], Women's Museum Wiesbaden, 1998.

7 Gimbutas, *The Civilization of the Goddess*, p. 352.

8 M. Mies, *Krieg ohne Grenzen: Die neue Kolonisierung der Welt*, Papyrossa Verlag , Cologne, 2005.

19 SARAH FISHER

1 S. Singh, J. E. Darroch and L.S. Ashford, *Adding It Up: Costs and Benefits of Investing in Sexual and Reproductive Health 2014*, Guttmacher Institute and United Nations Population Fund (UNFPA), 2014. Women with an unmet need for contraception are sexually active women of reproductive age (15-49) who want to avoid pregnancy but are not using a modern method of contraception.

2   UNICEF, *The State of the World's Children 2011, Adolescence: An Age of Opportunity*, UNICEF, New York, 2011.

3   UNICEF, *The State of the World's Children 2009: Maternal and Newborn Health*, UNICEF, New York, 2008.

4   K. Newman, S. Fisher, S. Mayhew et al., 'Population, sexual and reproductive health, rights and sustainable development: forging a common agenda', *Reproductive Health Matters*, 22(43), 2014, pp. 53–64.

5   S. Fisher and K. Newman, 'People, population, and climate change: opportunities for advancing climate resilience and reproductive rights', RH Reality Check, 27 October 2011, rhrealitycheck.org/article/2011/10/27/population-and-climate-change-opportunities-for-advancing-climate-resilience-and-reproductive-rights/, accessed 2 September 2014.

6   J. Cleland, A. Conde-Agudelo, H. Peterson et al., 'Contraception and health', *The Lancet*, 380, 2012, pp. 149–56; J. Cleland, S. Bernstein, A. Ezeh et al., 'Family planning: the unfinished agenda', *The Lancet*, 368(18), 2006, pp. 1810–27.

7   UNFPA, *Fact Sheet: Adolescent Girls' Sexual and Reproductive Health Needs*, 2012, www.unfpa.org/webdav/site/global/shared/documents/Reproductive%20Health/Fact%20Sheets/Adolescent%20Girls%20SRHealth_UNFPA%20Fact%20Sheet_July%205%202012.pdf, accessed 19 September 2014.

8   United Nations, Department of Economic and Social Affairs, Population Division, *World Population Prospects: The 2015 Revision, Key Findings and Advance Tables*, Working Paper no. ESA/P/WP.241, UN, New York, 2015.

9   World Health Organization and United Nations Children Fund, 'Progress on sanitation and drinking-water 2010 update', WHO, Geneva, 2011.

10 United Nations Food and Agriculture Organization, *The State of Food and Agriculture 2010–11*, FAO, Rome, 2011.

11 United Nations Environment Programme, *Women and the Environment*, UN, New York, 2004.

12 M. Wan, C. J. P. Colfer and B. Powell 'Forests, women and health: opportunities and challenges for conservation', *International Forestry Review*, 13(3), 2011, pp. 369–87.

13 Organisation for Economic Co-operation and Development, *Environmental Policy and Household Behaviour: Review of Evidence in the Areas of Energy, Food, Transport, Waste and Water*, OECD, Paris, 2008.

14 K. Norgaard and R. York, 'Gender equality and state environmentalism', *Gender and Society*, 19(4), 2005, pp. 506–22.

15 B. Agarwal, *Gender and Green Governance: The Political Economy of Women's Presence within and beyond Community Forestry*, OUP, Oxford, 2010.

16 World Bank, *Linking Sustainability with Demand, Gender, and Poverty*, World Bank, Washington, DC, 2001.

17 World Bank, *World Development Report 2012: Gender Equality and Development*, World Bank, Washington, DC, 2011.

18 Wan et al., 'Forests, women and health'.

19 Newman et al., 'Population, sexual and reproductive health, rights and sustainable development'.

20 See psda.org.uk .

21 Friends of the Earth, *Global Population, Consumption and Rights*, 2013, www.foe.co.uk/sites/default/files/downloads/population_friends_of_the.pdf, accessed 6 September 2014.

22 R. De Souza, 'Resilience, integrated development and family planning: building long-term solutions', *Reproductive Health Matters*, 22(43), 2014, pp. 75–83; V. Mohan and T. Shellard, 'Providing family planning services to remote communities in areas of high biodiversity through a Population-Health-Environment programme in Madagascar', *Reproductive Health Matters*, 22(43), 2014, pp. 93–103.

23 See phe-ethiopia.org.

20 KATE METCALF AND COLLEAGUES

All Women's Environmental Network resources are available at wen.org.uk/all-resources

1 Women's Environmental Network, *No Laughing Matter. Stress incontinence and the environment*, 2004.

2 Women's Environmental Network, *Pretty Nasty – questions & answers about phthalates*, 2003.

3 Women's Environmental Network, *Getting Lippy. Cosmetics, toiletries and the environment*, 2003.

4 Women's Environmental Network, *Toxic Tour: What's in my cosmetics?*, 2003.

5 Women's Institute and Women's Environmental Network, *Women's Manifesto on Climate Change*, 2007.

6 Women's Environmental Network, *Gender and the Climate Change Agenda. The impacts of climate change on women and public policy*, 2010.

7 Women's Environmental Network, *Why Women and Climate Change?*, 2010.

8 Greater London Authority, *English Indices of Deprivation. A London perspective*, June 2011.

9 Fawcett Society, *A Fawcett Society Briefing on Ethnic Minority Women, Poverty and Inequality*, 2008.

10 ONS, *Population Estimates for UK, England, Wales, Scotland and Northern Ireland, mid 2006*, Office for National Statistics, London, 2006.

11 K. Metcalf et al., 'Community food growing and the role of women in the alternative economy in Tower Hamlets', *Journal of the Local Economy Policy Unit*, Special Issue: 'Women and the local economy', 27(8), 2012.

12 Ibid.

13 J. Ward and R. Spacey, *Dare to Dream: Learning journeys of Bangladeshi, Pakistani and Somali women*, NIACE, Leicester, 2008.

14 O. Varley-Winter, 'Roots to work: developing employability through community food-growing and urban agriculture projects', Summary Report, City & Guilds Centre for Skills and Development, London, 2011.

15 L. E. Baker, 'Tending cultural gardens and food landscapes in downtown Toronto', *Geographical Review*, 94(3), 2004, pp. 305–25.

16 S. Hayes, *Radical Homemakers: Reclaiming Domesticity from a Consumer Culture*, Left to Write Press, Richmondville, NY, 2010.

17 N. Charles and M. Kerr, *Women, Food, and Families*, Manchester University Press, Manchester, 1988.

18 M. L. DeVault, *Feeding the Family: The Social Organization of Caring as Gendered Work*, University of Chicago Press, Chicago, IL, 1994; K. Wiig and C. Smith, 'The art of grocery shopping on a food stamp budget: factors influencing the food choices of low-income women as they try to make ends meet', *Public Health Nutrition*, 12(10), 2009, pp. 1726–34; V. Inglis, 'Does modifying the household food budget predict changes in the healthfulness of purchasing choices among low- and high-income women?', *Appetite*, 52(2), 2009, pp. 273–9.

23 EMMA HOWARD BOYD

1 Ruth Sunderland, 'We cannot return to the old macho ways', *Observer*, 15 February 2009, www.theguardian com/business/2009/feb/15/gender-recession-credit-crunch

2 Ibid.

3 www.boardsforum.co.uk/boardwatch.html

4 www.moraldna.org/wp-content/uploads/2014/10/The-MoralD-NA-of-Performance-Infographic-October-2014.pdf

5 www.gov.uk/government/uploads/system/uploads/attachment_data/file/31480/11-745-women-on-boards.pdf

6 30% Club, 'Diversity and stewardship – next steps', November 2012.

7 www.cbi.org.uk/media-centre/press-releases/2014/06/we-need-a-uk-target-on-reducing-gender-pay-gap-cbi/

8 www.frc.org.uk/Our-Work/Publications/Accounting-and-Reporting-Policy/Guidance-on-the-Strategic-Report.pdf

9 For example, www.mckinsey.com/client_service/organization/latest_thinking/unlocking_the_full_potential

10 Grant Thornton, 'Women in business: the value of diversity', September 2015, www.grantthornton.global/en/insights/articles/diverse-boards-in-india-uk-and-us-outperform-male-only-peers-by-us$655bn

11 McKinsey Global Institute, 'The power of parity: How advancing women's equality can add $12 trillion to global growth', September 2015, www.mckinsey.com/insights/growth/how_advancing_womens_equality_

can_add_12_trillion_to_global_growth?cid=mckwomen-eml-alt-mgi-mck-oth-1509

12 responsiblebusiness.haas.berkeley.edu/Women_Create_Sustainable_Value_FINAL_10_2012.pdf. By K. A. McElhaney and S. Mobasseri, UC Berkeley Haas School of Business. Research sponsored by KPMG with Women Corporate Directors (WCD).

13 30percentclub.org/wp-content/uploads/2014/11/2014-Survey-of-Women-on-Boards-1.pdf

14 www.catalyst.org/system/files/companies_behaving_responsibly_gender_diversity_on_boards.pdf

15 A. Capezio and A. Mavisakalyan, 'Women in the boardroom and fraud: Evidence from Australia', *Australian Journal of Management* 07/2015, July 2015.